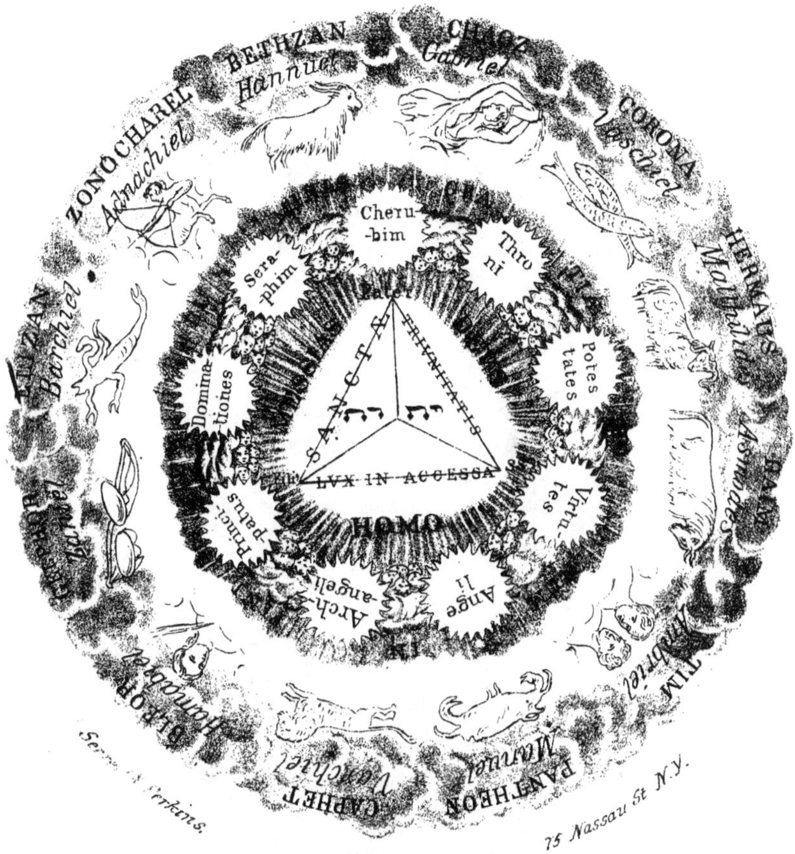

A pictorial representation of the angelic orders, according to the views of the Rabbins and Fathers, the ancient Sophists and Magi. The name of the Angel-Prince, and that of his subordinate, being placed over the sign of the Zodiac, which, astrologically, they govern, in conjunction with an hieroglyphic of the Trinity, encircled by the celestial hierarchy of the Scriptures

ANGELOLOGY.

——oo——

REMARKS AND REFLECTIONS

TOUCHING THE

AGENCY AND MINISTRATION

OF

HOLY ANGELS;

WITH REFERENCE TO THEIR

History, Rank, Titles, Attributes, Characteristics, Residence, Society, Employments and Pursuits;

INTERSPERSED WITH

TRADITIONAL PARTICULARS RESPECTING THEM.

BY GEORGE CLAYTON, Jr.

Luke, xxii, 43.

"Are they not all ministering spirits."—*St. Paul.*
"To thee all angels cry aloud—Cherubim and Seraphim."—*Com. Prayer.*
"Magna opera Domini, exquisita in omnes voluntates ejus."—*The Vulgate.*

Embellished with original Illustrations.

PUBLISHED FOR THE AUTHOR

BY HENRY KERNOT, 633 BROADWAY, N. Y.

1851.

TO

MY ESTEEMED FRIEND,

MR. GEORGE C. MORGAN;

The following pages are respectfully inscribed,—the ennobling subject which they embrace, having been considered at his request;

ACCOMPANIED WITH THE

CHRISTIAN HOPE,

OF GREETING HIM AMIDST

"THE GENERAL ASSEMBLY OF THE JUST,

AND THE

INNUMERABLE COMPANY OF

ANGELS,"

IN THE BEATIFIC VISION "OF THE CITY

OF THE

LIVING GOD;"

GLORIFIED IN THE RESPLENDENT RADIATIONS

OF THE

HOLY SHEKINAH

OF A

Celestial Immortality.

CORRECTIONS.

Page 32, line 19, for *applied*, read apply.
" 45, line 12, for *their*, read the.
" 61, line 21, for *beautiful*, read beatific.
" 62, line 29, for *by*, read but.
" 63, line 18, before *chambers*, insert *his*.
" 101, line 30, for *consolitary*, read consolatory.
" 170, line 12, for *aereal*, read aerial.
" " line 23, for *inscrutible*, read inscrutable.
" 177, line 2, for *the skies*, read heaven.
" 178, line 22, for *sanitary*, read sanitive.
" 180, line 30, before *Christ*, insert *of*.
" 190, line 12, for *prosperity*, read posterity.
" 205, line 4, for *invoking*, read involving.

PREFACE.

—— πίστις, ἐλπὶς, ἀγάπη τα τρία ταῦτα·
μείζων δὲ τούτων ἡ ἀγάπη.—1 Cor. xiii. 13.

The transcendent dignity and overwhelming grandeur of the sublime and glorious subject of investigating the nature and attributes, the characteristics and ministrations of Holy Angels,—encompassed by the admonitory and awful silence of the Scriptures,—evidently appear to have deterred even writers of philosophic research and lofty intellectual endowments, from imparting that plenitude of devotional consideration, to which, so attractive and cardinal a doctrine of divine revelation is, assuredly, entitled; to wit,—the special ministry and appointed agency of Angelic Intelligences, in reference to the wondrous economy of Redemption, and the mighty achievements of Omnipotent purpose, in executing the moral government of the universe.

A prefatory and deferential apology seems, therefore, requisite to atone for the apparently presumptuous temerity of the present production, unless justified or softened by the circumstances of its origination,—the appropriateness or fulfilment of its design.

Having prefixed, at the desire of a friend, a few remarks to the "Narrative of a Summer's Excursion, amidst the romantic and picturesque scenery of Nature," containing an allusion to a discourse touching the "Ministry of Angels," he was further requested, to contribute some observations on that inviting and majestic theme.

Conscious of disqualification and the absence of all suitable and sufficient preparation for the specific consideration of so delightful and elevating a topic, the request was declined,—but, subsequent meditation led to a train of contemplation which heightened in interest and enjoyment as he pondered upon the doctrine, in the magnitude of its importance, as bearing upon the selected instrumentality and chosen medium of the condescension of Jehovah in his terrestrial intercourse and transactions with lapsed and sinful humanity, in connection with the urgent beatitude of angelic association and pursuits,—as his reflections starting from the celebration, according to the Mosaic narrative, of the Creation, proceeded, in biblical vision, along the illumed and extended vista of prophecy, the mysterious and radiant avenue of redeeming Mercy, to the apocalyptic revelations of the millennial reign and foredoomed overthrow of "the prince of the power of the air and all spiritual wickednesses," towards the final consummation of all things, at the arrival of the bright morning of the resurrection and the solemn assize of the judgment day, upon the august descent and re-appearance of "the righteous judge of the quick and the dead," attended by the resplendent retinue of heaven, to conduct the predestinated ascension of the best to the eternal mansion of celestial glory!

As regards the annexed *compend*, it is alike the dictate of prudence and propriety to state,—that it does not arrogate originality of ideas or extent of research; that it has been chiefly prepared, during the past few months, in those interstices of thought which have accrued in the brief intervals of a secular vocation which did not admit of a continuous or comprehensive reading, the advantageous retirement of the study, or the auxiliary exercises of the secret closet of meditation; nevertheless, in all frankness, he considers it his duty to declare,—in the hope that others may derive a similar benefit—that the mental process which it has required, together with the agreeable and instructive fellowship of the religious sentiments of the practical piety of various authors, has proved—in his own experience—peculiarly profitable,—driving away those *Promethean* vultures of distrust and despondency which constantly hover around the mind, whilst environed by an accumulation of uncontrollable evils,—the tormenting oppression of physical melancholy, aggravated by the cureless corrosion of internal grief, the perturbing vexations of *social* injustice, the inflicted wrongs of administrative turpitude and judicial malversation, the unprovoked injuries of clerical detraction and dishonor, and the mischievous devices of a Janus-faced and heartless hypocrisy.

Mr. S. T. Coleridge, with his characteristic intuition, has observed, "*That the communicativeness of our nature leads us to describe our own sorrows,*"—an ægis which, if it do not protect the writer from the allegation of having trespassed beyond the boundary of a becoming decorum, in his figurative representation of *The Escort of Angels*, (including other emblematical designs,) he confidently turns for shelter, (regardless of the barbed missiles of a flippant censure or witless derision to which it may expose him,) to the remembered fidelity of the conjugal attachment of an expectant, though a disembodied affection, as well as the sympathetic sensibility of a Christian candor—having had to traverse, unattended by earthly alleviations, amidst sickness and seclusion, desertion and dejection, darkened by the tenebrious assaults of Satanic suggestions,† the *via dolorosa* of domestic and fraternal bereavement, as, in quick succession, from the relentless aim of the "insatiable archer,"

> "Thrice the arrow flew,
> And thrice his peace was slain"—

he would still fain cherish—and devoutly recommend to others, by

---

* The pain of my corporeal sufferings is greatly relieved, by the comforting hope of an anticipated re-union or recognition in the blessedness of heaven; and by divine aid, endeavor so to bring up in the nurture and admonition of the Lord, my left dear little ones, that in God's time, they may follow after me.

One of her last death-bed sayings.

† The devil ever consorts with our solitude, and is that unruly rebel that musters up those disordered motions which accompany our sequestered imaginations.

Sir Thos. Browne—*Religio-Medici.*

virtue of its soothing and edifying tendency, under the pressure of similar afflictive dispensations,*—the salutary and animating belief, that he was sustained—during the probationary discipline of providential appointment,—by the gentle and sympathetic† whispers of angel voices as they vibrated on the silver chords of the golden harp of the gospel, in unison with the melodious and enrapturing tones of divine promises and scriptural consolation.

As behooveth him,—with reverential humility, he commends this imperfect tribute of adoring gratitude to the gracious benediction of the *Great Angel* of the everlasting covenant, who, whilst He tabernacled "in the flesh for us men and our salvation," singled out, from amidst the thronging multitude, by the divinity of His omniscience, the remaining mites of the widow's *penury*; recording on the page of inspiration, that as the offering of her repentant faith and "love

---

* They teach the soul by woe subdued,
That sweetest flowers do lie
Hid in the green, thick, tangled wood,
Of dark Adversity.

CAROLINE MAY—*Proem to Treasured Thoughts.*

—Being an admirable and a choice selection of striking and sterling, elegant and edifying extracts,—pithy, practical, and pious observations gleaned from the writings of eminent authors, in the diversified departments of theology, philosophy, and general literature.

† I do think that many mysteries ascribed to our own inventions have been the courteous revelations of spirits, or the charitable premonitions of good angels, which forerun our calamities; for those noble essences in heaven have a friendly regard unto their fellow-nature on earth.

SIR THOS. BROWNE—*Religio-Medici.*

unfeigned," they were a larger donative, than the munificent and united gifts of those, who, from the vain promptings of an ostentatious superfluity, cast in out of their *abundance* into the treasury of the temple of the Jewish synagogue.

To Him—the Lord of Angels—

"Whose frown can disappoint the *proudest* page,
Whose approbation prosper even *mine*."

"O Everlasting God, who hast ordained the services of angels and men in a wonderful order; mercifully grant, that as thy holy angels always do thee service in heaven, so by thy appointment they may succor and defend us on earth, through Jesus Christ our Lord."

Collect for St. Michael and All Angels.

ILLUSTRATIONS.

WOOD CUTS.

PROEMIAL.

——— But, oh! the exceeding grace
Of God Most High, that loves his creatures so,
And all his works with mercy doth embrace,
That blessed *Angels* he sends to and fro,—
How oft do they their silver bowers leave,
To come to succor us, that succor want!
And all for love, and nothing for reward:
Oh! why should God in heaven to man have such regard!

Spencer.

——— Man he made, and for him built
Magnificent this world, and earth his seat,
Him Lord pronounc'd; and, oh! indignity!
Subjected to his service *Angel-wings*,
And flaming ministers to watch and tend
Their earthly charge.

Milton's Paradise Lost, b. ix.

When Thou, attended gloriously from heaven,
Shalt in the sky appear, and from Thee send
The summoning *Archangels* to proclaim
Thy dread tribunal! forthwith from all winds
The living, and forthwith the cited dead
Of all past ages, to the general doom
Shall hasten.

Id. b. iii.

INTRODUCTION.

Bright Angels, with adoring face,
  In all their shining forms,
Stand waiting, round the throne of grace,
  For gifts to mortal worms.—Dr. Watts,
altered and accommodated.

Are they not all ministering spirits, sent forth to minister for them who shall be heirs of salvation?—Hebrews 1 : 14.

The works of the Lord are great, sought out of all them that have pleasure therein. Psalm cxi. 2.—Invoking the guiding afflatus of that sacred Inspiration which animated the fervid exclamation of the pious and philosophic Psalmist, whilst contemplating in the secret chamber of rapt meditation, the mighty and mysterious operations of Jehovah, displayed in the wondrous works of the visible creation, the retributive procedures of a special providence, the revealed and prophetic glories connected with the gracious economy of Redemption—would we seek to introduce—by a few preliminary observations, sustained by the collated remarks and collateral opinions of diverse authors—to the reader's serious and believing attention, the ennobling and inviting subject attempted in the succeeding pages, prompted by the sincere desire and humble hope, that it may be canvassed in such a manner, as in no wise to invalidate its manifest attractions, elevating sublimity, consolatory support, devotional and edifying tendency.

That a theme, so pregnant with the noblest sentiments and divinest considerations should have been treated with such marked indifference, cannot certainly be justified, on the alleged plea, that the perversion or abuse of any doctrine revealed in the volume of Inspiration, founded either upon the danger of the idolatrous or interdicted worship of angels,* or, the impenetrable mysteriousness by which it

* ———the Roman Church doth ill,
When they adore within their churches still,
Saints, Images, and Pictures much unfitting,
As thereby great idolatry committing;
And as for miracles, they further say,
That such are wrought amongst them every day;
Some handle hot coals, without scorching, can,
And maids bear children———

THOMAS HEYWOOD, *Hierarchie of the Angells*, 1653.

There seems to have been in the kingdom of Judah an uninterrupted contest between the worshippers of Jehovah and those of idols, resisting all the appeals of their prophets, the miracles of Elijah and Elisha, the judgments of God, the continued fulfillment of various predictions, and every other evidence of the truth of their Scriptures.—DR. GEORGE TOWNSEND, *Notes on Witch of Endor.*

The history of the Jews is the record of a continual struggle between pure Theism supported by the most terrible sanctions, and the strangely fascinis enveloped to our finite reason and degenerated faculties; and which disregard is fully substantiated, not merely by the prevailing slight of professing believers in the Bible, but also corroborated by the printed testimony of several pious, learned, and distinguished theologians who have adorned the various denominations of our common Christianity.

In a scarce, valuable, and anonymous treatise entitled "*Pneumatologia*,* or a Discourse on Angels," published in the year 1701, from the pen of a writer, who, to the rare endowment of a lucid judgment, unites the erudition of the scholar, the acuteness of the philosopher, the piety of a saint, and occasionally, the persuasive eloquence of the rhetorician; in a well written recommendatory preface by a Mr. George Hammond, the following appropriate remarks occur: "The subject here undertaken to be treated upon, is certainly very high and noble in itself, and exceedingly useful for us, to be acquainted withal, in regard there is so much spoken of the angels and their ministry in the Holy Scriptures. For that which is written therein, is written for our learning. It is then a matter which deserves to be soberly inquired into. What may be the reason why the Scripture-

ating desire of having some visible and tangible object of adoration. Upon the same principle or inclination may be explained, the strong tendency of the multitude in all ages and nations, to idolatry.—MACAULAY'S *Review of Milton.*

The angelical nature, though it is a secret for the most part to us till we come to heaven; yet it is such a secret as we may modestly inquire into and seek to know so far as it is revealed, either in nature or the Scriptures.—*Pneumatologia.*

* I beg to avail myself of this opportunity, to tender my respectful acknowledgments to the Rev. Mr. Cady for his obliging permission to consult some curious old theological *tomes* belonging to the library of the Episcopal Theological Seminary, which were not to be met with in any other of the public libraries of this city.

doctrine concerning angels is no more attended to? For it is, in our time, but sparingly treated upon; and not so frequently and deeply in the thoughts of Christians, as it should be; and consequently not improved by the children of God to their growth in faith, holiness, and comfort as might be. Let me be pardoned, if I offer my conjecture in two instances: (1.) The bold, curious, and confident speculations touching the angels, both in elder times, and in the days of the schoolmen, who intruded into things not seen, vainly puffed up by their fleshly minds. This makes way for a voluntary humility, and issued in the worshipping of angels. And some (it is probable), that they might avoid this rock, have thought it dangerous to be inquisitive into these things, which are taught in the Scripture of Truth concerning them. (2). The irreligiousness and skepticism* of materialists and sadducees, who deny, or pretend to doubt whether there are, indeed, any immaterial beings, at all. And if there be no separate spirits, as to their existence, there can be nothing spoken, concerning such, that is to be regarded." Further adding: "The worthy author, how much soever he extols the dignity of angels and their wonderful properties, yet he still leaves them and their ministrations under the sovereign will and command of God, and Jesus Christ their head, to whom they devote themselves and their services."

Archbishop Tillotson observes, "The doctrine of angels is not a peculiar one of the Jewish or Christian religion, but the general doctrine of all religions that ever were, and therefore cannot be objected against by any but atheists. And yet I know not whence it comes to pass, that this great

* The first great errors that infested the Christian Church were those of the Gnostics, who pretended into a very sublime γνωσις, or Mystic Theology, which was no other than a corrupt complex of Orphic, Pythagoric, and Judaic infusion.—GALE, *Court of the Gentiles*, 1676.

truth, which is so comfortable to mankind, is so very little understood by us. Perhaps the corruption of so great a part of the Christian church in the point of worshipping the angels, may have run us so far into the other extreme, as scarcely to acknowledge any benefit by them. But surely, we may believe they do us good without any obligation to pray to them ; and may own them as the ministers of God's providence without making them the objects of our worship."

The devout *Bishop Hall*, likewise, respecting the neglect of this sublime and glorious doctrine, to which he refers in his "Tractate Concerning the Invisible World," thus rebukingly soliloquizes in one of his searching meditations. "The good Lord forgive me, for that I have suffered myself so much to forget his Divine presence, and so the presence of his angels. It is, I confess, my great sin that I have filled mine eyes with other objects, and have been slack in returning praises to my God, for the continued assistance of those blessed and beneficent spirits. Oh! that the dust and clay were so washed out of mine eyes, that I might behold, together with the presence, the numbers, the beauties and excellencies of those ever present guardians." With regard to the reprehensible oversight of the valid claims of this interesting doctrine of Revelation, the late excellent Rev. Mr. Bickersteth has thrown out the following judicious and forcible intimations and requisitions. "No part of divine truth can be neglected without spiritual loss, and it is too evident that the deep and mysterious doctrine of Revelation respecting evil spirits and good angels, has been far too much disregarded in our age. This has arisen, on the one hand, from the wide spread of infidel principles, and on the other from the unscriptural, idolatrous and extravagant attention paid to this subject in the Church of Rome, in which good angels are worshipped, and the evil spirits brought forward to foster delusions. But we gain no solid victory over Popery, by omitting the truths which have been corrupted and abused. Our duty is rather to take forth the precious from the vile, and hold fast the simple and plain truth revealed for us and our children; thus shall we be as God's mouth to the people." Equally applicable are his additional observations, as bearing, with fearful apprehension upon the fatal tendency of those vicious theories, fraudulent manœuvres, baneful and debasing delusions which attend the black retinue of the "Legion" of modern pretenders to a familiar intercourse, criminal and intriguing connection with supernatural agencies and spiritual beings, which disgrace the character of the present day, stultifying the understanding of infidel advocates, as well as ensnaring their imbecile devotees into the entanglements of a moral blindness and fearful perdition.* In view of these threatened

* To the sober mind, it is painful to reflect, that a talented and popular clergyman of this city should have countenanced, by his attendance, the Satanic imposture, to converse with "*the spirits of the Rochester knockings;*" and which became so barefaced a fraud as even to be denounced by their recent agrarian and socialist advocate. Has it not the appearance of a wicked hypocrisy for a preacher of the gospel of Christ to visit such blasphemous exhibitions, in impious disregard to the spirit and abiding moral obligations of that interdict of divine authority recorded in Deut. xviii. 10, 11. "*There shall not be found among you any one that maketh his son or his daughter to pass through the fire, or that useth divination, or an observer of times, or an enchanter, or a witch, or a charmer, or a consulter with familiar spirits, or a wizard, or a necromancer.*" The puerile plea of curiosity is no valid excuse. Was it not the indulgence of a forbidden and unhallowed curiosity which forfeited Paradise, "brought death into the world and all our woe," and required the sacrificial atonement and piacular sufferings of the bleeding victim on the ignominious Cross of Calvary! Moreover, why does it not more frequently occur to the thoughts of the professed adherents of the "pure and undefiled religion" of Christianity that to attend on the Sabbath, the lectures and discourses of declaimers of heterodox sentiments, who desecrate the sacred hours of the Lord's day in defending the infidel claims of the

evils, he fills, with an urgent breath, the warning trumpet of serious admonitions and sagacious foresight, sounded forth in the following expostulation. " Looking at the signs of the times, and the long neglect and unnatural denial of all angelic ministrations or spiritual influence, and at the express predictions of false Christs and false prophets, *who shall show signs and wonders, insomuch that if it were possible, they should deceive the very elect*, and that when men *receive not the love of the truth that they might be saved, for this cause God shall send among them strong delusions that they should believe a lie.* I cannot but think there is a painful prospect of a sudden recoil and religious revulsion from the present unbelief and misbelief, to an unnatural and undistinguishing credulity, when antichrist shall appear in his latest form, " with signs and lying wonders." I would, therefore, leave an earnest caution on the minds of my readers. *Beloved, believe not every spirit, but try the spirits, whether they are of God.* The Scriptures have forewarned us beforehand that we may not be *led away with the error of the wicked and fall from our own steadfastness.*"

In the fervid expressions of devotion, actuated by the ardent enthusiasm of a genuine Christian philosophy, Mr. John Reynolds, in his disquisition or " Inquiries concerning the state and economy of the angelical worlds," printed in 1723, thus proceeds, " And surely we shall find in the angelical system such heights and depths, as will raise our admiration of that God, whose fiat created the various worlds he has made, and the beautiful administrations he has

founders of antichristian systems, that by so doing, they virtually belie the profession of their faith, commit an awful affront on their avowed Redeemer, and are verily guilty of a criminal violation of the fourth commandment of the decalogue ! G. C.

chosen and ordained. No wonder we meet with inscrutable mysteries connected with the nature and order, laws and ministry of those incorporeal attendants that surround and applaud the Throne. Our inquisitive minds are apt to wonder that a door or casement is not opened for our clearer prospects into the celestial world, toward which we are called to travel. We admire, when these natives of heaven appeared, so often, in the primitive world, and came sometimes, (one would think) upon lower offices and services; that when so many inspired messengers came from God; yea, that when the Lord Himself came from heaven, to teach us how to get there, they would none of them tell us more of the world from whence they came, or to which they would invite us; and that they no more particularly describe the state, the inhabitants, employments, and felicities that are there. But they came not, it seems, to gratify our curiosity; but to direct us safely thither. An early thirst of undue knowledge soon ruined our race in the head of it, and it is not now to be indulged. Our greatest business and felicity are not to return to angels, (though they will be exceeding good company,) but to Him that made (and can make blessed) both them and us; and therefore the most the Lord of heaven tells us of them, (though he knew their essence, their regimen and offices so well) is, that they are glad when any one of us is reduced to repentance, and reconciled to God; and therefore set in a fair way to their world, their enjoyments, and society. There we shall know them as much as we shall desire. In the mean time we are to walk by faith and hope in that light that has been afforded us. And it will be our wisdom, as well as our duty, not barely to be content with, but to be thankful for that measure of supernatural revelation, that Divine wisdom has thought fit to vouchsafe to us; which will suffice to guide us to life and immortality, without any one's coming from the dead or descending from the world of native life and immortality." These important reflections, though well adapted to suppress the pruriency of that curiosity of the human mind, consequent on our degenerate condition, respecting those abstruse points of inquiry enshrined in the silence of Divine wisdom, yet, sufficient is revealed to excite our wondering admiration, as well as promote our edification, and also afford supporting comfort as we prosecute our toilsome pilgrimage through the wilderness of this vain world, till we have attained to the blissful associations and society of angels, and reached the bright and eternal residences of those illustrious and celestial immortals, for as Dr. Owen justly remarks: "It is the height of ingratitude not to search after what may be known of this great privilege and mercy whereof we are made partakers in the ministry of angels. God hath neither appointed or revealed it for nothing. He expects a revenue of praise and glory for it; and how can we bless him for it when we know nothing about it? This ministry then of angels, is that which with sobriety we are, in a way of duty, to inquire into. Let us on this account glorify God and be thankful. Great is the privilege, manifold are the blessings and benefits that we are made partakers of by this ministry of angels. What shall we render for them and to them? Shall we go and bow ourselves down to the angels themselves and pay our homage of obedience to them? They all cry out with one accord: "See you do it not, we are your fellow-servants." What shall we then do? Why, say they, worship God! Glorify and praise him, who is God of all angels; who sends them unto whom they minister in all they do for us. Let us bless God, I say, for the ministry of angels."

In an exceedingly able and very orthodox article contributed by Professor Moses Stuart to the Bibliotheca Sacra, he starts with this exegetical interrogatory. "Of what importance can the doctrine respecting good and evil angels be to us? We owe them, it is said, no duty of homage or worship, and as they are invisible beings, if they exist at all, we can never decide with any certainty whether or when they interpose in our behalf or interfere for the sake of injuring us? We have therefore no interest in this matter.

"I cannot accede to such a view of the subject; the Scriptures have taught us, that the original holy and happy condition of our race was essentially changed by the interference and crafty malignity of Satan. The necessity of the redemption of the Son of God stands inseparably connected with this. The atonement, the nucleus and centre of Christianity proper, is, in some important respects, a consequence of Satan's interference; or in other words it was rendered necessary by the tempter when he assailed our first parents. Nor is this all which may be truly and properly said in regard to this subject. If there are good angels, the voluntary ministers of God's will; or evil ones who are the executioners of his justice, or examples in their sufferings of the proper desert of sin; then, these facts are important to us, inasmuch as they cast light upon God's providential government of the world—a subject of deep interest to all moral and accountable beings.

"There is another point of view in which we may contemplate this subject. The Scriptures of the Old and New Testament are filled with passages that have respect to angels good or evil. Some of these passages are involved in not a little obscurity as presented to us, because we are not sufficiently familiar with the Hebrew modes of expression and thought to appreciate at once the full meaning of the sacred writers. If now it be true that a proper attention to the angelology of the Scriptures will help us to explain these, and especially in case it will render most of the obscure passages in question altogether intelligible, then attention to this subject cannot be fairly deemed unimportant."

Sufficient, it is presumed, has now been advanced, with the support of suitable authorities, fairly to ward off the unmeaning cavils of a determined or disguised scepticism, as well as abash the daring buffoonery* of a profane derision, to whose impiety the subject may be exposed, reinforced by the scoffing irreligion of those who ridicule, as superlatively absurd, the idea, and reject, alike, the internal and historic evidences of the veritable existence of immaterial beings, those real, though invisible instruments, who unceasingly carry forward the merciful protection, benevolent designs, mysterious operations and punitive judgments of the Supreme Governor of the moral, and the Almighty Creator and Upholder of the material universe ; inasmuch as the belief of their actuality is classed by them amongst those intangible objects of sense, whose nature and essence, mode or vehicle of communication with the inhabitants of this lower world are beyond the limited comprehension of the finite and degenerate faculties of the human mind† :—

* A medical satirist, indulging "in jestings not convenient," pertly inquired of me, "*If I had ever caught an angel and dissected him*"! Such an extraordinary and perplexing case of profound sagacity, brimstone wit and abstruse morality, unquestionably comes clear of all exceptions and demurrers, within the tenebrious jurisdiction of the Areopagus of Pandemonium.
G. C.

† Metaphysicians incline to universal skepticism, finding in the vast regions of philosophy we can, to adopt an homely phrase, scarcely see beyond our noses; have dwelt with something like exultation on the incapacity of man's intellect to overcome the difficulties which surround the most indubitable truths.—St. John, *Prelim. Disc. to Browne's Religio.*

despising the assistance and illumination of that faith* of celestial birth, by which alone they obtain a willing and beneficial reception into the intellect and heart; as she stands erect and unmoved, in the modest attitude of persuasive virtue,† upon the broad base of Inspiration, pointing, with

* Reason is a rebel unto Faith, and considers her propositions as absurd. There are a set of heads, that can credit the relations of mariners, yet question the testimonies of St. Paul; and peremptorily maintain the traditions of Ælian or Pliny, yet in histories of Scripture raise queries and objections; believing no more than they can parallel in human authors.—Sir Thomas Browne, *Religico Medicii.*

To believe only possibilities is not faith, but mere philosophy; many things are true in divinity which are neither inducible by reason, nor confirmable by sense; and many things in philosophy confirmable by sense, yet not inducible by reason.—Id, *Christian Morals.*

The skeptic denies the realities of faith, as the blind might deny the beauty of color, or the deaf the harmony of sound.—Slack, *Ministry of the Beautiful.*

The wisest of us, which is the holiest, see somewhat by the eye of faith—faith being the end of wisdom, the great lesson of the universe.—Id.

Faith only can raise us above this little daily life, and worldly business; that only can give the soul such a direction to higher things, and to objects and ideas which alone have value and importance,—and amidst the circling causes of appearances and events, is an immovable pole.—M. Von Humboldt, *Thoughts, &c., of a Statesman.*

Never yet did there exist a full faith on the divine word which did not expand the intellect, while it purified the heart; which did not multiply the aims and objects of the understanding, while it fixed and simplified those of the desires and passions.—Coleridge's *Aids to Reflection.*

Faith subsists in the synthesis of the Reason and the individual Will. Faith is the source and sum, the energy and principle of the fidelity of man to God, by the subordination of his human will, in all provinces of his nature, to his reason, as the sum of spiritual Truth, representing and manifesting the Will Divine.—Id, *Confessions of an Inquiring Mind.*

† Infidel France, in the height and frenzy of her barbarities and wickedness on throwing off the recognition of the divine authority of the Supreme and Moral Governor of the Universe, substituted as the idol of national worship a worse than pagan object in the gross exhibition of the nude prostitute of an egregiously depraved imagination as the unnatural, unphilosophical and lying representative of the "Goddess of Reason." For this, and other abominations, fearful jud ments are still suspended over her. G. C.

a serene and attractive countenance, to the "living oracles" of immutable and eternal Truth;—repudiating her sacred claims and glorious hopes, so vividly described in the sublime definition of an apostle, as "the confident expectation of things hoped for, the conviction of things which are not seen;" being the only rational medium by which *we understand the worlds were framed by the word of God, so that things which are seen were not made of those things which do appear;* whilst by the assurances of her enlightened apprehensions, she enables us to realize the amazing scenes of the invisible and eternal world,—to await, with patience, the predicted destruction of the present fabric of this terrestial globe,—to anticipate the anxious resurrection of the redeemed in Christ,—to be prepared for the awful solemnities of the final judgment,—to espy in the resplendent perspective of eternity, "the new heavens and new earth" of the upper kingdom and sanctuary, welcomed by the "innumerable company of angels" beatified in the unfading grandeur, inconceivable felicities and immortal youth of the heavenly state;

"—— Where, the blest immortals,
In love's pure beauty stand;
Alluring us, through faith's translucent portals,
Into the better land."

Such exalting beatitude, ethereal sympathies, and brilliant prospects constitute the imperishable inheritance of the children of Faith; confirmed by the cheering smiles of an approving providence, and the sustaining promises of Divine asssurance as they advance along the irradiated thoroughfare of obedience and holiness to the "pearly gates" of the city of the heavenly Jerusalem! During their career on earth, they are surrounded by the fiery "chariots" and "horsemen" of the host of spiritual and benignant agencies who take a deep interest in their welfare, strewing their path with the bright and fragrant flowers of peace and joy, and refreshing their fainting souls with the sweetest music of celestial melody. Wisely, therefore, does it behoove every tempted child of fallen Adam, to heed the momentous admonition of Lord Bacon, in the philosophy of his religion, "Not to seek the living among the dead, but, soberly, to render unto faith the things that are faith's."

By a different description of minds, or the lukewarm professors of a nominal Christianity, the discussion or expression of a belief, in the varied circumstances, in which the specific instrumentality of angelic beings has been, and is still employed, as connected with the believer's present welfare and eternal destiny, will be probably demurred to, on the shallow ground, that the subject is of too speculative a character to be of any essential service in promoting the practice of religious duties or stimulating to the more fervid exercises and frequent communion of devotional piety; but, on the contrary, rather to be discountenanced, from its obvious tendency to foster the fatal delusions of a fanatical presumption and forbidden curiosity, rashly intruding themselves into those arcana of nature and the secrets of the spiritual world, which it has pleased an all-wise God to conceal within the veil of impenetrable mysteries; yet, who, nevertheless, with an earnestness and devotion that would honor a martyr's zeal, and the characteristic inconsistencies of a superficial faith advocate and revel in the most startling absurdities of modern Mesmerism, the sublimated hallucinations of a frenzied Swedenborg, and the insidious neology and transcendentalism of the German school of Divinity.

To the multifarious and antagonistic demurrers of vain hypotheses, assuredly, it is not requisite to offer an extended reply; forasmuch as the authority and facts of the Bible which relate the embassy and appearance of angels, during the Adamic, patriarchal, and Mosaic economy—the fulfillment of prophecy when they announced the glad tidings of redemption for mankind—the corroborative declarations of the Great Teacher, whilst in the days of his humiliation He sojourned upon this earth, respecting them; together with that angelic succor which sympathized with the agonized Redeemer in the sorrowful garden of Gethsemane—their overpowering splendor which confounded the affrighted soldiery of the guarded sepulchre; and their gracious information to the desponding Magdalene, as she stood in the attitude and anguish of pensive grief, beside the virgin and vacated tomb of the risen Saviour—their frequent interposition chronicled in the history of the lives and missions of the apostles, in their behalf, as the first heralds of the gospel of salvation, and toward the martyred disciples of the Prince of Peace—their attendance and commission to execute the final dispensation of Jehovah, at the consummation of all things, on the exit of time, revealed in the awful disclosures of the apocalypse of St. John, fully answer, and solemnly rebuke the futility of all such opposing objections, and make manifest the serious temerity of such willful and questioning misbelief.*

With humble sincerity, it is hoped, in the ensuing pages, that no statement will be advanced, opinion adduced, or

* Purely speculative opinions are of little value except so far as they tend to promote the moral objects and a saving belief in the truth of Christianity.—FOSTER, *Christian Morals.*

We repel that philosophizing spirit which consists in resolving all the extraordinary phenomena recorded in the Bible into the mere effect of natural causes. Nothing can be more contemptible than such presumption of philosophy.—*Idem.*

speculation presented, of "private interpretation," that will not bear the sanction of Scripture warrant; the Bible being the only acknowledged standard of authority—the only infallible oracle of our faith. From this living fountain of Divine Truth, whose crystal stream issues from, and circulates around, the throne of inspiring wisdom and all-sufficient grace, would we draw pure, and copious draughts of spiritual knowledge.* With reverential gratitude would we heed the bright lamp of Inspiration, suspended by the golden chain of redeeming love, from the footstool of forgiving mercy, whose guiding and radiant beams, illumining the dreary passage of this wilderness-world, and gilding the gloomy entrance to the valley of the shadow of death, reflect their extended effulgence upon the beautiful portals of the everlasting gates of the celestial city, surrounded by the attendant and glittering train of the angelic messengers of the Majesty of heaven!

Happy, therefore, thrice happy they, who in the attainment of the divine science of spiritual discoveries applied this Holy Book as an effective repellant to the subtle magnetism of Satanic suggestions, and as the safest and most certain non-conductor of the latent electricity of those fallacious theories, too abundantly generated, in the charged batteries of the secret laboratory of a depraved heart and perverted reason!

Controlled by the foregoing determination, with the invoked guidance of the divine blessing, will we endeavor to prosecute an inquiry into the revealed history, exalted rank,

* It is an admirable observation closing an introduction pointing out the pre-requisites for the correct composition and essential enjoyment of Divine Poetry, prefixed to the poem on the Messiah by the devout, though too rhapsodical, Klopstock: "It requires more than the knowledge of mythology to understand and feel the beauties of Homer, and much more than philosophy to relish the sublime graces of Revelation."—G. C.

transcendent attributes, moral virtues, attractive lineaments, and heavenly habitudes of those noble and illustrious beings —*the ministering and adoring angels of Jehovah.*

We pause to insert the following extracts from the notes of Dr. George Townsend's *Historical and Chronological Arrangement of the New Testament*, a work preeminently deserving of a place in every Christian's library; and which cannot but be read with intense interest and persuasive impression.

"The doctrine of the ministry of angels, so much esteemed by the primitive church, as well as by the most eminent and pious Christians of all ages, has now become one of those which, without any one well-founded argument, is to be reasoned away. The repeated appearance of angels, both in the old and new dispensations, seems designed to point out to us the near, though mysterious, connection of the invisible state with that which we now inhabit. And what can be more consolatory to the believer, than the idea, corroborated by numerous passages in the Scripture, than the belief, that the angels of heaven are around us, the ministering spirits of God for our good, watching over us, and fulfilling the wisdom of his providence! Why should the opinion be disclaimed? Angels were present at the creation; they have been repeatedly manifested to man. To Isaiah the seraphim appeared veiling their faces with wide-spreading wings. The form that was visible to Ezekiel had the semblance of a lambent flame, enveloping what seemed its body. To the women they appeared in shining garments, and to the keepers of the sepulchre as lightning, with raiment white as snow. They are the happy possessors of that blessedness to which the spirits of the departed hope to be admitted. And they shall be again visible in their thousands of thousands at that magnificent and glorious triumph, when the Ancient of Days shall sit on the throne of his glory, and the assembled universe be summoned before his high tribunal. Is it impossible, then, that they are invisible yet efficient agents in many of those innumerable events which are attended with moral and religious benefit to individuals and to the world; which are but too generally ascribed to incidental circumstances, or the well-laid plans of human policy?

"The soul of man is gifted with powers and properties which are distinct from the human body, and which it possesses in common with superior beings. I cannot, therefore, believe that idea to be irrational, which represents the manner of our present union with the invisible world by the following ingenious and curious image. Suppose a number of lighted lamps were placed in a room, one of which only was covered with an earthen vessel; the lamp so encumbered, as soon as the covering was either broken or removed, would find itself in the same state and condition with the other lamps. So it may be with the accountable spirit of man. The earthen vessel, the body, may be broken by violence, or silently destroyed by sickness or age, but, as soon as the veil or the covering of the body is removed, the unfettered spirit finds itself the companion of kindred spirits, which, though unseen, are continually surrounding it. The time is not far hence, when we shall know even as we are known; in the meantime, the very attempt to speculate on these things elevates and purifies the mind.

"The German commentators of the self-named liberal class, en deavor to explain away every miracle recorded in the New Testament, by representing them as natural events which have only been considered as miraculous by the misapprehending of the Hebraisms of the inspired writers.

"The explanation of Hezelius is so singular, that it may appear doubtful whether in his eagerness to remove the opinions of a miraculous interference by an angel, he does not establish a still greater miracle. He thinks that a flash of lightning penetrated the prison in the night, and melted the chains of St. Peter without injuring him. The apostle rose up, and saw the soldiers who guarded him struck prostrate to the ground by the force of the lightning. He passed them as if led by the flash of lightning, and escaped from the prison before he perceived that he had been liberated by the providence of God. So completely, however, has the skeptical philosophy of the day pervaded society, that even among professed Christians, he would now be esteemed a visionary, who should venture to declare his belief in this most favorite tenet of the ancient church. The early fathers regarded the ministry of angels as a consoling and beautiful doctrine, and so much at that time was it held in veneration, that the founders of Christianity cautioned their early converts against permitting their reverence to degenerate into adoration. We now go to the opposite extreme, and seldom think of their existence; yet what is to be found in this belief, even if the Scriptures had not revealed it, which is contrary to our reason? We believe in our own existence, and in the existence of God; is it utterly improbable, then, that between us, who are so inferior, and the Creator, who is so wonderful and incomprehensible, infinite gradations of beings should exist, some of whom are employed in executing the will of the Deity toward finite creatures? Does not God act even by human means in the visible government of the affairs of the earth? what absurdity, then, can be discovered in the opinion that the spiritual nature of man should be under the guardianship of spiritual beings? This, in fact, was a doctrine universally received till it became perverted and degraded by vain and idle speculations,—till it became so encumbered with absurdities, that the belief itself was rejected. Some writers on this subject went so far as to imagine they could ascertain the orders of a hierarchy, and could even assert the numbers of each rank. Others changed the office and ministry of angels, investing them with independent control over the works of God, an opinion strongly and justly reprobated by the most eminent authorities. And because in the original Hebrew that which executes the will of the

Deity is sometimes called an "angel," whether it be winds or storms, fire or air; many again have transformed the angels in the Old Testament into obedient elements, accomplishing the designs of Providence, according to which hypothesis, the aged patriarch must have prayed that the blessings of an element might descend upon his grandchildren. The Messiah must have been created a little lower than the winds and the floods, who, in like manner, were commanded to worship him; and, again, when the superiority of Christ is declared, the passage must be rendered: 'To which of the elements said he at any time, sit thou on my right hand, until I make thy foes my footstool.' Leaving all such fantastic and unreasonable interpretations out of the question, let us turn to that interpretation of Scripture on this point, which has been acknowledged by all classes and divisions of Christians, from the time of the apostles to the present day. From the evidence of Revelation, we have grounds for believing that angels are spirits superior to mankind, some of whom have lost, while others have preserved, the state of happiness in which they were primarily created, and that these are now opposed to each other. With the precise cause of the fall of the evil angels we are not made acquainted. We only know that they retain the remembrance of their original condition; that they are powerful, though under restraint; that gradations of superiority and influence exist among them; that they acknowledge a superior head, and that they are destined to eternal punishment.

"Of good angels, we learn, that they continue in their primeval dignity. They are endued with great power, and because they are employed in the constant execution of the decrees of Providence, they have received the name of messengers or angels. They are called the armies and the hosts of heaven; in innumerable companies they surround the throne of Deity; they are made partakers of his glory and rejoice to fulfill his will.

"Their office, as ministering angels to the sincere and accepted worshippers of our common God, is more fully and accurately related. Through the whole volume of revelation we read of the agency of superior beings in the affairs of mankind. They were stationed at the tree of life in paradise. In Jacob's vision of the ladder, they are represented as ascending and descending upon earth. They appeared to the patriarchs, to Abraham, to Lot, to Jacob, and they were made alike the ministers of both the vengeance and mercy of God. They were intrusted with the destruction of the cities of the plain. 'And the angel of the Lord went out and smote in the camp of Sennacherib a hundred and fourscore and five thousand.' (2 Kings xix : 35.) God sent an angel to Jerusalem to destroy it—who was seen between the earth and the heaven, having a drawn sword in his hand, stretched out over Jerusalem. In the New Testament, they announced the birth of Christ, and of his forerunner; they became visible to the shepherds, and proclaimed the glad tidings of salvation to the senseless world. They are interested for, and sympathize with, man; for 'there is joy in heaven over one sinner that repenteth.' They were the watchful and anxious attendants of Christ in his human nature. They ministered to him after his triumph in the wilderness and his agony in the garden. As they announced his birth, so also they proclaimed his resurrection, his ascension, and his future return to judgment. They were made the spiritual means of communication between God and man. They were the divine witnesses of the whole scheme of Redemption. By an angel Joseph was warned to flee into Egypt. (Matt. ii. 13.) By an angel Cornelius was directed to the house of Peter. (Acts x. 3–22.) By an angel that apostle was released from prison. And by the ministry of an angel were signified to St. John those things which should be hereafter.. In his last and mysterions revelation, the agency of superior beings is uniformly asserted, and they are represented as fulfilling the most solemn decrees of omnipotence. They are represented as standing on the four corners of the earth, as having the seal of the living God, as offering on the golden altar the incense and prayers of the saints, as holding the key of the bottomless pit; and as executing the vengeance of God upon the visible creation, and upon all those who have not the seal of God upon their foreheads; all which, though metaphorical expressions, imply the probable agency of these invisible beings in the affairs of the world. And when time shall be no more, these holy beings who have sympathized with man here, and been witnesses of his actions, and the infinite mercies of his almighty Creator and Redeemer, will be the accusing or approving spectators of the sentence passed upon him in eternity; for our Savior has expressly declared, that 'whosoever shall confess me before men, him shall the Son of Man also confess before the angels of God. But he that denied me before men shall be denied before the angels of God."—Dr. Townsend, *Notes on the New Testament.*

HISTORY AND NATURE.

UPON the threshold of our intricate yet interesting and delectable subject,—approved by the united testimony and sanction of Revelation, Religion and Reason, that divinely-appointed triumvirate for the moral and mental government of man's social and spiritual nature,—would we conspicuously inscribe the Christian sentiment and judicious admonition of Lord Lyttleton, that, "God is pleased, in this present world, to appropriate and proportion our knowledge, not to our pride and curiosity, but to our wants and condition."

The peculiar brevity, transcendent simplicity and instructive reserve which distinguish and dignify the Mosaic narrative, in reference to the primordial origin of all existences, and the vivific operations of the workmanship of omnipotence in the production of this material world, associated with the incorporeal and unseen presence of the subtle vitalities of spiritual beings, plainly and evidently declare, that "it is the glory of God,* to whom belong secret things,† in their profound and fathomless depth,‡ to conceal" from the unhallowed temerity of mortal intrusion, those incomprehensible mysteries which envelope the elemental principles of organic life, and the essential attributes of spiritual essences! For, notwithstanding the remarkable endow-

* Proverbs xxv. 2. † Deut. xxix. 29. ‡ Romans xi. 33.

ments and capacious faculties of the human intellect, is not the imperfect attainment of our knowledge, in connection with the sublime and astonishing exhibitions of divine power, and benevolence and wisdom, admirably calculated to promote a beneficial tendency upon the mind, with respect to the fear, and homage and adoration due towards, and the sense of our entire dependence upon, the constant care and protection, as well as providential supplies of the almighty Creator of "the heaven and the earth"? True! with the first elements, the bases, the essences, of matter and spirit, and all things contained in the circumference or presented in the phenomena of being, the prying attempts of the most penetrative, enlarged and gifted understandings cannot cope. With their properties, qualities, combinations, affinities, component parts, specific influences and peculiar effects, however, much has been recently elicited by the aid, and brought to light in the surprising and splendid discoveries of the searching science of modern chemistry; but, beyond this separating line of the demarcation of experience and knowledge, Reason is strictly forbidden to trespass, though to Faith, in the joyous hope of a believing expectation, guided by the gracious disclosures of Inspiration, she is encouraged to a nearer and more anxious approach to the Supreme Cause of all causes.

This sacred and majestic laconicism is likewise applied to the early history and society of mankind, giving but very slight information to what extent the arts and sciences flourished in primeval time; and withholding any very minute description of those excessive vices and artificial refinements of wickedness which provoked the awful punishment of divine displeasure, resulting in that watery destruction which overwhelmed and swept the entire antediluvian race from off the surface of the polluted earth! So, with regard to the inherent principles and hidden workings of nature in the curious machinery of the material universe, the invisible inhabitants and the secret agencies of the ethereal world, the communications of the Bible are circumscribed by divine " wisdom and knowledge," in correspondence with the necessities and limitation* of our finite faculties, mental apprehensions, moral condition, immortal desires and eternal destiny, either in the blissful perfection of Heaven, or the dolorous perdition of Hell!

The unevangelical disquisitions of some theologico-geologists to quadrate the discoveries of modern science with the infallible truth of God's word and the requisitions of a divine faith, it is to be apprehended, are calculated to produce a most unfavorable tendency on the proud and unenlightened mind. The observation of Dr. Anderson, in his recently published work entitled *The Course of Creation*, receives its own approbation. " The wisdom of man will be confounded when it tries to fathom the methods and devices of the divine Artificer in originating his works. His safety will often be in distrusting his own understanding, in not magnifying overmuch the ingenuity of his own speculations; and in sometimes believing that even science will be exalted by approximating to, rather than departing from, the literalities of Scripture."

Indeed, it is well for Philosophy to kindle her torch, and Reason to light her lamp, at the pure and brilliant flame, which ever burns with a steady and undiminished lustre upon the ethereal altar of the sacred temple of immutable and

* " We know but little of the invisible world, or of the manner in which the disembodied spirit continues to exist; our understanding and our apprehension are so limited in this stage of existence, that we cannot comprehend one-half of those truths which both our senses, our reason and revelation compel us to approve."—Dr. Geo. Townsend, *Note on Witch of Endor.*

eternal Truth. The mind but once convinced upon the testimony of authentic history, and other demonstrative evidences of the inspiration of the Bible, whatever difficulties may arise, or apparent contradictions may present themselves to its oracular declarations, in the recent discoveries of science, must not be allowed, even, for a single moment, to interfere with the valid and established claims of a divine Revelation. The obscure province of Reason and the bright regions of Faith are too remote, and the specific objects of the one, are too distinct and dissimilar from the heavenly aspirations of the other, and a holy faith can never succumb to the vain and haughty pretensions of the former, because, in her loftiest altitude she will never be able to reach the sublimities of the latter. The very instant that reason is permitted the ascendant, Faith, also, loses her virtue, her validity, her essence,—being at once lifeless, and bereft of her vitality upon the withdrawn favor and protection of her offended God. To suppose a Revelation devoid of mysteries, involves the paradox of identifying the temple without its presiding God. Neither can I justify the bold assertion of the pompous philosophy of our quaint physician, in his Religio Medici, *that in his religion there were not impossibilities* (incomprehensibilities) *enough to satisfy his faith :* when I reflect upon the incomprehensibility of the self-existent Jehovah, who inhabiteth the immensurability of the circle of eternity, whose presence fills all space ; at whose fiat came forth, "out of nothing," the beautiful fabric of this fair creation,—the mysterious hypostasis of the holy trinity of the Godhead,—the permitted introduction of moral evil into this sin-disordered world,—the prophetic incarnation of Deity to impart validity to the atonement of the Redemption, in the substitution of the innocent for the guilty, typified in the sanguinary rites of the Aaronic priesthood and ceremonial, to answer the demands of moral law and harmonize the essential attributes of the divine character,—the wonderful and needful operations of the Holy Ghost, in Regeneration, by the constant descent of the enlightening, consolatory, and sanctifying influences of the promised Paraclete,—the revealed resurrection of the body, having been resolved into its original dust, to receive the irreversible sentence of its destiny,—during the transforming and purifying process of the conflagrant flames of a blazing universe,—in the presence of the august assize of an assembled world, before the solemn tribunal of the omniscient scrutiny and righteous decision of the Angel-Jehovah Judge, upon the indictment of every thought, imagination and action,—every idle word and vain conversation, misapplied time and misimproved means of grace;—in this awful whirlwind of mental emotion and spiritual consternation, "the small still voice" of Faith alone restores the tranquillity of my mind, and sustains my overwhelmed and fainting spirit; whilst the thrilling apostrophe of St. Paul, "O the depth of the riches both of the wisdom and knowledge of God! how unsearchable are his judgments, and his ways past finding out!" suits my agitated feelings best, elevates me, awhile, to the "third heaven" of his supercelestial vision, or supports me in the contemplation of his unutterable spiritual experience; arresting the erratic inclinations of unbelief, and bidding her return, from whence she had wandered, to the orbit of faith in the solar system of Christianity, obscured in the penumbra of doubts, and amidst the gravitating influences of centrifugal temptation, which, but for the polarizing attractions of the MYSTIC CROSS, would draw my oscillating soul away, from completing the epicycle of Christian duties and moral responsibilities and conscientious monitions belonging to that nebulous sphere in which Providence has appointed me to revolve, as my terrestrial axis.*

Provided our investigations are conducted with the obedience of a biblical faith, and the humility of a reverential submission, in the reception of the revealed verities enshrined in the sanctuary of inspired truth; it is, certainly, the privileged duty and peculiar delight of the enlightened mind and sanctified heart, soberly to examine the sacred and mysterious chain of divine operations which link, in harmonious union, the wonderful economy of nature, the intercommunication of spiritual and heavenly intelligences, with the in-

* I believe that our estranged and divided ashes shall unite again; that our separated dust, after so many pilgrimages and transformations into parts of minerals, plants, animals, elements—shall, at the voice of God, return into their primitive shapes, and join again to make up their primary and predestinated forms. As at the creation, there was a separation of that confused mass into its pieces; so at the destruction thereof there shall be a separation into its distinct individuals. As, at the creation of the world, all the distinct species which we behold lay involved in one mass, till the fruitful voice of God, separated the united multitude into several species; so at the last day, when these corrupted relics shall be scattered in the wilderness of forms, and seem to have forgot their proper habits, God, by a powerful voice, shall command them back again into their proper shapes, and call them out by their single individuals; then shall appear the fertility of Adam, and the magic of that sperm that hath dilated into so many millions. I have often beheld as a miracle that artificial resurrection and revivification of mercury, how being mortified into a thousand shapes, it assumes again its own and returns into its numerical self. This is that mystical philosophy from whence no true scholar becomes an atheist; but from the visible effects of nature grows up a real divine; and beholds, not in a dream, as Ezekiel, but in an ocular and a visible object, the types of his resurrection.

The life and spirit of all our actions is the resurrection, and a stable apprehension that our ashes shall enjoy the fruit of our pious endeavors; without this, all religion is a fallacy, and those impieties of Lucian, Euripides, and Julian, are no blasphemies, but sensible verities, and atheists have been the only philosophers. How shall the dead rise is no question of my faith; to believe only possibilities is not faith but mere philosophy.—Sir T. Browne.

scrutable scheme and saving dispensation of Redemption. In the expansive and luminous firmament of celestial realities, the cheering and radiant doctrine of the appointed ministration and particular offices of unfallen angels, shines forth with a most vivid, attractive and transparent brightness; assuring us that the invisible and commissioned cohorts which attend and surround the sapphire throne of Deity are constantly dispatched,—passing the flaming boundaries of their own locality and habitation in the distant regions of ethereal glory,—and especially intrusted with benevolent embassies of love and mercy, grace and consolation to those "who shall be their heirs of salvation"!

Postponing, to the sequel, the presentation of a variety of relevant observations and irrefragable proofs demonstrative of the Inspiration of the Bible, we assume the rationality and necessity of yielding an implicit belief to the infallible truth of Divine testimony, as the only safe and solid basis of unimpeachable authority, upon which to establish the doctrine and dogma of the real existence and ordained ministration of angelic intelligences; illustrated by those appropriate and convincing facts recorded in the sacred Scriptures, which will exhibit to prominent view, the superlative excellence, supreme importance, and delightful character of the subject that we now advance to canvass in diametrical opposition to those impious negations,—originating in the natural enmity of the human heart toward a holy and a righteous God, and the stiff-necked pride of the perverted intellect, as regards the revealed method of a sinner's acceptance in the sight of Jehovah, realized in the atonement, the mediation, and the economy of salvation,—which have affronted the declarations of Holy Writ, and the faith and hopes of Christianity from the days of the disputatious and scornful Jews of the Sadducean sect, down to the present time of the pertinacious and infidel deism of modern materiality, or the profligate pretensions of a profane mesmerism; disguised in the *protean* assumptions of a pseudo-philosophy, as presented in the multiform appearances of metamorphizing theories, chameleon beliefs, atheistical principles, practice and systems.*

Amidst the chaos of the phantasmagoric fictions and discordant speculations,—evidently based upon distorted traditions of the Mosaic narrative of the *genesis* or origin of the solar system of the visible world,—which have disfigured the pagan descriptions of the cosmogony of this earth, together with those philosophic theories upon whose unsubstantial foundations are constructed the mythological theogonies of the more polished and enlightened nations of Greece and Rome;

* No savage worshipping the most preposterous idol, ever believed greater absurdities, than a modern sceptic, who makes his small modicum of reason the standard by which to measure the boundless universe. Christianity in the past was not limited by eighteen and a half centuries, which we call its era. It illumined the earliest ages, it burned brighter in the soul of Plato, than in most minds now. The good and wise of all ages have been of one faith. The loftiest truth is never circumscribed by man's intellect. The deepest truths of religion and philosophy are made known to us by appeals to our sympathy.

Nature will not allow man to intellectualize himself into infidelity. Every grand prospect, every burst of melody carries conviction to the heart that truth is eternal, and man destined for immortality.

Let the keenest intellect soar to its sublimest heights, and when it has found some great truth among the loftiest Alps of reason, if it sink deep into the heart of the discoverer, he will be able to bring it home to the hearts of others, not as a discovery of science, but as a verity of faith.—SLACK, *Ministry of the Beautiful.*

To thoughtful observators the whole world is a phylactery, and everything we see an item of the wisdom, power, or goodness of God. Words cannot exceed, when they cannot express enough. Even the most winged thoughts fall at the setting out, and reach not the portal of Divinity.—SIR THOMAS BROWNE, *passim.*

Serrell & Perkins, No. 75 Nassau. Drawn by Perkins

THE CREATION,

Celebrated by Angels.

the only clear ray of light and information which Jehovah has condescended to vouchsafe, respecting the creation of spiritual and angelic beings is preserved and conveyed through the medium of that most ancient and authentic of all books,—whose supposed author was the Jewish lawgiver—the book of Job, where in the seventh verse of the thirty-eighth chapter, they are represented, under the appellation and character of the *sons of God*, as celebrating the stupendous and magnificent display of the power, and benevolence, and wisdom of the Deity, in the glorious exhibition and appearance of the visible and various works of a completed universe, having received the complacent approbation of the Almighty Architect, as they sprang up innumerable, under the omnific influence of the uncreated beam of the Sun of Righteousness, along the shining banks of the crystal river of life, on the bright morning of everlasting day, instinct with the unfading youth of immortality!—

> "From multitudes of angels, with a shout
> Loud as from numbers without number, burst
> Forth blessed voices, uttering joy.
> * * * * * *
> All these with ceaseless praise his works behold
> Both day and night—
> Singing their great Creator."—Milton.

Beyond the boundary line of inspired information, with which divine wisdom, as it were, has fenced in, this sublime and inscrutable subject, it is vain for mortal intellect to try to traverse, by attempting the irrational, presumptuous, and indevout endeavor to penetrate through the veil of the intentional silence of unrevealed mystery—for as much as any additional knowledge, if it were attainable by the unaided effort of our finite comprehension, we cannot perceive, would either promote our happiness, deepen our penitence, advance our holiness, establish our faith, superinduce greater spirituality of mind, or more effectually secure our salvation; whilst from the reserve of the Mosaic account, which makes no mention of angels, the design of the Jewish lawgiver, is, therefore, obviously intended to prefer a practical confutation of the ancient and prevalent idolatry of Sabeism, or the worship of sun, moon, and stars, evidently referred to by the venerable and renowned patriarch Job: *If I beheld the sun when it shined, or the moon walking in brightness; and my heart hath been secretly enticed, or my mouth kissed my hand.*

Equally futile, fabulous and fantastical are those speculations which have been indulged to adjust and determine the precise period of the creation of angelical intelligences; for some, in the foolishness of their mental conception, aiming "to be wise above what is written," have supposed they were created on the same day with the "heaven and the earth;" implying that Moses included them under those terms, in the declaration that *In the beginning God created the heavens and the earth;* others, that he intended them under the epithet light,* which God created on the first day, comprehending under that expression both angels

* When light was commanded, then were the angels created. That when God separated the light from the darkness, by that disunion, is to be understood, the dreadful and terrible judgments of God against the Devil and his angels, who, from being angels of light, by reason of their pride and rebellion were converted into Devils of darkness. At the same time, the matter of the four elements with spiritual creatures was produced, viz., those spiritual and corporeal bodies which were created in the beginning of time. Life, wisdom, and Light designate the angels who are said to have been first created, by virtue of their excellency and dignity, and especially ordained to contemplate, praise, and magnify Almighty God's liberality and goodness throughout all generations.

It was a beautiful superstition,—perhaps a true one—that of the luminous nature of the soul. Light with its kindred agencies is the most spiritual of physical existences.—SLACK, *Ministry of the Beautiful.*

and souls; and also, that the soul of Adam was created before his body, like as the angels were, and afterwards breathed and divinely infused into him.

The Hebrews, likewise, held the conceit, that they were created on the second day; and that God consulted them, saying, *Let us make man in our image, after our likeness;* others, again, maintain the opinion that they were called into existence on the fifth day.* Origen, with some of the Greek and Latin fathers, believed they were created before the formation of the world, and which sentiment they think derives some countenance from that passage of Job: *Where wast thou when I laid the foundations of the earth?"*

Plato† considered the angels as the first born and first fruits of God's creation; upon the hypothesis that spiritual beings preceded, in priority of existence, corporeal bodies, and that the Great Parent employed them as ministers for the procreation of others. Aristotle maintains a similar opinion, speaking of them as the original movers of the universe; holding, also, the notion that the heavens were eternal, together with all empyreal souls and intelligent substances.

The supposition has likewise been favored by some modern divines, that angelic beings were created a long period antece-

* But to determine the day and year of this time (creation of angels) is not only convincible and statute madness, but also manifest impiety.—Sir Thomas Browne.

† Pythagoras used to entertain his disciples with stating the various generations and transmigrations his soul had undergone before it entered his body, borrowing his notion of its preexistence from the east, and its gradual descent into this dark and material world from that region of spirits and light which it is supposed to have once inhabited, and to which, after a long lapse of purification, it will return. This belief, under various symbolical forms, may be easily traced in almost all the oriental theogonies.

dent to the formation of our earth,—a series of ages before the construction of the solar system; but at what era in the mysterious revolutions and immeasurable cycles of eternity, Divine Revelation has not disclosed; suggesting the idea that the Supreme Being of infinite power, wisdom, and benevolence, would not have remained inactive during this incomprehensible interval of illimitable space, leaving so vast and inert a vacuum in the immeasurable regions of his boundless kingdom, to be unoccupied by intelligent creatures, as inconsistent with the operations and character of the omnipotent Creator, and as tending to reflect discredit upon the unimpeachable and living oracles of God.

Modern, like ancient Sådducism, impiously denies the reality of the existence of angels, arising, forsooth, from the invisibility of their intangibile nature; a negative which, upon this absurd hypothesis, is likewise applicable with awful temerity, to the irrefragable truth of the very existence of the Deity, whose ubiquity we cannot apprehend, either by our visual organs or mental faculties; whilst the demonstrative refutation of St. Paul declares: *That the invisible things of him from the creation of the world are clearly seen, being understood by those things that are made, even his eternal power and Godhead; so that they are without excuse.* The pointed reproof of our Saviour—in addition to his other declarations,—to the affrighted and disbelieving disciples, confirms the same position, *a spirit has not flesh and bones as ye see me have.* The belief of their existence, however, has prevailed from the earliest period of mankind, conveyed through the medium of traditions which have long been corrupted alike by Jewish Rabbies and learned pagans. The imaginary beings which human fancy has offered to our notice, have been but the superior representations of our race under the name of *Genii*, *Demons*, *Dii*, or gods of the ancient eastern sages, down to the *Fairies*, *Sylphs* and *Elves* of modern credulity; invested by a disordered and impure imagination, with corresponding powers and attributes, dispositions and demeanor; in striking contrast to the essential particulars, extraordinary faculties, and preeminent attributes which adorn and constitute those transcendently pure, benevolent, illustrious and celestial beings described, in the sacred volume, as the constant attendants and commissioned ambassadors, and selected agents appointed to execute the gracious and punitive purposes of Omnipotence upon the throne of universal empire.

The positive existence, the ready attendance, and protective guardianship of angelical intelligences was frequently alluded to, by the Messiah, during the humiliation of his terrestrial sojourn, as well as corroborated by the declarations and visions of the apostles and St. John the Revelator. The Old and New Testament abound with references to the visible appearances and actual interpositions of angels. It was a cherub, armed with a flaming sword, that was stationed as a guard at the entrance of the terrestrial paradise—angels appeared to Abraham, in his tent—to Lot, and forewarned him of the impending destruction of Sodom and Gomorrah, those guilty and devoted cities of the plain—it was an angel that pointed out to the disconsolate Hagar, the spring of water, to relieve the extremity of her thirst—they were angels that ascended and descended on the mystic ladder for the encouragement of the patriarch Jacob—it was an angel which opposed Balaam, in his wicked career and avaricious project, threatening to slay his she-ass which found a rebuking tongue to resent the prophet's cruelty—the archangel Gabriel visited Daniel, in Babylon, appeared to Zechariah, the father of John the Baptist, the forerunner of the Redeemer of the world, and also announced to Mary, the consecrated virgin-mother, the birth of the long expected Messiah, as well as his nativity to the shepherds, who were peacefully attending their flocks—and also probably pointed out the phenomenon of a particular star, which directed the Magi to the manger which cradled the infant Christ, at Bethlehem—it was an angel that warned Joseph, in a dream, to retire, with the holy family, into Egypt, and escape the barbarous stratagem of Herod—they were angels who attended upon our Saviour after his temptation in the wilderness; and an angel descended from heaven to administer to his agony in the sorrowful garden of Olives; and after his resurrection, angels appeared to the holy women who came to the consecrated tomb to embalm his body—angels were seen by the apostles after the Resurrection of the ascended Saviour—the angel of the Lord delivered the apostles from their prisons—the law was given to Moses by the ministration of angels; but without extending the enumeration, evidential of their real existence and diverse operations as revealed in the Scriptures, we will only add, that the belief of this attractive doctrine has obtained amongst the Mahometans, Greeks, Romans, and other nations of the earth,—under every imaginable form, use, and worship, in strict correspondence with the respective systems of their senseless idolatry, the theories of their pseudo-philosophy, and the delusions of their debasing superstitions.

We have now reached a point in our reflections, from which we shall not deem it expedient to venture into the imaginative and hazardous regions of abstract speculations, and which has provoked the curiosity, taxed the ingenuity, and exercised the girded efforts of the loftiest intellects, whether in the character of the philosopher, the metaphysician, the moralist, or the theologian; and therefore, it behooves us to observe the utmost Christian circumspection while treating of the supposed constitution of angelical natures, in reference either to the immateriality or corporeity of their subsistence, the mode of their intercourse with, or those vehicles of communication in which they have appeared to the apostate inhabitants of this sublunary planet, lest in the daring excursion beyond the precincts of biblical ethics and Scriptural information, we incur the analogical penalty of that reiterated interdict which guarded the sanctified Mount, upon the delivery and enactment of the Decalogue, from the unhallowed gaze and forbidden intrusion of the children of Israel, as it trembled amidst the thunder and lightnings, the smoking cloud and reverberating voice of the trumpet waxing louder and louder, increasing the terrific solemnity of the distant and august scenery which glorified the sacred and awful summit of Sinai!

A very brief survey, then, of the opinions which have been entertained on this difficult subject will be sufficient; as any ineffective attempt at critical inquiries on so abstruse a matter would be alike vain, dissatisfactory and unprofitable.

The ancient philosophers, including the peripatetics of the Grecian schools, considered that angels or demons (for these appellatives were employed synonymously) were composed of two qualities, corporeal and incorporeal, corresponding to the body and soul of man; the only difference being, that the souls of angels never descended into such gross and terrestrial bodies as the human, and are invariably invested with aerial or fiery substances; classifying their genii into *demons*, *angels* and *heroes*, of which distinction, those were esteemed angels whose appropriate sphere was placed nearest to the heavens: others, giving them also, a double substance—igneous and ethereal—slightly varying in their representations, viz., that by their empyreal essence they were enabled to contemplate God, but by their material element they became visible to men.

The fathers of the church supposed angels to be possessed of subtle, ethereal, and aerial bodies, making this difference between good and evil angels, to wit, the former being clothed with a radiant splendor, and the latter with a dark fuliginous obscurity—the good angels being constituted of transcendently refined substances which always accompanied their development to mortal vision, and which they believe was only the phlogistic or ethereal essence belonging to their nature.*

The specific nature of angels, whether pure spirits divested of all corporeal vehicles, has been a controversy of long standing, not only among the ancient philosophers, but of the Christian fathers; whilst Divine Revelation has maintained an admonitory silence upon this mysterious theme of human investigation. The nature of angels is expressed in the Scriptures by the epithet "*spirit.*" They are of a *spiritual* nature, not compounded of parts as bodies are,

* Angelical bodies send forth rays and splendors such as would dazzle mortal eyes, and cannot be borne by them; but the demoniac body, though it seemeth to have been such once (from Isaias calling him, that fell from heaven, Lucifer), yet it is now dark and obscure, foul and squalid, and grievous to behold, it being deprived of its cognate light and beauty. Again, the angelical body is so devoid of gross matter that it can pass through any solid thing, it being indeed more impassible than the sunbeams; for though these can permeate pellucid bodies, yet are they hindered by earthy and opaque substances by which they are refracted; whereas the angelical body is such, as that there is nothing that can resist or exclude it.—Cudworth, *Intellectual System.*

The angels are not subject to any change, saith St. Bazil, for amongst them there is neither child, young man nor old; but in the same state in which they were created in the beginning, in that they everlastingly remain; the substance of their proper nature being permanent in simplicity and immutability. By nature angels were created mutable, but by contemplation immutable.—Heywood, *Hierarchie.*

and yet they are not simple and uncompounded as God is, who is a spirit.

To the human mind it is difficult to entertain a proper perception of a spirit. Even in our endeavors to impart our individual and inadequate conceptions of the varied operations of Deity, we are confined to the imperfect medium of anthropological expressions; whilst the apostle Paul, in his striking illustrations of the doctrine of the resurrection, drawn from the analogies of the material world, makes the distinction of terrestrial and celestial bodies :—*There is a natural body and there is a spiritual body.* " From angels being called spirits, it is not necessary to conclude that they have no body, nor material frame at all ; to be entirely immaterial, is probably peculiar to the Father of spirits, to whom we cannot attribute a body without impiety, and involving ourselves in absurdities. When the term spirit is employed to denote the angelical nature, it is most natural to take it in a lower sense, to denote their exemption from those gross and earthly bodies which the inhabitants of this world possess. Their bodies are spiritual bodies, "for there is a natural body, and there is a spiritual body;" the latter of which the righteous are to receive at the resurrection, who are to be made equal to the angels.

" Whether there is in the universe any being purely spiritual, and perfectly detached from matter, except the Great Supreme, is a question, perhaps, not easy to solve, nor is the solution of it at all essential to our present inquiry. ' God is a spirit,' and we cannot conceive of any portion or modification of matter, as entering into his essence without being betrayed into contradiction and absurdity. In regard to every other class of being, it is conjectured, that the thinking principle is united to some corporeal vehicle through which it derives its perceptions, and by which it operates;

while perfect spirituality, utterly separate from matter in any possible state, is the exclusive attribute of the Deity. When angels are spoken of as spirits, this mode of expression may possibly denote no more, than that the material vehicle with which they are united, is of a nature highly subtle and refined, at a great remove from flesh and blood which compose the bodily frame. Who will presume to set limits to creative power in the organization of matter, or affirm that it is not, in the hand of its Author, susceptible of a refinement which shall completely exclude it from the notice of the senses? He who compares the subtlety and velocity of light with grosser substances, which are found in the material system, will be reluctant to assign any bounds to the possible modification of matter, much more affirm there can be none beyond the comprehension of our corporeal organs."*

But if in physics there are unfathomable depths, is it not reasonable to expect that in the obscure regions of ontological investigations—in that science particularly conversant with God and spiritual essences, that we shall be stopped, at almost every step, by phenomena beyond our comprehension? "It is childish," remarks John Foster, "to babble about the "impossibilities of religion," until we understand the entire scheme of the intellectual and physical world—until we can explain who we are, whence we are, and wherefore we are. Until we know what laws govern the elements, mould them into sentient forms, and again after a season, dissolve those warm and beautiful structures, and give their dust to the wind. Until we can decide the nature of that mysterious principle which we term life, discover how in some it becomes a fountain of motion, in others, of passion, intellectuality, and all those marvellous phenomena which we ob-

* Robert Hall.

serve in ourselves and others. Until we can determine in what consists the invisible chain we denominate *affection*, that binds us not only to the living but to the dead, to forms long passed away, to minds translated beyond the stars, and the utmost bourne of the visible creation. Until then, let us be humble, nor mutter even in the secrecy of our hearts; considering how very imperfectly we comprehend even our present existence, notwithstanding our experience of, and intimacy with it. Diminutive as we are, we nevertheless involve a world of mystery.* The acutest, the profoundest investigations have been baffled. What is life? How continued? and if we had the means of pursuing the inquiry into our future state, it may be presumed, that every mystery would be aggravated. It is true that the 'Great Revealer of secrets' could have told us by revelation some things respecting the future state which we might in some superficial general manner have understood. For example: whether the disembodied spirit will have a material vehicle? whether there will be a distinct formal process of judgment on it at death? In what place it shall dwell till the resur-

* There is surely a piece of divinity in us, something that was before the elements, and owes no homage to the sun. Nature tells me that I am an image of God, as well as the Scriptures. He that understands not that much, hath not his introduction, his first lesson, and yet is to begin the alphabet of man.—Sir Thomas Browne.

Man has the whole world in counterpoint to hm, but he contains an entire world within himself. Now, for the first at the apex of the living pyramid, it is man and nature; but man himself is a syllepsis, a compendium of nature—the Microcosm. In man, the centripetal and individualizing tendency of all nature is itself concentred and individualized—he is a revelation of nature.—S. T. Coleridge, *Theory of Life.*

All souls existed from the beginning in the divine soul; all individuality which is, has been, or will be, had its pre-existence in creative being.—Slack, *Ministry of the Beautiful.*

rection? Whether it will, during that interval, be apprised of the transactions on earth? Whether it will have sensible intimate communications with superior spirits? Whether it will have a clearer, vaster manifestation of the grand scene of the creation? Whether it will have a luminous foresight of what it will become at the resurrection? When, and of what kind will be the local habitation of the hereafter? Of what the employments will chiefly consist?"

Such overwhelming realities—such grand and incomprehensible probabilities, so mysteriously veiled, are calculated to attract, whilst they confound and elude the scrutiny of the severest investigations of scientific and metaphysical research,—as they stand aloof, like the mystic and awful recess in the innermost pavilion of the Jewish temple! Yet, is not the moral intention of Divine wisdom and grace sufficiently apparent, in that concealment with which God has been pleased to screen, from the intrusion of mortal presumption, the imbecility and limitation of human faculties, of a fuller knowledge of the mysteries of the organic world, the specific nature of angelical beings, the inscrutable decrees of almighty purpose and sovereign grace, and the inconceivable wonders of the future state, that in our present sinful and spiritual condition, attended with the religious responsibilities of this probationary scene of existence, Faith should unceasingly operate as the active principle upon the stimulating anticipations of our hopes, the devout aspirations of our hearts, and the practical demeanor of our lives? This obvious appointment of faith, to be an actuating principle, upon the interior thoughts and outward actions, is partly, because it cannot be otherwise, and partly, because to be governed by the inspired declaration and revealed will of Jehovah, constitute the vital and energetic essence of all those obligations binding upon his intelligent and amenable creatures.

The conjecture that angels—these pure intelligences and transcendently dignified *spirits*, assume corporeal forms, only on particular occasions, which, as soon as they are fulfilled, they throw off the transient medium which they required—the vehicle of their visibility returning to the source from whence it originated; Dr. Dick, in his Philosophy and Theory of a *Future State*, pronounces "a mere assumption, destitute of any rational or spiritual argument to substantiate the truth. There is no passage of Scripture, with which I am acquainted," he remarks, "that makes such an assertion." The passage in Psalm civ. 4, "Who maketh his angels spirits, and his ministers a flaming fire," has been frequently quoted for this purpose, but it has no reference to any opinion that may be formed on this point. Although the passage were considered as referring to angels, it would not prove that they were immaterial substances, for, while they are designated *spirits*, which is equally applicable to *men*, as well as to angels—they are also said to be a "flaming fire," which is a *material* substance. This passage seems to have no particular reference to either opinion; but if considered as expressing the attributes of angels, its plain meaning is, that they are endowed with *wonderful activity*—that they move with the swiftness of the winds, and operate with the force and energy of flaming fire; or, in other words, that He, in whose service they are engaged, and who directs their movements, employs them with the strength of the winds and with the rapidity of lightning. In every instance in which angels have been sent on embassies to mankind, they have displayed *sensible* qualities. They exhibited a *definite form*, somewhat analagous to that of man, and *color* and *splendor*, which were perceptible by the organ of vision—they emitted *sounds*, which struck the organs of hearing,—they produced the harmonies of *music*, and sang sublime sentiments which were uttered in articulate words—they were distinctly heard and recognized by the persons to whom they were sent—Luke ii. 14—and they exerted their power over the sense of *feeling*; for the angel who appeared to Peter in the prison, "*smote* him on the side, and *raised him up*." In these instances angels manifested themselves to men through the medium of the three principal senses, by which we recognize the properties of material objects; and why, then, should we consider them as purely immaterial substances, having no connection with the visible universe? We have no knowledge of angels but from Revelation; and all the descriptions it gives of these beings, leads us to conclude, that they are connected with the world of matter as well as of mind, and are furnished with organical vehicles, composed of some refined material substance suitable to their nature and employments. When Christ shall appear the second time, we are told, that he is to come, not only in the glory of his Father, but also in the "glory of his holy angels," who will minister unto him, and increase the splendor of his appearance. Now, the glory which the angels will display, must be *visible*, and, consequently, material; otherwise, it would present no glory or lustre to their view. An assemblage of purely spiritual beings, however numerous, and however exalted in point of intelligence, would be mere inanity, in a sense intended to exhibit *a visible* display of the Divine supremacy and grandeur. The vehicles, or bodies of angels, are, doubtless, of a much finer mould than the bodies of men; but although they were at all times invisible through such organs of vision as we possess, it would form no proof that they were destitute of such corporeal frames.

The air we breathe is a *material* substance, yet it is *invisible ;* and there are substances whose rarity is more than ten times greater than that of the air of our atmosphere. Hydrogen gas is more than twelve times lighter than common atmospheric air. If, therefore, an organized body were framed of a material substance similar to air or hydrogen gas, it would in general be invisible ; but in certain circumstances, might reflect the rays of light, and become visible, as certain of the lighter gaseous bodies are found to do. This is, in some measure, exemplified in the case of *animalculæ*, whose bodies are imperceptible to the naked eye, and yet are regularly organized material substances, endowed with all the functions requisite for life, motion, and enjoyment." To whose striking suggestions may not inappropriately be added, the acute observations of a kindred philosopher and that original thinker, Sir Thomas Browne. "Intuitive perception in spiritual beings may, perhaps, hold some analogy unto vision, but yet how they see us or one another, what eyes, what light, or what perception is requisite unto their intuition, is yet dark unto our apprehension,—and even how they see God, or how unto our glorified eyes, the beautiful vision will be celebrated, another world must tell us, when our perceptions will be new, and we may hope to behold invisibles.

"Again, desert not thy title to a divine particle and union with invisibles. Acquaint thyself with the choragium of the stars, and consider the vast expansion beyond them. Let intellectual tubes give thee a glance of things which visive organs reach not. Have a glimpse of incomprehensibilities, and thoughts of things which thought but tenderly touch. Lodge immaterialities in thy head, ascend unto invisibles, fill thy spirit with spirituals, with the mysteries of faith, the magnalities of religion, and thy life with the honor of

God, without which, though giants in wealth and dignity, we are but dwarfs and pigmies in humanity, and may hold a pitiful rank in that triple division of mankind, heroes, men, and beasts. For though human souls are said to be equal, yet, is there no small inequality in their operations; some maintain the allowable station of men, many are far below it; and some have been so divine as to approach the apogeum of their natures, and to be in the very confinium of spirits."

Leaving the obscure frontiers and uncertain boundaries of doubtful speculations, we gladly re-enter the clearer atmosphere and reascend to the brighter scenes and more brilliant prospects which belong to the ethereal region of a satisfying belief and the sublimer decisions of the metaphysics of a biblical faith—recalled and re-animated by the exciting expostulation of St. Paul's glorious interrogatory, realizing the promise of our hope, the foundation of our faith, the perfection of holiness, and the victory of Redemption. *Why should it be thought incredible with you, that God should raise the dead?*—or the thrilling and magnanimous challenge of the valiant warrior, the apostolic champion of the MYSTIC CROSS. *Where is the wise, where is the scribe, where is the disputer of this world? Hath not God made foolish the wisdom of this world? For after all that, in the wisdom of God, the world by wisdom knew not God, it pleased God by the foolishness of preaching to save them that* BELIEVE.

NOTE.—We ought not to attempt to draw down or submit the mysteries of God to our reason, by contrariwise to raise and advance our reason to divine truth.—LORD BACON, *Advancement of Learning.*

Nothing contributes more to prove the spirituality of man, than the exalted delight which he is able to derive from the operations of his intellect or his fancy.—KNOX, *Winter Evenings.*

By spiritualizing the corporeal works of God, there may accrue to the pious soul uses far more valuable than they can afford the body.—BOYLE.

The annexed particulars have been selected from Allen's *Modern Judaism*;—a most entertaining and instructive work, displaying an elaborate and extensive research into rabbinical literature, and a familiar acquaintance with Jewish traditions;—on account of the very extraordinary fictions, and representations and discrepancies which they embrace respecting the creation, other circumstances and events of the angelical world.

TRADITIONARY AND ANECDOTICAL.

"The rabbinical writings abound with traditions concerning angels. Of the time of their creation different accounts are given by different rabbies; who have endeavored to support their respective statements by the citation of texts of Scripture, which they wish their readers to accept as decisive proofs of what they have taken upon themselves to affirm. To the question, 'When were the angels created?' Rabbi Jochanan answered, 'The angels were created on the second day; this is what is written;' 'who layeth the beams of chambers in the waters; who maketh the clouds his chariot; who walketh upon the wings of the wind; who maketh his angels spirits.'—Psalm civ. 3, 4. Rabbi Chanina said, 'The angels were created on the fifth day; this is what is found written.' 'And fowl that may fly about the earth;' and, 'with twain, he did fly.'—Gen. i. 20, Isaiah vi. 2. Rabbi Luliani maintains the orthodoxy of both these statements. 'They who follow the opinion of Rabbi Chanina, and those who adhere to that of Rabbi Jochanan, all agree that the angels were not created on the first day, that it might not be said Michael spread out the firmament in the south, Gabriel in the north, and the holy and blessed God in the middle; but "I am the Lord that maketh all things, that stretcheth forth the heavens above, that spreadeth abroad the earth by myself."—Isaiah xxiv. 24. Rabbi Bechai harmonizes them. 'There are some angels who continue forever, namely, those who were created on the second day: but others perish, according to the explanation of our rabbies of blessed memory, who say that the holy and the blessed God created daily a multitude of angels who sing an anthem to his praise and glory, and then perish; and they are those who were created on the fifth day.' Another rabbi contradicts them all. 'Before the creation of the world, the blessed God created the shape of the holy angels, who were the beginning of all created beings, and were derived from a glance of his glory.' The description of Daniel, 'A fiery stream issued and came forth before him;' 'thousand thousands minister unto him,' is supposed by Jaechiades to represent angels as emanations from the divine essence. He means to say, that they are of the very substance of that divine light which is of the same nature with the throne of glory; and because they are supporters of the throne, which is flaming fire, that is, pure light; though there can be no doubt, but that the light of the throne is a more transcendent light, because it is with God, himself, and emanated from him the first of any; whereas the angels were created afterwards, being seraphs, and a stream of fire, that is, light drawn from the first light.' But this comment is at variance with the Talmud, which from the same text had extracted the doctrine of a daily creation of angels who immediately sing an anthem and then expire; that standard of Jewish orthodoxy not confirming this production of celestial ephemera to one particular day, as Rabbi Bechia does, but extending it to every day. 'Every day ministering angels are created out of the river Dinor or fiery stream, Daniel vii. 10, and they sing an anthem and cease to exist; as it is written; "They are new every morning; great is thy faithfulness. Lam. iii. 23. One book of high authority asserts all angels to be short-lived creatures of a single day. "The emperor Adrian (let his bones be pounded) once asked Rabbi Joshua, the son of Chanina: you say that none of the multitude of angels above do praise God twice, but the holy and blessed God creates every day in heaven, a multitude of angels who sing an anthem before him and then perish." And Rabbi Joshua answered him; "yea, we do say so." Another represents some angels as exempted from this fate. The holy and blessed God creates every day a multitude of angels, and they sing a hymn; except Michael and Gabriel and the princes of the chariot and the Metraton and Sandalphon, and their equals, who remain in their glory with which they were invested in the six days' creation of the world, and their names are never changed. After their hymn of praise the "ephemeral angels return again to the river Dinor, which is the place of their creation, and is derived from the sweat of those animals which are under the throne of glory, which sweat because they carry the throne of God." Some angels are said to be created from fire; others from water; others from wind; but from the sixth verse of the thirty-third psalm, Rabbi Jonathan inferred that there is an angel created by every word that proceeds out of the mouth of God." Angels are described as differing greatly in magnitude and stature. The Talmud declares one angel to be taller than another by as many miles as a man would travel in a journey of five hundred years. One rabbi affirms, "that four classes of ministering angels sing praises in the presence of the holy and blessed God. The first class, at the head of which is Michael, is on the right hand; the second, under Gabriel, on the left; the third, under Uriel, before him; the fourth, under Raphael, behind him; and the divine Majesty is in the midst, seated on a throne high and lifted up." The distance at which the angels stand from the divine Majesty, is pretended to be stated by the famous Rabbi Akiba, almost with the geometrical exactness of an actual admeasurement. High rabbinical authority affirms that angels were consulted respecting the creation of man; that they divided into two parties, some strongly recommending his creation, and others loudly protesting against it; that while they were in a fierce pursuit on the subject God made Adam without their knowledge, and then informed them that their contentions were useless, for that man was already created.

Whatever satisfaction or dissatisfaction was produced in the angelic council by this decision, it was, long after, arranged at the bar of rabbinical scrutiny, and judgment was formally pronounced against the Creator. The following anecdote of piety and sapience is recorded in the Talmud. "The wise men say that for a number of years the school of Shammai and the school of Hillel disputed amongst themselves; some asserting that it would have been better if man had not been created; others contending that it was better for man to have been created. The votes being at length collected and counted, the majority were of opinion that it would have been better if man had not been created; but that now since he had been created, it was his duty to lead a virtuous life. Another rabbinical author asserts that the angels were previously consulted about the creation of the world. Among the Jews it is a received opinion, that the world was created on the first day of the month Tisri, and that on this day God sits in judgment on mankind; when three books are opened, of the righteous who observe the precepts, of the middling, and presumptuously wicked. The righteous are instantly written to everlasting life, and the wicked assigned to the burning fire. Those whose works are equal, remain in a state of suspense till the day of atonement. If, however, they forsake their evil works, and manifest repentance, their portion, ultimately, will be with the righteous; but if reformation do not intervene, death will be their destination."

The following additional traditionary and anecdotical statement of the diverse opinions and strange speculations which have been entertained by various writers, together with some curious particulars respecting the formation of the world, the creation and intercourse of angels, the first pair, the apostasy, Paradise, the nature of the soul, &c., may not be regarded as altogether uninteresting.

Some have imagined that the angels were created at the

same time that Adam was made; while others have again considered the speculation as inconsistent or unworthy of belief from the supposition that sufficient time was not allowed for the obedience and probation of the angels in which to manifest their respective characters and moral dispositions. From the period of Adam's creation to the time of his fall, ten days were supposed to have transpired, which has undergone the following singular and descriptive calculation. Adam it appears was created on the sixth day, which was Saturday, the next being the Sabbath; which no doubt he observed and sanctified by worship; for, it is said, God ceased from his labor on that day and rested. On Monday, the animals were brought, in procession, by pairs, before him, to receive their appropriate names. On Tuesday, finding himself still companionless, God caused him to fall into a deep sleep, and took from his side the famous rib from which was produced the mother of mankind. Wednesday was occupied by Adam and Eve in forming one another's acquaintance, and selecting a suitable resting-place for the approaching night. Thursday was noted for the giving of the divine law expressing the conditions of life and death. On Friday they were shown the garden and trees of Paradise and instructed in what manner to dress and cultivate them. On Saturday they commenced their agreeable labors, unattended, however, by fatigue, indulging themselves in delightful conversation, in the examination and comparison of the beautiful objects of Paradise, and from which originated all the social happiness of the globe. On the Sabbath, they rested. Adam, with his heaven-given bride, celebrated the second Sabbath of the creation, employing its sacred hours in recounting the history of their first thoughts, and complacent interviews with angelic spirits, referring to the power and wisdom and benevolence of their Maker, and other suitable acts of devotion and holy aspirations. On Monday, they again resumed their attention to the garden of Eden, ascertaining the different kinds of fruits most delicious to their taste, beguiling their occupation by their happy conversation. Their language was imparted to them by Inspiration, and was the most comprehensive, eloquent and musical that could possibly salute the ears of immortals, resonant with the melody of heaven. On Tuesday, they became excursive in their imaginations, and desirous of knowing further respecting the extent and productions of Paradise, to wonder at its immensity, luxuriate in the profusion of its bounty, and look over its battlements to the country beyond or beneath it. The first pair, now separated from one another in the extensive grounds of the garden of Eden, but with greeting smiles met one another, at every opening of the enchanting scenery through which they wandered. As inclination actuated our first parents, so they were attracted by the fascinating objects which surrounded them. A beautiful stream, which formed a cascade, that dashed its transparent waters over a ledge of diamonds, arrested the notice and charmed the ears of our primogenitor Adam. During this time, Eve had seen at a distance, on a mount, the most gorgeous landscape of blushing roses, golden fruited trees, and luscious vines; while thousands of birds of Paradise feather the fragrant air with their burnished wings, warbling ethereal songs in harmony with the Æolian zephyrs of the atmosphere. Enchanted with the beauty of the surrounding loveliness, unobserved and unsuspected by Adam, who remained in fixed admiration by the iridescent cascade of the head waters of the Euphrates, Eve stole away. Surprised by the sportive play of a glittering fish in the silvery stream, which had not passed before him on the day he had designated the animals, he looked around to communicate his joyful astonishment to his fair helpmate, but discovered she had strayed away from his side. Not doubting of soon finding her, he strolled gently down the stream, when passing by a delicious grove of oranges, he saw her afar, descending a grassy acclivity, having in her hands the very fruit of the forbidden tree, of which she soon prevailed upon him to eat;

"Whose mortal taste
Brought death into the world, and all our woe,
With loss of Eden."

This disastrous event completed the tenth day, including the Saturday of his creation.

The comparative extent of Eve's delinquency in proportion to Adam's guilt, has also exercised the elaborate ingenuity of the commentators, and they mostly agree that since she was not created when the prohibition was issued, she could not therefore have heard it, a conclusion confirmed by the inaccurate manner in which she reports it to the serpent; her share in the crime of disobedience is consequently considerably lighter than Adam's. In corroboration of this view of the matter, it is asserted that the Deity addressed his reproaches to Adam, alone, for having partaken of the forbidden fruit; whilst the gallantry of one annotator upon the words "I will put enmity between thee and woman," affirms the proof, that the sex from that period, became enlisted into the service of heaven as the chief foe and obstacle, which the Spirit of Evil would have to contend with in his inroads on this world.

"The fall of Adam by frail Eve entic'd,
Was his own death, ours, and the death of Christ;
In whose backsliding may be apprehended
Offenders three, three *offences*, three *offended*.
The three *offenders* that mankind still grieve
Were Satan, Adam, and our grandam Eve;
The three *offences* that sin first advanced
Were *malice*, weakness, and blind *ignorance;*
The three *offended* to whom this was done,
The Holy Spirit, Father, and the Son.
Thus in the devilish Alcoran 'tis said
God i' the beginning four things made,
And those with his own hands: the first a *pen*,
Which all things from the first to the last, both when
And how they were created (writes at large;)
The second thing he took into his charge
Was the man *Adam*, and the self-same day

He fashioned him of parti-colored clay,
And that's the reason (neither think it strange)
That in men's faces there is still such change
And contrariety in look and hair,
Some black, some brown, some tawny and some fair;
The third a *throne*, his majesty to grace;
The fourth for souls a blessed resting place
Called *Paradise.*————
As yet for instance, before man's creation,
The earth had solid and a firm foundation,
And was inhabited in time forepast,
By devils first, then angels, Adam last."

—HEYWOOD, *Hierarchie of Angells.*

Whether Eve was created in Paradise or not, has caused much controversy amongst the fathers and theologians. With respect to Adam, it is agreed, that he was created *outside* and put into Eden, to undergo the temptation which issued in his fall. Some of the commentators inquire with considerable warmth, why should woman, the ignoble creature of the two, be created *inside?* To which query, others again reply, that it was but a fair tribute to her beauty and purity that it should be so, and that in compliment to her, if the scene of creation was not already Paradise, on that event (her creation), it became so immediately. Josephus is amongst the number who believe she was made *outside.* The generality of the sentiments of the fathers upon this difficult subject is in favor of her being produced *inside* Paradise. The Rabbies have made some strange additions to the Mosaic account of the fall. They assert that Eve perceiving, by certain indications, that in consequence of eating the forbidden fruit, she must certainly die, thereupon determined that her husband should partake of the same, and amiably informed him that he must perish with her; urging him to taste of the interdicted fruit. Meeting her solicitations with repeated refusals, she tore off a branch from the tree, and belabored him without mercy, until he was induced to comply with her request; saying, this was the accusation preferred by Adam in his reply to Jehovah, "The woman whom thou gavest to be with me, she gave me of the tree (that is, according to rabbinical interpretation, she cudgeled me with a bough of the tree) and I did eat." Some divines count Adam thirty years old at his creation, because they suppose him created in the perfect age and stature of man. Adam is represented as having been created of such an enormous height that he reached from earth to heaven. When the ministering angels saw him, they trembled and feared. What did they do? They all went up before God in the upper habitation and said, 'Lord of the Universe! There are two powers in the world.' Then God laid his hand upon Adam's head and reduced him to a thousand cubits; other rabbies affirm him to have been reduced to nine hundred cubits,—two hundred cubits—one hundred cubits in stature. They further mention, that in the hour in which God created the first man, he made a double person, male and female, with two faces, but joined them behind. That he afterwards cut asunder this two-fold person, thereby forming a man and a wo man; and made a back for each. Not satisfied with converting Adam into a monster, the rabbies have degraded him into the similitude of an ape; gravely asserting that the creator made him with a tail, resembling an ourang-outang (Lord Monboddo's theory) but afterwards cut it off to increase his beauty. The following serio-comico description is too curious to be omitted. Adam and Eve being buried in the cave of Machpelah, this altercation is said to have happened between them. About twelve hundred years after their death, when Abraham was preparing to bury Sarah in the double cave, they arose, feeling unwilling to remain there any longer. They said, 'We have always been ashamed and confounded before the blessed God on account of the sin we have committed, and you are come to increase our disgrace, for your good works overwhelm us.' Abraham answered: 'I promise that I will intercede with God for you, that you may not be confounded any more.' And so Adam returned to his place; but Eve, by no means satisfied with this, would not re-enter; whereupon Abraham, without losing much time, carried her, with his own hands, to Adam, and buried Sarah and Eve together. The grotesque notion was also held by some of the rabbies, that angels have bodies, which if cut, with admirable skill, would soon come together again, like the property of vermicular substances.

Amongst their ridiculous fables, the Rabbins mention as the descendants of Sammael, who was a fallen seraph, Adam and Eve. When the blessed God created the first man, whom he formed alone, without a companion, he said, 'It is not good that the man should be alone,' and therefore he created a woman and named her Lilith. They immediately began to contend with each other for superiority. The man said it behooves thee to be obedient, I am to rule over thee. The woman replied, we are on a perfect equality, for we were both formed out of the same earth. So neither would submit to the other. Lilith seeing this, uttered the *Shem-hamp-horath*, that is, pronounced the name of Jehovah, and instantly flew away through the air. Adam then addressed himself to God and said, 'Lord of the Universe! the woman whom thou gavest me has flown away from me.' God immediately dispatched three angels, Sennoi, Sansennoi, and Sammangeloph to bring back the fugitive. He said to them: If she consent to return, well; but if not, you are to leave her, after declaring to her that a hundred of her children shall die every day. These angels then pursued her, and found her in the midst of the sea, in the mighty waters in which the Egyptians were to be afterwards destroyed. They made known to her the divine message, but she refused to return. They threatened unless she would return to drown her in the sea. She then said, Let me go; for I was created for no other purpose than to debilitate and destroy infants; my power over the males will extend to eight days, and over the females to twenty days after their birth. On hearing this, the angels were proceeding to seize her, and carry her back to Adam by force, but Lilith swore by the name of the living God, that she would refrain from doing any injury to infants, whenever and wherever she should find those angels or their names or their pictures, on parchment or paper, or on whatever else they might be written or drawn, and she consented to the punishment denounced against her by God, that a hundred of her children should die every day. Hence it is that every day witnesses the death of a hundred young demons of her progeny. And for this reason, we write the names of these angels on slips of paper or parchment, and bind them upon infants, that Lilith, on seeing them, may remember her oath, and may abstain from doing our infants any injury. Another rabbinical writer says, 'I have also heard, that when the child laughs in its sleep in the night of the Sabbath or of the new moon, the Lilith laughs and toys with it, and that its proper father or mother, or any one that sees the infant laugh, to tap it on the nose and say, Hence, begone, cursed Lilith, for thy abode is not here, which should be said three times, and each repetition should be accompanied with a pat on the nose. This is of great benefit because it is in the power of Lilith to destroy children whenever she pleases.'

Some of the ancient divines held the opinion, that the creation of the angels was concealed from Moses, lest any man should apprehend (like some heretics of old) that they aided and assisted God in the formation of the world, when they only appeared as spectators; lest they should be deified, and the honor due to the Creator be conferred upon the creature.

The schoolmen placed Paradise in the east, because the east is the nobler quarter, the right hand being more noble than the left, and the east being on the right. The period during which our first parents enjoyed their state of innocence, is as much disputed as the site of Paradise. Some extend the period to one hundred years, others, contract it to three hours; and a few, grant seven years. Cedrenus and Chrysostom place the fall on the evening of the day, in which Adam was created; and there are others who assign to the *Protoplasti* (as our first parents have been named), as many years of paradisiacal beat-

4*

itude, as were occupied by our Saviour's ministry on earth. The jesuit, Hardouin, places the terrestrial paradise in Palestine, intersected by the Jordan, and not far north from Enon, near Salim, in which John baptized. Different speculations have situated paradise in the third, fourth, or in the lunar heaven, in the moon itself, in a mountain near the lunar heaven, in the middle region of the air, without and above, and beneath the earth, in a place where the ken of man can never reach, under the arctic pole, in that spot of Tartary now occupied by the Caspian seas, in the extreme south, in a land of fire, in the east, on the banks of the Ganges, in Ceylon, in China, in an uninhabited place beyond the east, in America, in Africa, under the equator, above the mountains of the moon, from which the Nile is supposed to arise, in Armenia, in Mesopotamia, Assyria, Persia, in Babylonia, and in Arabia. The *Gannath*, or happy garden of the Mahommedans, is compared to Paradise, irrigated by rivers of incorruptible water, streams of milk, pleasant wine, and clarified honey; containing flowing fountains, and abounding with all kinds of fruit, furnished with couches lined with embroidered silk, and covered with beautiful carpets interwoven with gold. Beauteous damsels, pure virgins with complexions like rubies and pearls, attended by youth with goblets of flowing wine. With the Mussulmen, it is a disputed question whether the future Paradise is already created or whether it will be created hereafter. The orthodox maintain that its locality is in the seventh heaven under the throne of God: that its soils consist of the finest wheat flour, or of the purest musk, or of saffron; its stones are pearls, and jacinths; the walls of its buildings are enriched with gold and silver, and the trunks of all its trees are of gold. The most remarkable tree in the palace of Mahommed is the *Tuba*, the tree of happiness, extending its boughs to the abode of every true believer. It affords grapes, dates, and pomegranates more luscious than ever regaled mortal palate, upon its twigs are ready dressed birds, silken mantles and horses with rich housings, all like fairy gifts in a pantomime, will burst from its opening fruits at a wish. The black-eyed damsels or Houris are formed of pure musk; some of the pavilions in which they reside are sixty miles square. Eight gates will lead to Paradise, and the first entertainment of the blessed, will be the whole earth presented as a single cake of bread, the ox Balâm and the fish Nûn, the lobes of whose liver will suffice for seventy thousand men. The very meanest will have eighty thousand servants and seventy-two Houris, besides all the wives whom they married when living. Whenever he eats, three hundred attendants will serve his table, with three hundred golden dishes at once. Wine, not forbidden in Paradise, will be supplied in equal variety and abundance. Perpetual youth will be the portion of the glorified inhabitants, who, at whatever age they may die, will be raised with the power and vigor of a man of thirty, and their stature will be increased to equal that of Adam, who measured sixty cubits.

Respecting the soul, the heathens supposed it was a coruscation of the sphere or particle of the Deity, and had an existence anterior to the foundation of the heavens. The modern Jews maintained the preexistence of the soul, considering it an emanation of the Deity, and eternal in its nature.

The Chaldeans represented the soul as originally endowed with wings, which fall away when it shrinks from its native element, and must be produced before it can hope to return. Some disciples of Zoroaster once inquired of him, "How the wings of the soul might be made to grow again." "By sprinkling them," he replied, "with the waters of life." "But where are those waters to be found?" they asked. "In the garden of God," replied Zoroaster.

The mythology of the Persians has allegorized the same doctrine in the history of those genii who strayed from their dwellings in the stars, and obscured their original nature by mixture with the material spheres; while the Egyptians connecting it with the ascent and descent of the sun in the Zodiac, consider autumn as emblematical of the soul's decline toward darkness, and the reappearance of spring as its return to life and light.

The Rabbinical fictions of the loves of Uzziel and the Schamchazai, may represent the fall of the soul from its original purity, and the loss of light and happiness which it suffers in the pursuit of the world's perishable pleasure; and the punishment both from conscience and divine justice with which impurity, pride, and presumptuous inquiry into the awful secrets of nature are sure to be visited.

The ancients fancied that impure souls, after their departure out of the body, wandered up and down, for a certain space, in their spirituous, vaporous, and airy body, appearing about sepulchres and haunting their former habitations.

The Arabians held the opinion that the souls of men perished with their bodies, but should yet be raised again at the last day.

It was forbidden by the Council of Iliberit, in the year 313, to kindle a candle in a burying ground, lest it should disturb the souls of the departed. And that the dead, whose bodies were not decently interred, could not enter the world of spirits, but would have to wander about on the earth, was the general belief in Homer's time.

Origen supposed that God would not persist in his vengeance forever, but after a definite time of his wrath, he would release the damned soul from torture. He imagined it to exist anterior to the body, which as its earthly prison, would not rise again.

Pythagoras entertained the opinion of a three-fold constitution of the soul. The stoics, however, repudiated the idea of triple souls, or a triad of the mind.

The Rabbies divided the soul into three compartments—the seats of reason,—of appetite,—and of the passions.

They also held the conceit, that there is a heaven or treasury of souls called *Gelph*, from which God furnishes children, before their birth. On the sixth day of their existence, souls are described as having the honor of being consulted regarding their future incarnation into bodies. When the Creator said, 'Let us make man,' &c., he addressed the souls, and did not force them into the body, as a prison, without their consent. That in their original and glorious state, for centuries they enjoy the utmost happiness previously to their being embodied; and might again realize the same felicity after death; rendering the resurrection of the dead needless. The descent into and occupation of the body, however, is represented as not always perfectly voluntary. Take the following specimen of the union of the spirit to the embryo body. God beckons to the angel who is set over spirits, and says to him, Pray send me such a spirit. Presently he appears before Jehovah, and worships in his presence. Then says Jehovah to him: Betake thyself to this matter. Instantly the spirit excuses himself, and says unto him: Governor of the world, I am fully satisfied with the world in which I have existed from the day I was created; if it please thee, do not oblige me to betake myself unto this putrid matter, for I am holy and pure. Jehovah says unto him, The world into which I am going to send thee, is better than the world whence thou art; besides, when I formed thee, I did not make thee but for this matter; whereupon, God immediately coerces him, whether willing or unwilling, into the midst of the matter.

The foregoing, and many other vagaries, even more extravagant, which might be adduced from Talmudical and Rabbinical writings, are taken, be it remembered, from books which the Jews hold more sacred than the Bible of the Old Testament; and painful is the reflection, that such puerile fancies should still becloud the understandings, in connection with that awful delusion and disbelief which still paralyze the heart of Israel—once the peculiar and favorite people of Jehovah, to whom appertained the law, the prophets and the covenants—and of whom as concerning the flesh, Christ came, who is over all, God blessed forever.—Romans ix. 5.

RANKS AND TITLES.

In the prosecution of our inquiries, under the second division of our delightful theme, we are not forbidden the appropriate and auxiliary application of the law or principle of analogy, which we have previously employed ; provided we invade not the sacred jurisdiction, nor trespass beyond the permitted boundary of an evangelical Faith,— on whose awful *Peniel* of solemn mysteries, wrestling Reason, Jacob-like, oft adventures with her sublime truths, a determined encounter ; refusing to surrender, until the *Angel* of the covenant, at the *day-dreak* of spiritual illumination, touching the sinew of bold presumption, and checking the inquiry of vain curiosity, commands her to proceed onwards, though with the halting step of human frailty, in the toilsome and troublous journey of mortality, having achieved, in the glorious contest, the benediction and assurance of Divine aid and protection, as the victory of prevailing prayer.

The interdict of Scripture is not suspended over the supposition, that in the stupendous operations of Deity, a vast and boundless scale of beings exist, confirmed to the hallowed and modest inspection of Reason, as established by the developments and discoveries of science, and further sanctioned by the inspired declaration of apostolic authority, "*That one star differeth from another star in glory ;*" whilst in the expanse of devout contemplation, wonders are presented exceeding the utmost ken of mortal faculties, and the still more astonishing and brighter perceptions of angelic intelligences—*Canst thou by searching find out God? Canst thou find out the Almighty unto perfection!*

Any attempt, how ingenious soever or plausible, to fathom the amazing and awful machinery of the Divine Architect, beyond the precincts of Revelation, is not only vain and unprofitable, but obvious impiety; and it is on this principle that we indignantly reject, notwithstanding his pretended illuminations, the absurd supernaturalism of the Swedenborg theory of the intimate correspondency of terrestrial things, with the celestial economy; as being in direct opposition to the sacred averment of Inspiration, that *Eye hath not seèn, nor ear heard, neither have entered into the heart of man, the things which God has prepared for them that love him*, as a daring encroachment upon the invisible and resplendent domains of a genuine Faith.

The subtle efforts, also, of another class of theorists, are equally objectionable, who would endeavor to reconcile the verities and mysteries of Christianity with the infidel notion of an eternal series; so ably considered and refuted in the following observation, of one of the strongest intellects, since the days of the Royal Preacher, which has appeared in gladiatorial conflict upon the capacious arena, of the splendid amphitheatre of metaphysical controversy and ethical science.

Soame Jenyns, in his *Free Inquiry*,—and to whose theory corresponded that of Pope* and Lord Bolingbroke,—

* "See through this air, this ocean, and this earth,
All matter quick, and bursting into birth;
Above, how high progressive life may go!
Around, how wide! how deep extend below!
Vast chain of being! which from God began
Natures ethereal, human, angel, man,

broached the hypothesis, that there exists a vast and finely graduated chain of being, from Infinity to non-enity—from God to nothing; and that to exclude a single link out of the

Beast, bird, fish, insect,—what our eye can see,
No glass can reach; from Infinite to thee,
From thee to nothing. On superior powers
Were we to press, inferior might on ours;
Or in the full creation leaves a void,
Where one step broken, the great scales, destroyed
From nature's chain, whatever link you strike,
Tenth, or tenth thousandth, breaks the chain alike."

Essay on Man.

For there is in this universe a scale of creatures, rising not disorderly or in confusion, but with a comely method and proportion. Between creatures of mere existence and things of life, there is a large disproportion of nature; between plants and animals and creatures of sense, a wider difference; between them and man a far greater; and if the proportion held between man and angels there should be yet greater.—SIR THOMAS BROWNE, *Religio.*

Writers have not been wanting who enforce the doctrine of necessity with regard to all the phenomena of nature, as concatenated in a chain of iron mechanism, and affirm that an unbroken chain of gradually advancing organization has been evolved from the crystal to the globule, and thence through the successive stages of the polypus, the mollusk, the insect, the fish, the reptile, the bird, and the beast, up to the monkey and man. But while, on the other hand, we avoid being led away by the dazzling generality, or being offended with a wild speculation, reckless alike of inductive facts and of moral consequences, let us not reject a principle which, when viewed, in subservient relation to other principles, may prove to exist, and to have a place in the reality of things.—HARRIS, *Pre-Adamite Earth.*

All the leading nations of the heathen world have fallen upon the belief of intermediate beings between man and the Great Supreme. The Dii Minores of the Latins and Greeks; the multitude of inferior gods amongst the Egyptians; the Amshaspands and Izeds, and Defs of Zoroaster and the Persians; the innumerable subordinate deities of the Hindoos, as well as other nations, all substantiate the propensity of the human mind to inculcate the doctrine of the existence of an order of intermediate beings between man and the Supreme.

concatenation would be destructive of the beauty and perfection of the whole. Dr. Johnson, however, asserted in opposition to this sentiment, "That this chain, from the very nature of things, must be incomplete at both ends—that between that which does, and that which does not exist, there must be an infinite difference, that chain, therefore, cannot be attached to *nothing*." The moralist further demonstrated, "That between the greatest of finite existences, and the adorable Infinite, there must exist another illimitable void,—that between unlimitedness and the limited, there must evidently appear an inevitable separation in nature and qualities, in relation to the existent and non-existent. He also asserted, that not only is it incomplete at both ends, but that we must view it as nearly incomplete, in many of its intermediate links, as well as at the terminal ones; that it is already a broken chain, seeing that between its various classes of existence, myriads of intervening existences might be produced by graduating more minutely what must necessarily be capable of infinite gradation; and that to base an infidel theory on the imaginary completeness of what is positively incomplete, and the impossibility of a gap existing in what is already replete with vacuities, is just to base one absurdity upon another.

"The scale of existence from Infinity to nothing cannot possibly have being. The highest being not infinite, must be at an infinite distance from Infinity. Cheyne, who, with the desire inherent in mathematicians, to reduce everything to mathematical images, considering all existences as a *cone*, and allowing the basis is at an infinite distance from the body, in this distance between finite and infinite, there will be room for an infinite series of indefinable existences.

"Between the lowest positive existence and nothing, whenever we suppose actual existence to cease, is another chasm infinitely deep, where there is room, again, for endless orders of subordinate nature, continued forever and ever, and yet infinitely superior to non-existence. To these meditative excursions humanity is unequal. But we may inquire, not of our Maker, but of each other, since on the one side, creation, whenever it stops, must pause infinitely below Infinity, and on the other, infinitely above nothing, what necessity there is, that it should proceed so far either way—that being, so high or so low, should ever have existed. We may interrogate, but can any created wisdom supply an adequate rejoinder !"

Dr. Dick observes : " When we consider the variety of original forms and intellectual capacities which abound in our terrestrial systems, and that there is an infinite gap in the scale of being between the human mind and the Supreme Intelligence, it appears quite conformable to the magnificent harmony of the universe, and to the wisdom and beneficence of its Almighty Author, to suppose, there are beings within the range of his dominion as far superior to man in the comprehension and extent of mental and corporeal powers, as man is, in these respects, superior to the visible, despicable insect; and that these beings, in point of number, may exceed all human calculation and comprehension. The idea is corroborated by several intimations contained in the records of revelation, where we have presented to our view a class of intelligences, endowed with physical energies, power of rapid motion, and a grasp of intellect incomparably superior to those which are possessed by any of the beings which belong to our sublunary system."

Furthermore. In the scale wheresoever it begins or ends are infinite hiatus. At whatever distance we conceive the next order of being elevated above man, there is room for an intervenient order of beings between them; and if for one, then an infinite concatenation of other orders, since everything that admits of more or less, and consequently all the parts of that which admit them, may be infinitely subdivided; so that as far as we can judge, there may be room in the vacuity between any two steps of the scale, or between any two points of the cone of being, for the infinite exertion of infinite power.

A becoming apprehension of the glorious attributes and moral perfection of God inclines to the conviction that He would take pleasure in calling into existence beings bearing a nearer resemblance to the spirituality of the divine nature, and renders it, therefore, not improbable, that Jehovah would create more than one order of intelligent and holy beings to reflect the glories of the Godhead, and celebrate with the seraphic praises of eternity the infinite benevolence and wisdom, and holiness of the incomprehensible I AM. Upon this supposition several philosophic writers have suggested that the planets are inhabited by rational beings as harmonizing with the arrangements of creative power, visible in the uniformity and developments of the natural world; and a similar inference has been drawn by theologians respecting the multitude and rank and precedency of the glorious inhabitants of the heavenly state.

The hypothesis is not without foundation, that a variety of orders prevail amongst the illustrious inhabitants of the celestial world, as consonant with the exhibitions and manifestations of almighty design and purpose, illustrated by an appeal to the physical constitution of the material universe which connects the solar system with others of a similar nature, and these not improbably, with some still greater and more magnificent central system, around which they revolve, and to which they are subordinate. What, therefore, is true and applicable with respect to the physical universe by the parity of analogy, may be correct in reference to the great moral universe, in which Deity is represented as the central and all-influencing Sun.

"It is highly probable, independent of Revelation, that there are many orders of beings superior to man. To suppose our own species to be the highest production of Divine power would indicate irrational and puerile presumption. When we consider the infinite variety of creatures presented to our notice in the descending scale between us and nothing, it is agreeable to analogy to conceive the number is not less of those which are above us; the probability of which is enhanced by the discoveries now made of the extent of the universe, and of the existence of bodies compared to which the globe we inhabit is but a spot. While there are known to be material systems immensely superior in magnitude to that with which we are conversant, what should lead us to doubt that there are in the intellectual world beings possessing an equal mental superiority? It surely will not be pretended that there are any properties discernible in man that mark him out as the most transcendent workmanship of the Deity, the masterpiece of almighty power; or that there is any ground for supposing creative energy suspended its operations here, rather than at any other point in its progress. The distance between us and nothing is infinite, yet the interval is occupied and filled up with innumerable orders of sensitive beings; how improbable is it, then, that the distance between us and Deity, which is infinite, is an empty void! Were all the secrets of the material world laid open, and the whole structure of the human mind, with all the laws of thought, volition and emotion perfectly developed and explained, we should not be a step nearer to a solution of the question, under present consideration, nor at all more qualified to determine the number and orders of superior intelligences, or what station they occupied, or the faculties by which they are distinguished."*

* Robert Hall, *Personality of Satan.*

An order of angels is as consentaneous with the natural apprehension of our minds, as the orders of beings lower than man, are with the observations of our senses.—PROF. STUART, *Bibliotheca Sacra.*

In the works of creation with which we are acquainted, we find a regular gradation pervading the whole; from the rudest specimen of brute matter, up to man, the lord and ruler of the lower world. Minerals, vegetables, and animals rise regularly in dignity, one above the other; the lowest species of these kingdoms of nature ascend, but little above the highest in that immediately beneath it; and no where do we find wide transitions or gaps in the scale of existence. It can scarcely be believed, therefore, that the interval between man and the Supreme Being, which presents such a wide chasm, is totally unpeopled. It is more natural to suppose that the interval is filled up by numerous orders of intelligent creatures, to whom the blessing of existence has been imparted by the Creator, and who are, in a variety of ways, subservient to the accomplishment of the purposes of providence.—*Idem.*

How natural does the thought seem which suggested itself to the profound mind of Cuvier, when indulging in a similar review of the wonders and analogies of nature. Has the last scene in the series arisen, or has Deity expended his infinitude of resources and reached the ultimate state of progression at which perfection can arrive? The philosopher hesitated, and then decided in the negative, for he was too intimately acquainted with the works of the omnipotent Creator to think of limiting his power; and he could therefore anticipate a coming period in which man would have to resign his post of honor to some nobler and wiser creature—the monarch of a better and higher world. How well it is to be permitted to indulge in the expansion of Cuvier's thought, without sharing in the melancholy of Cuvier's feelings,—to be enabled to look forward to the coming of a new heaven and a new earth, not in horror, but in hope,—to be encouraged to believe in the system of unending progression, but to entertain no fear of the degradation or deposition of man! The adorable Monarch of the future, with all his unsummed perfection, has already passed into the heavens, flesh of our flesh and bone of our bone, and Enoch and Elias are there with him—fit representatives of that dominant race, which no other race shall ever supplant or succeed, and to whose onward and upward march the deep echoes of eternity shall never cease to respond.—HUGH MILLER, *Footprints of the Creator.*

Attracted by the rich luxuriance, and inviting landscapes of the panoramic scenery of beautiful illustrations, brave thought, curious and speculative theories, by which the pleasing investigation of our sublime subject has been surrounded, we have been detained beyond our intention; and proceed to show, so far as Revelation warrants, the pre-eminent dignity and exalted station which angelic beings sustain in the boundless empire of creation, irradiated in the dazzling glories of the reflected magnificence of the divine presence and the majestic display of Almighty wisdom and benevolence.

From the various representations which are given in the sacred pages of Holy Writ, respecting these celestial beings, as bearing the character, and fulfilling their exalted destination as attendants around the throne of the Most High, as the illustrious ambassadors of his will, and the appointed executioners of his purposes throughout the domains of universal empire; in connection with the transcendent attributes with which they are endowed, we cannot hesitate in determining, that they hold the highest rank and elevation in the scale of created intelligences. In the heavenly and supernatural visions vouchsafed to Isaiah, Ezekiel, Daniel, and St. John, they spoke of their overpowering resplendency, in the most exalted terms of inspired description, and with emotions of consternation and horror, indicative of their surprising grandeur. Mortal dialect fails to afford an adequate expression of their greatness and beauty, by allusions to earthly delineations and distinctions, describing them as the top, flowers, and the masterpieces of creation, the cream of all intelligent excellency, the nobles and princes of the universe, the body-guard of Jehovah, and the cabinet council of the Great Supreme,—the miniatures of God. Even imagination, in her loftiest poetical strains, surrenders the attempt as presumptuous and vain; whilst the different and numerous titles attributed to them in the Scriptures, will further establish the pre-eminency of their distinction amongst spiritual existences.

SERAPHIM*; is the title applied, and in the Scriptures specified only, by Isaiah, in his overpowering vision recorded in the sixth chapter of his prophecy, as denominating the highest order of the celestial hierarchy, and as their name indicates, from the Hebrew epithet, *burners* or *burning ones*, "glowing with a pure and serene, intense and immortal flame of divine love; returning, without ceasing, the light and warmth which they have received from the great central Sun of the universe; reflecting with supreme beauty the image of that divine Luminary." In the entranced visions of the prophet Ezekiel, and St. John the Divine, the *living creatures* mentioned, if not precisely identical, present a most striking and very close resemblance. As the symbolical figures in the Holy of Holies were called cherubim, from their proximity to the Divine Presence, so Isaiah appropriates to these glorious beings which he beheld in the spirit, the term of *Seraphim*, to de-

* Dionysius makes the following arrangement in the precedency of angels; giving the first place to the angels of love, called Seraphim; the second, to the angels of light, styled Cherubim; and to the third, in their respective rotation, as angels of knowledge, illumination, office and authority, under the terms, thrones, principalities, dominions, powers, virtues, &c.

The Platonists divided angels into three classes. *Supercelestes*, which stand in the presence of Jehovah; *Celestes*, who are appointed to govern the stars; *Subcelestes*, commissioned to rule over kingdoms, cities, and particular persons.

Cardinal Hugo, a famous divine of the twelfth century, distributes the heavenly angels into three classes or hierarchies, each of which he subdivides into three orders. In the highest are cherubim, seraphim, and thrones; in the middle class are dominions, principalities, and powers; in the lowest are virtues, arch-angels and angels.

note their flaming, dazzling appearance; the idea being naturally suggested by the splendid effulgence of the golden cherubs, when they reflected the glory of God in the tabernacle of Israel; and in which belief the Jewish commentators agree: "This is *Mercăvah*, which is the name they give to Ezekiel's vision of the living creatures and the wheels; and this appears by the name *Seraphim*, which signifies burning. So Ezekiel's living creatures are said to be like burning coals of fire."

Dr. Owen regards the *seraphim* as a distinct order of angelic beings. The generally received opinion of the Jews maintain, that those visions of the glory of God granted to Isaiah and Ezekiel were the same, and that Ezekiel saw nothing but what Isaiah saw also; only they say, that Ezekiel saw the glory of God and his majesty, as a countryman, who admires all the splendor of the court of a king; Isaiah, as a courtier, who took notice only of the person of the king himself. Isaiah calling the glorious ministers of God, *seraphim*, from their nature compared to fire and light; Ezekiel, *cherubim*, from their speed in the accomplishment of their duties. Isaiah saw his vision as in the temple. "*I saw the Lord sitting upon a throne, high and lifted up, and his train filled the temple.*" Aben Ezra and Kimchi, suppose that he saw the throne of God in heaven, and only his train of glory descending into the temple; yet it is more probable that he saw the throne itself in the temple, his train spreading abroad to the filling of the whole house; for the temple is called "The throne of his glory," Jer. xiv. 21; and, "A glorious high throne," chap. xvii. 12; that is, a throne high and lifted up, as in this place. Ezekiel saw his vision abroad in the open field, by the river Chebar; chap. i. 3. Isaiah saw first the Lord himself, and then his glorious attendants. Ezekiel saw first the chariot of his glory and then God above it. Isaiah's seraphims had six wings, with two thereof they covered their faces, which Ezekiel's cherubim had not; and that because Isaiah's vision represented Christ, referred to by the Evangelist John: *These things said Esaias, when he saw his glory, and spake of him,* involving the mystery of the calling of the Gentiles and the rejection of the Jews, and which the angels were not able to look into,—Eph. iii. 9, 10; and were therefore said to cover their faces with their wings, as not being able to look into the depths of those mysteries; but in Ezekiel's vision, when they attended the will of God in the works of his providence, they looked upon them with open face."*

* Amongst the directions of Jehovah given to Moses, he was commanded to make figures of cherubim of solid gold, with which to decorate the mercy-seat of the tabernacle.—Exodus xxv. 18–22. Solomon also, ornamented the altar-piece of his magnificent temple, with immense figures of cherubim.—2 Chron. iii. 13, 14. We have no account, that there was ever made any sculptured or pictorial representations of seraphim. Sir Robert Ker Porter, however, in his travels in the East, found in Persia an ancient relic, on one side of a square column at Mourg Aub, purporting some resemblance; but it was conjectured to have intended some superior spirit, probably the tutelary genius of the country. It is supposed to have been about the age of Cyrus, the conqueror of Babylon, and to furnish the best, if not the only ancient representation of the seraphim of Scripture. The figure is of the human form, with the wings attached; two of which fall to the feet, and two others rise above the head, which is covered with a symbolical mitre surrounded by horns. The figure faces the temple, with uplifted hands and open, standing in a benedictive attitude. Sir Robert, remarks, "With the exception of the mitre, there is no thing I have seen or read of, which bears so strong a resemblance to the whole figure on the pillar as the ministering or guardian angels described under the name of cherubim, by the different writers in the Bible; and if we are to ascribe these creations to Cyrus, how readily may he have found the models of his genii, either in the spoils of the temple of Jerusalem, which he saw among the treasures of Babylon, or from Jewish descriptions, in the very word of prophecy, which mentions

5

Though their name and title are not declared by the apostle John, it seems clear that the mysterious beings, who in vision were beheld by him when in exile in the isle of Patmos, were *seraphim.* His description corresponding to that of Isaiah's, "*In the midst of the throne, and round about the throne, were four living creatures, full of eyes before and behind. And the four living creatures had each of them six wings about him; and they were full of eyes within; and they rest not day or night, saying, Holy, holy, holy, Lord God Almighty, which was, and is, and is to come.*—Rev. iv. 6–8. "The Lord sitting upon a throne," as in human form, is declared by the apostle to have been Christ in his glory. He alone has manifested the Godhead to men; for, *No man hath seen God at any time; the only-begotten Son who is in the bosom of the Father, he hath declared him.*—John i. 18. This august emblematical scene relates, therefore, to the pre-existent glory of the Son of God, as our Redeemer.

The "throne high and lifted up," the Rev. Mr. Scott, in his Commentary, observes, "seems to have been the place of the mercy-seat, over which the glory of the Lord used to appear, and where he reigned as the God of Israel over the whole earth; and as an exterior symbol of his majesty," his train or the skirts of his robes filled the whole temple. "Above," or rather *over against,* this throne stood the seraphim, the burning ones, the most glorious of

him by name, and which doubtless would be in the possession of Daniel, and open to the eye of the monarch, to whom it so immediately referred."

In Sweden, about the year 1334, there was a military order instituted with the title of Seraphim; but dormant from the period of the Reformation until 1748. It derived its name from the golden fringes, embroidered with cherubim, whereof the collars of the order were composed. The number of knights, besides the king, and members of the royal family, being limited to twenty-four.

the angelic order. They stood as employed in celebrating his praises, and preparing to execute his mandates. Each of them had six wings; "with twain he covered his face;" an emblem of his inability steadfastly to behold, or fully to comprehend, all the glory of the Lord, and of profound reverence and adoring awe. "With twain he covered his feet," denoting humility, as conscious that he and his services were unworthy the notice of the Lord, or even of the other seraphim in the presence of the Lord. "And with twain he did fly," representing their prompt celerity and alacrity in executing the will of God; at the same time, they sang aloud, responsive to each other, "Holy, holy, holy, is the Lord of Hosts." This three-fold repetition has generally and justly been supposed to refer to the three Divine Persons in the Trinity, and to the holiness displayed in the great work of redemption.* For the seraphim seem to celebrate to the Lord's holy hatred of sin, as displayed both in the salvation of the gospel, and in the punishment of its opposers; in which respect the whole earth, "as well as the heavens has been or will be filled with his glory. While this solemn hymn of praise was echoed from one to another of the angelic worshippers, the *post* or *pillars* of the porch of the temple shook at every response, and the whole house was filled with smoke, or thick darkness, as when it was dedicated by Solomon."—1 Kings viii. 10–14.

The Jews say that this treble ascription of praise refers to the three worlds, as if it were, Holy, is Jehovah in the world of spirits; holy, in the middle world of the stars and other heavenly bodies; and holy, upon earth which we inhabit. But leaving this fanciful interpretation, every

* In glorious imitation of this solemn ascription of praise and homage by the angelic hosts, is said to have originated the practice of chanting or responsive worship in the Protestant Episcopal service and communion.

Christian will readily acknowledge that the mystery of the Trinity of the sacred persons in the adorable Godhead, is the evident mystery contained in this triple celebration of the glory and holiness of Jehovah.

In the book of Numbers, xxi. 6, 8, the fiery serpents there mentioned are called seraphim, either from their color, or from their rage, or the effects of their venomous bite, which produced the most painful inflammation attended with insatiable thirst. Their luminous appearance, when flying, in the air, presented a shining form like fire ; and as beings of the highest order in the celestial hierarchy, are styled " angels of the presence," from Isaiah vi. 2, 6 ; the prominency which has been given to the serpent in ancient worship and idolatry is doubtless founded on their symbolical character. The brazen serpent raised by Moses in the wilderness, was typical of the expected Messiah, the Saviour of mankind, and so recognized by those of the Israelites whose faith realized the saving remedy for all sin in the redemption of Christ. For proof of which they adduce that passage in John iii. 14 : "*And as Moses lifted up the serpent in the wilderness, even so must the Son of Man be lifted up.*" Some writers having indulged the conceit that the brazen serpent exhibited the shape of the cross, formed by the appearance of its wings, which resembled, however, more those of the web-like texture of the bat, than the feathers of a bird. Some of the Christian fathers and early commentators, suggest the idea, that the success of the arch-fiend over Eve, in the temptation of the garden of Eden, was mainly attributable to his assumption of the similitude of this splendid and illustrious figure, which she had observed always attended the majesty and manifestation of the divine glory or shechinah, mistaking the voice of the serpent which addressed her as one of the Sons of God. *Istum fuisse serpentem cui Eva ut filio dei crediderat.*

CHERUBIM, is also another title by which the angels of God are designated; its etymon being derived from the Hebrew, and signifies, *fulness of knowledge.* According to some expositors the term is taken from a Chaldaic word denoting *youth.* Others, give it the meaning of *swiftness of flight,* as angels have usually appeared with the appendage of wings. Others, again, attribute to it the same root as Rabbi, *a teacher,* implying the extent of knowledge and vast intelligence possessed by angels, represented also by eyes in the mysterious and apocalyptic visions of Ezekiel and St. John. *Full of eyes round about, and before, and behind, and within.*

The first mention of cherubim recorded in the Scripture, is in 3d chapter of Genesis and 24th verse,* from which we learn they were divinely appointed as sentinels to guard the approach to the garden of Eden immediately upon the disobedience and apostacy of our first parents.

Respecting the history, the character, the nature and the design of the cherubim, much ingenuity has been exercised, learning expended, and an abundance of theological controversy and speculative explanations indulged. Those which Moses, by divine authority, was commanded to prepare and place at each end of the mercy-seat or propitiatory, and which overshadowed the ark, with expanded wings, in the most holy place of the Jewish tabernacle,

* The fiery flying serpent, whose body moving in the air resembled the vibration of a sword, like flaming fire, was appointed with the cherubim to guard the entrance of the garden of Eden. Cherubim and seraphim are frequently mentioned in Scripture as attendants upon the Divine Majesty or Shechinah; which appeared here in great glory, at the passage into the garden of Paradise, as well as in aftertimes, at the door of the tabernacle of the congregation of Israel, to their great astonishment.—PATRICK.

were very splendid figures, made of pure and solid, beaten and burnished gold.—Exodus xxv. 18, 19. The original import of their name, together with their form or shape, excepting that they were *alata animata*, winged creatures, is not definitely ascertained. The opinion of Grotius, that they resembled the figure of a calf, or the supposition of Bochart and Spencer, that they partook more of the character of the bull, than anything else, is as groundless as it is infelicitous.* Josephus states that they were extraordinary creatures, of a figure unknown to mankind. The opinions of critics founded upon the 10th verse of the 1st chapter of Ezekiel were, that they were figures composed of various creatures, as a man, a lion, an ox, and an eagle. But we are not furnished with any decided evidence that the figures placed in the Holy of Holies in the tabernacle were of the same description as those symbolical representations which appeared, in a vision, to the prophet Ezekiel. The contrary rather seems to be indicated, inasmuch as they looked down upon the mercy-seat, which is an attitude not well adapted for a four-faced animal, like the

* All the multiform animals which appear in connection with Idolatry owe their origin to the cherubim; being misrepresentations of the doctrines or mysteries retained in the legends of these "overshadowers of the mercy-seat." The satyrs, sphinxes, chimera, &c., which have been introduced and interwoven into every system of pagan idolatry, probably originated from the misunderstood remembrance of these Hebraic symbols.

The cherubim mentioned by the sacred historian, were the sum and substance of the second and patriarchal dispensation, as the Jews truly confess the ark with the mercy-seat and cherubim to have been the whole Levitical service. There can be no doubt but these sacred emblems were carefully preserved by Adam and his believing posterity to the times of Noah, and from him to Moses.—PARKHURST, *Lexicon.*

The cherubim may be traced on the insignia of the armies of the Israelites. The standard of Reuben was the figure of a man; Judah's, that of a lion; Ephraim's, that of an ox; and Dan's, that of an eagle.

emblematical cherubim which Ezekiel beheld. The cherubim of the sanctuary were two in number, one at each end of the mercy-seat, which, with the ark, was placed exactly in the middle, between the north and south sides of the tabernacle. It was here that atonement was made and God rendered propitious, by the high priest sprinkling the blood upon and before the mercy-seat.—Lev. xvi. 14, 15. Here the glory of God was manifested, and here, he met the high priest, and through him, maintained intercourse with his chosen people.—Exodus xxv. 22; Numb. vii. 89. From hence he gave forth his oracles; whence the whole place was called *debir*, from the root *debar*, which signifies to speak, because God who dwelt between the cherubim, declared his mind from hence, when he was consulted, by the high priest, with *urim* and *thummin*. These cherubim had feet whereon they stood, and which were joined in one continued beaten work to the ends of the mercy-seat, covering the ark, so that they were entirely over and above it. Those in the tabernacle were wrought solid gold, but of small dimensions; whilst those in the magnificent temple of Solomon were of great magnitude, fabricated from the wood of the olive tree, or *tree of oil*, overlaid with gold, and whose expanded wings extending the entire breadth of the oracle or altar piece, being twenty cubits broad.—1 Kings vi. 23–28; 2 Chron. iii. 10–13.

They are also styled *cherubim of glory*, not from the beauty or excellency of the material of which they are composed, but from constituting a glorious symbol of the Divine Presence or Shechinah which rested between them. As this glory resided in the inner tabernacle, and as the figures of the cherubim represented the angels who surrounded the manifestation of the Divine Presence in the world above, that tabernacle was rendered a suitable emblem or image of the court of heaven, in which light it is alluded to throughout St. Paul's epistle to the Hebrews.*

The disciples of Mr. Hutchinson strenuously contended that the cherubim are emblematical representations of Jehovah himself, or rather of the Trinity of persons in the Godhead, with man received into the divine essence. To which objections have been raised;—that God being a pure spirit, without parts or passion, perfectly separate and remote from all matter, should require Moses to make material

* The most generally received opinions respecting the cherubim are, either that they were hieroglyphics of the Trinity, as they appear in the works of creation, providence, and redemption; or that they represent the character and office of the ministers of religion; or were descriptive of the general history of the church. The subject is intricate, but one leading idea runs through all the interpretations, namely, that they have evident reference to the plan of redemption, for they are allowed to be descriptive either of its divine authors, its divinely commissioned human instruments, or its general history.—WM. BROWN.

Cherubim were introduced into the tabernacle and the temple, and appear to have been considered as the emblems of the visible church.—TOWNSEND, *Notes Old Test.*

The word translated flaming sword, imports a bright flame of waving fire. That this appearance was permanent at the gate of Paradise, and supposed to be the same glory which was manifested to Moses in the Burning Bush. Under the Levitical institution the cherubic symbols and the burning flame were united both in the tabernacle and the temple; the cherubim being considered as emblems of the visible church, and the burning flame symbolical of the Divine Presence. The human form in Ezekiel's vision was a representation of the Angel-Jehovah; the head and protector of the visible church. From this Divine personage, out of the midst of the flame, between the cherubim, the prophet received his commission; and is the same mysterious and sacred Being who had appeared unto Adam, Abraham, Isaac, Jacob and Moses, Isaiah, Ezekiel, "the school of the seers," under the Judaic, and prophetic economy as well as to the apostles, St. John, in the isle of Patmos, and the primitive saints, under the Christian dispensation, and who will descend to the Judgment, with the glory of heaven, surrounded by the resplendent train of attendant angels.

and visible images of himself is highly improbable, and counter to the repeated interdictions to the Israelites, as well as the more direct prohibition enacted in the second command of the decalogue delivered from the summit of Mount Sinai, amidst thunder and lightnings, blackness, and tempest, and the awful voice of the trumpet waxing louder and louder, "*Thou shalt not make unto thee any graven image, or likeness of anything that is in heaven above, or the earth beneath, or the waters under the earth.*"* Add to this, that in all places in Scripture where the cherubim are specified, God is expressly distinguished from them. *The Lord placed at each end of the Garden cherubim, and a flaming sword. He rode upon a cherub and did fly. He sitteth between the cherubim. The glory of the God of Israel was gone up from the cherub, whereupon he was to the threshold of the house. Then the glory of the Lord went up from the cherub, and stood over the threshold of the house; and the house was filled with the cloud, and the court was full of the brightness of the Lord's glory.* And again, *Then the glory of the Lord*

* Within the sanctuary of the temple at Jerusalem were the figures of the cherubim. These figures combined, in one body, a man, a bull, a lion, and an eagle, in which the form of the bull predominated. The calves which Jeroboam set up, were intended to represent these cherubim, and were either the entire figure of the cherubim, or in the shape of an ox or a calf, or perhaps, only having the head of a calf, in which case Jeroboam would merely have been guilty of schism and not idolatry. But he had no sooner set up the golden calves than he gave them the names of the Egyptian idols, declaring the cherubim to be the bulls Apis and Mneois, and pronounced them the deliverers of Israel from the thraldom of Egypt, requiring them to be received with similar rites, as those with which Jehovah was worshipped at Jerusalem. In this manner Jeroboam caused Israel to commit the heinous sin of idolatry. Hosea x. 5: Styles the idols of Jeroboam "the calves of Beth-aven." Aven was the same as the Egyptian deity Aun or On. Aven, Aun or On, was the sun, the same as Osiris. The worship of the calves, therefore, must have been, virtually, that of the sun.

departed from the threshold of the house, and stood over the cherubim.

In all the foregoing passages the glory of the Lord, that is, the shekinah, the sublime symbol of his presence is carefully distinguished from the cherubim; without the slightest intimation being afforded, that they were images or emblematical representations of the incomprehensible Jehovah. Mr. Parkhurst's elaborate attempt to sustain Mr. Hutchinson's sentiments, involve contradiction, and are much too fanciful for the sobriety of Christian judgment to obtain a ready reception.

In conformity with the opinions of many eminent divines, the cherubim are supposed to represent the angels that surrounded the Divine Presence in heaven; and accordingly their faces were directed towards the mercy-seat where God was declared to dwell; whose glory the angels in the tabernacle of the upper sanctuary always behold, and upon which their eyes are continually fixed, as they are also on Christ, the true propitiatory, which mystery of Redemption, *They desire to look into*, and evidently signified by the cherubim being turned inward, and their eyes steadfastly fixed, in the attitude of inspection, on the mercy-seat.

In Ezekiel's vision, the cherubic figures are obviously connected with the dispensations of providence, and they have, therefore, appropriate forms emblematical of strength, wisdom, swiftness, and constancy, requisite for holy angels, as ministering spirits to execute the designs of God; but in the sanctuary they are associated with the administration of the purposes of grace, and accordingly appear more properly in the representative character of adoring angels.

Some commentators have agreed that zōa, *or the living ones* (mistranslated "beasts,") are hieroglyphical representations, not of the characteristics of angels, but those of genuine Christians during the suffering and active periods of the Church of Christ. The first a lion, signifying their undaunted courage in undergoing the torture of martyrdom; the second, a calf, indicative of unwearied patience and constant labor; the third, having the face of a man, expressive of circumspection, prudence, and compassion; the fourth, a flying eagle, to imply activity, penetration, and vigor—representing, likewise, the extensive ministration of angels, in whatever appertains to the providential events and circumstances attending the progress of Christianity.

The wheels which composed a part of the august machinery of Ezekiel's vision, have been regarded as representing the throne of the Deity. The involution of the wheels intimate, their rolling every way, with the perfect freedom of locomotion, showing how well adapted were the forms of the cherubim for the service of conducting the throne—*their faces turning every way.*

The eyes* in the wheels are significant of the dispensations of Providence controlled by infinite wisdom; and the glittering splendid hues or tints radiated from them, fitly represent the dazzling brightness of those illustrious and attendant spirits that encircle the divine majesty of Jehovah.

A modern divine† considers that "there is no foundation in the Scripture for the opinion that cherubim and seraphim are distinct orders of angels. The two names are merely distinctive of two attributes attaching to the same order of

* It would not be far from the truth to say, that these eyes were of the nature of those we call *eyes* in the peacock's feathers, that is, they were spots peculiarly embellished with colors or streaks, like those of the golden pheasant of China.—TAYLOR.

† Dr. Henderson.

beings—their *nearness* to Jehovah, and the *glorious effulgence* of their celestial nature."

Dean Woodhouse, in his translation of the Apocalypse, pronounces with much confidence a similar opinion, stating that the description of *living creatures* in Rev. iv. 6, is improperly rendered, and which he proceeds to prove by a comparison of several particulars; and that the living creatures of Saint John, are the same celestial intelligences with those described by Isaiah and Ezekiel, showing by the resemblance of the description, that the seraphim of Isaiah and the cherubim of Ezekiel are reconciled in the similitude or character of the *living creatures* of St. John's apocalyptic vision, to wit: 1st. The number of *living creatures* is the same as described by the prophet; but Ezekiel already intimates the indistinctness of the vision, and the difficulty of expressing by similitudes taken from earthly things; for he says, "As it were the likeness of four living creatures."

2. Here both writers concur in expressing this indistinctness. John says, "In the midst of the throne, and round about the throne," as if he could not fix the exact station of these heavenly attendants. Ezekiel says, "In the midst," and at the same time expresses the uncertainty of their position.

3. The abundance of eyes is the same in both writers, though not described exactly in the same manner. From both, it appears that no part of these heavenly ministers are without eyes. The eyes, that wonderful part of animal creation, the inlets of knowledge and intelligence, are innumerable, and thus express infinite superiority of understanding to anything which is earthly.

In the vision of Ezekiel, the cherubim had each four wings; in that of Isaiah and Saint John, they have six.

With reference to the propriety of the difference, Grotius remarks, that "the seraphim of Isaiah have twc more wings than the cherubim of Ezekiel, because they are represented as being more immediately in the presence of God; and therefore each of them is furnished with *twain to cover his face* before such transcendent brightness." Here, also, what was wanting in Ezekiel's description is supplied by that of Isaiah. The seraphim sung the praises of God without intermission.

After this comparison of concordant passages of Scripture, we shall have little hesitation in determining the nature and species of these *living creatures* of the Apocalypse. They are the same with those in Isaiah and Ezekiel; and Ezekiel has settled that point, by declaring expressly that they are *cherubim*, and that he knew them to be *cherubim*. They are the highest order of angelic beings, attending nearly upon the throne, and speaking thence with the voice of thunder, which is the voice of God. They are so near to the throne, so intermingled with its dazzling splendor, that human faculties must fail in attaining any precise and adequate idea of them.

Notwithstanding the confidence with which the Dean has supported his views regarding the identity of the *living creatures* seen by Ezekiel and those glorious spirits beheld in the vision of Isaiah, we leave them to the judgment of those who are conversant with the difficulties of reconciling the differences of theological controversy, and submit his diatessaron accordingly.

Withdrawing, from the turbid and agitated waters of polemical theology, how much serener, more delightful, consolitary and animating is the contemplation that these illustrious, resplendent, benevolent and sympathizing spirits are ever active on our behalf, and constantly interpose for our welfare, in every temptation, trial, affliction, seasons of despondency, privation, and sorrow;—softening to our over-powered spiritual apprehension, the insufferable glory and ineffable grandeur of the Divine Majesty,* by whom they are commissioned, with errands of mercy and grace, to carry forward the benignant purpose of almighty goodness, forbearance and loving-kindness, comprehended in the great and wonderful mystery of Godliness—the Redemption.†

* "A throne of pure and solid splendor framed,
On which the Monarch of Immensity,
With such intolerable brightness flamed,
That none of all the purest standers-by
Could, with cherubic or seraphic eyes,
His vast irradiations comprise."

BEAUMONT.

Where the bright seraphim in burning row,
Their loud uplifted trumpets blow,
And the cherubic host in thousand choirs,
Touch their immortal harps of golden wires.

MILTON.

† "The helmed cherubim,
And sworded seraphim,
Are seen in glittering ranks with wings displayed,
Harping in loud and solemn choir
With inexpressive notes to heaven's born heir."

MILTON, *The Nativity.*

"Yet far more faire be those bright cherubims,
Which all with golden wings are over dight,
And those eternal seraphims,
Which from their faces dart out fierce light."

SPENSER.

Perhaps when the Jewish nation shall be converted, and become believers in Christ, there may be such new effusion of the Spirit on men, or such a happy discovery some way made of the darker parts of the Mosaic economy, and the writings of the prophets, as may show us more of the resemblance, which God designed between the type of the law in the temple and priesthood, and their antitypes in the gospel, than has ever yet appeared;

For the angel of the Lord encampeth round about them that fear him and delivereth them. The chariots of God are twenty thousand, even thousand of angels.

In connection with the foregoing statement, it will be only requisite that we briefly enumerate the other titles of distinction by which the angelic Intelligences of the celestial hosts are designated in the sacred Scriptures.

Archangel.—The specification of this title is no where to be found in the Old Testament, and only mentioned twice in the New, being applied only to one personage, under the name of Michael. In St. Jude, where it is mentioned, Michael is represented as contending with the arch-fiend respecting the discovery of the body of Moses.* The other

and, among other things, the form of a cherub, as an attendance of angelic beings on the Majesty of God, in the Holy of Holies, may appear more conspicuously in its original truth and glory.—Dr. Watts.

* From an obscure passage in the New Testament, in which Michael the archangel is said to have contended with the devil, about the body oi Moses (Jude 7) we may collect, that he was buried by the ministry of angels, near the scene of the idolatry of the Israelites; but the spot was purposely concealed, lest his tomb might also be converted into an object of idolatrous worship among the Israelites, like the brazen serpent. Bethpeor lay in the lot of the Reubenites (Josh. xiii. 20). His death was announced by the Lord himself to Joshua, "Moses my servant is dead," (Josh. i. 2). So that there was no human witness of his decease; the account of which was probably added by Joshua from revelation.—Dr. Hales.

The same God, that by the hands of his angels carried up the soul of Moses to his glory, doth also, by the hands of his angels, convey his body down into the valley of Moab, to his sepulture. Those hands which had received the law from him, those eyes that had seen his presence, those lips which had conferred so often with him, that face that did so shine with the beams of his glory, may not be neglected when the soul is gone: He, that took charge of his birth and preservation in the reeds, takes charge of his carriage out of the world; the care of God ceaseth not over his own, either in death, or after it.—Bp. Hall.

Michael seems to be invested with a rank and power in the armies of instance in which it occurs is recorded in 1st Thessalonians iv. 16, where the term archangel is used in reference to the second advent of our Saviour at the last day, coming in his glory, and attended by the resplendent retinue of heaven; respecting which *Theoderet* has this striking and solemn apothegm. "That if the sound of the trumpet, when the law was given from Mount Sinai, was so dreadful to the Jews, that they said unto Moses, *Let not the Lord speak unto us, lest we die;* how terrible must be the sound of this trumpet (the archangel's) which will call all men to the final judgment." Whether in both these instances Jesus Christ may not be intended, is deserving of the consideration, and has attracted the notice of the biblical student. Bishop Horsley, besides other critics, confidently asserts, with much ability and ingenuity, that the reference in the passage in Jude is alone applicable to the Redeemer of mankind; for the word archangel simply indicates a superiority of command over the hierarchy of heaven. Some of the ancient writers, holding the singular conceit, that the rank over which Michael presides, is the eighth of the celestial orders,* affirming that Paul mentioned only a part of the heavenly choir, there being more of which he has not spoken. Others have imagined that the distinction of the title bears some allusion to the customs of oriental order observed in the courts of the Assyrian, Chaldean and Persian kings.

heaven, to which that of Satan seems to correspond amongst the infernal crew of fallen angels.

* The fathers entertained the opinion that the vacancies occasioned in the different orders of angels by the fall of Lucifer, were to be filled up from the human race. A council of the papacy backs the idea, that it was only the tenth order of the celestial Hierarchy that revolted and apostatized, and that, therefore, the promotions which occasionally take place are intended for the completion of that *grade* alone.

Michael, the archangel, tells Daniel that he is one of the chief princes in the court of the Almighty.

From the passages in the Bible which contain the name of Michael, he there appears, and is pointed out to our view as an angel of peculiar dignity and transcendent glory in the court of the Most High. Gabriel and Michael are the only proper names of angels recorded in the Holy Scriptures; and it has been argued from this circumstance, that all the multitudes of the angelic hosts have their appropriate distinctive appellations; and though to our finite comprehension such a conjecture presents an extreme difficulty, yet, the God "*who telleth the stars and calleth them all by their names*, and whose *understanding is infinite*, may have the name of each particular angel registered in the apocalyptic book of immortality.*

Some commentators suppose that those princes or angels, (Danl. x. 13,) who opposed Michael and Gabriel, were evil spirits, such as are described by St. Paul under the names of the *rulers of the darkness of this world*, having their residence in the lower regions of the air.—Ephes. ii. 2; vi. 12. These evil spirits are sometimes represented as a part of the heavenly host, both in respect to their original station, and because they are the instruments of Providence, and have a command over the inferior world, as far as God thinks fit to permit it.—(1 Kings xxii. 19; Job i. 6. They are likewise represented as accusers of good men before God, and as aggravating their faults, in order to have them delivered over to them, as the executioners of God's judgments, (Job i. 11; ii. 5; Rev. x. 12). It was

* After the captivity, the Jews borrowing the invention of the pagan nations, gave names to angels, and were scrupulously careful to retain them. In Tobit iii. 17, we find the name of Raphael; and in 2 Esdras iv. 1; i. 36, Uriel, or Jeremiel, an archangel.

the opinion of the Jews, that there are noxious and accusing spirits who fly about the air, and that there is no space between the earth and the firmament that is free from them, but the air is full of demons.

Various opinions have been given as to the dispute respecting the body of Moses in the martial contest between Michael and Satan. Some consider it has been taken from an apocryphal book, or a Jewish legend, and only mentioned as an illustration; but such a quotation hardly would have been made by an inspired penman. Others think that the body of Moses is a figurative expression for the Jewish people or polity, as Christians are called the body of Christ, and has reference to Zech. iii. 2. But it seems most reasonable to conclude that Moses was buried by the ministration of angels, Deut. xxxiv. 6, and the spot concealed, lest his remains should be made the object of idolatrous worship. *Lightfoot*, however, considers it a mere Jewish tradition, quoted by the apostle to meet the Jews on their own ground.

That the body of the Jews and their service, should be called the body of Moses, and that these words are to be referred to Zech. iii. 1, 2, seems not very probable, seeing in that prophet there is no mention of Michael or of the body, or the death of Moses, nor doth Onias speak of the body of Moses, (2 Macc. xv. 12), but *of the whole Jewish nation.*

Moreover, that Moses was not buried by the Jews, we learn from Scripture, which saith, *No man knoweth of his sepulchre unto this day*, and therefore Philo saith, he was buried not by men, but angels; that there was an altercation betwixt Michael the archangel, and Sammael the prince of Devils, about the body of Moses, we learn from the tradition of the Jews; and it is most probable it was not only that his sepulchre might be unknown, lest the Jews, who were prone to idolatry, should worship him; but about the ascent of it into heaven, he being taken away as Enoch and Elias were, and not dying the common death of men, (which Satan contended he ought to do, for killing the Egyptian), but disappearing only.

Hence the Jews say, "ascendit ad ministrandum Excelso," *that he ascended to minister to the Lord.* And Philo saith, God brought him near to himself, saying to him, *stand with me*, and that by the word of God he was *translated*, whence he was present with Elias at the transfiguration of our Lord.*

" *Lawrence* has translated from the Ethiopic, the book of Enoch (Jude 14), which was brought from Abyssinia by Bruce, and considers it to have been written by some Jew, a short time before the Christian era. It does not appear to have ever been received into the sacred canon; and the quotation of a single passage from it by St. Jude, as *Lawrence* observes, will not prove his approbation of the whole book, more than the quotations from uninspired writers by other apostles; but the book itself is interesting, as showing what were the Jewish opinions upon various points, before the birth of Christ. The passage quoted by St. Jude, forms what is called chap. 2 of the Book of Enoch, and is translated by *Lawrence* as follows: " Behold he comes with ten thousand of his saints, to execute judgment upon them, to destroy the wicked, and to reprove all the carnal for everything which the sinful and ungodly have done and committed against him."

In the testament of the twelve patriarchs, a similar fictitious or apocryphal work, about the beginning of the second century, the belief or practice seems to have existed, of the

Patrick.—*Annotations.*

invocation of intercessory angels, who made supplication on behalf of the righteous, and obtained the remission of their sins; and which fictions were deposited, as testimony before the angels of the presence of the Most High. In this spurious production Gabriel is represented as praying for those who dwell on earth, and supplicating the Lord of spirits.

ANGEL.—This name may be considered as a generical term applied to the various orders of intelligences belonging to the spiritual world, as well as those diversified agencies and ministrations which Jehovah has been pleased to employ as instruments in accomplishing the omnipotent purposes of His will, declared in the operations of nature; the procedures of his Providence, and the economy of Grace, as connected with the redemption of mankind. The term is derived from a Greek word αγγελος (angelos), signifying messenger; and in its most comprehensive acceptation is a name of office, not of nature:—*nomen non naturæ sed officii.* The most august and prominent personage to whom this name has been attached is the Angel-Jehovah, the Messenger of the everlasting Covenant—the Messiah.

In several places of the Old Testament we find mention of this sacred person, under the title of *Angel of the Lord,* styling himself JEHOVAH and GOD; exercising Divine prerogatives, manifesting Divine perfections, and claiming the homage which is due to Deity alone. "This person, therefore," remarks Dr. Hunter, in his *Sacred Biography,* "can be none other than the uncreated *Angel of the Covenant,* who, 'at *sundry times and in diverse manners,*' in maturing the work of redemption, assumed a sensible appearance; and at length, in the fulness of time, united his Divine nature to ours, and dwelt among men, and made them "to behold his glory, as the glory of the only-begotten of the Father, full of grace and truth.' "

To Adam appeared the " Angel Jehovah," in Paradise,* both before and after his transgression—although no specific or express mention is given of God being revealed to him in this character or relation before the apostacy; but as the Son of God " created all things visible and invisible," we believe that " the Lord God, who formed man of the dust of the ground, and breathed into his nostrils the breath of life, and man became a living soul," was the Angel Jehovah.

In the beginning of the third chapter of Exodus, the glorious individual who appeared to Moses, and spoke to him out of the burning bush, was this " Angel of the Covenant."—" Now Moses kept the flock of Jethro, the priest of Midian, and he led the flock to the mountain of God, even to Horeb. And the Angel of the Lord appeared unto him in a flame of fire, out of the midst of a bush. And when the Lord saw that he turned aside to see, God called unto him out of the midst of the bush. Moreover, he said, I am the God of thy Father, the God of Abraham, the God of Isaac, and the God of Jacob. And Moses hid his face, for he was afraid to look upon God. And God said unto Moses, I AM THAT I AM."

* Three things were necessary to be known by man, even in a state of innocence and purity, and they appear to have been revealed by the *voice*—the Angel Jehovah, which talked with our first parents, in Eden. These were—the right choice of food, the institution of marriage, and the use of language. The Angel Jehovah had been the guide and protector of man before the fall, and He afterwards becomes his Mediator and Judge. The Angel Jehovah commences a new dispensation, which, when it has passed through its three forms of the Patriarchal, Levitical, and Christian, will be terminated by reviving and perfecting the primeval happiness of mankind, in that future Paradise, of which the Garden of Eden was but a type and emblem.

The reply of Hagar, the handmaid of Sarah, contained in the narrative regarding her in the 16th chapter of Genesis, points out the angel which addressed her as the " Angel of the Covenant."—" *Thou God seest me.*"

One of the three heavenly messengers whom Abraham " entertained unawares," was the Angel of the Covenant, is evident from the name Jehovah, which the patriarch rendered, and the supplication made to him to avert the destruction of Sodom ; and it was the same Angel of the Lord who called to him out of heaven the second time, upon the obedience of his faith manifested in the sacrificial offering of his only son Isaac, when he received the assurance, " By Myself have I sworn, saith the Lord, for because thou hast done this thing, that in blessing I will bless thee,—because thou hast obeyed my voice."

It was the same glorious personage who appeared to Jacob in the mysterious conflict of Peniel—" For I have seen God face to face, and my life is preserved. Likewise unto Joshua, on succeeding Moses, as the leader of Israel, styling himself the " Captain of the host of the Lord ;" to Manoah, the father of Sampson. " And Manoah said unto his wife, We shall surely die, because we have seen God. But his wife said unto him, if the Lord were pleased to kill us, he would not have told us such things as these."—Judges, xiii. 16–23.

In various passages of the prophetic book of Zechariah, this Divine Person is described as being intimately acquainted with the counsels of the Most High, as presiding over the affairs of the world, directing the ministrations of superior intelligences ; as protecting, vindicating, and interceding for the oppressed Jewish church, as judging and triumphing over their enemies, as *sent* by the Lord of Hosts, and therefore repeatedly called " Jehovah." Passages evidently pointing out the Great "Angel" or "Messenger of Jehovah," respecting whom, Dr. J. Pye Smith, in his *Scripture Testimony*, observes—"that he claims uncontrolled sovereignty over the affairs of men; He has the attributes of omniscience and omnipresence; He performs works which only omnipotence could accomplish; He uses the awful formula by which the Deity, on various occasions, condescended to confirm the faith of those to whom the primitive revelations were given; He 'swears by HIMSELF;' He is the gracious Protector, and Saviour, the Redeemer from all evil, the Intercessor, and the author of the most desirable blessings; His favor is to be sought with the deepest solicitude, as that which is of the highest importance to the interests of men; He is the object of religious invocation; He is, in the most express manner, and repeatedly declared to be JEHOVAH, God, the ineffable I AM THAT I AM; yet this mysterious person is represented as *distinct* from God, and acting (as the term *Angel* imports) under a divine mission."

GODS; from the Hebrew, translated *elohim*, is a word, in several instances, applied to angels in the Scripture. So the inspired Psalmist calls upon and admonishes the mightiest and noblest of created beings to render cheerful and solemn homage to the Messiah, "*worship him all ye gods.*" Bishop Horne remarks, that this clause of the verse establishes "Christ's supremacy over all that are called gods in heaven or in earth, and who are hereby enjoined to pay adoration to him instead of claiming it for themselves." In Hebrews i. 6, St. Paul teaches us that the gods *elohim* in Psalm xcvii. 7, are angelic spirits. The Hebrew word *elohim*, is first employed in the Bible in Gen. i. 1, as the sacred name of God the creator, and though plural, it is joined to a singular verb, to inculcate, as many believe, the doctrine of the adorable Trinity.

The application of the term *elohim* or gods, to angels, commentators consider as denoting their power and authority as the delegated administrators of the divine government, in different parts of the world; as magistrates are appointed under kings to execute justice in assigned districts and provinces of their kingdoms. Judges and magistrates are, therefore, designated by the epithet *elohim* or gods, "God standeth in the congregation of the mighty, he judgeth amongst the gods."—Psalm lxxxii. 1. Rulers and judges are here intended, as is manifest from the following verses: "How long will ye judge unjustly, and accept the persons of the wicked? I have said ye are *gods;* and all of you shall die like men."—Verses 2, 6, 7.

SONS OF GOD, is another title applied to the angels who resemble in glory and effulgence the morning star, or as others suppose, on account of the luminous vehicles with which they are clothed. The morning star is distinguished for its peculiar brightness. What a grand appearance does the poetry of Job (xxxviii. 7) present to our view—ten thousand times ten thousand and thousand of thousands of glittering angels attending the birth of time, and hymning hallelujahs to the Almighty Creator.

The appellation also indicates their near relation to the Supreme Being in reference to His paternity, as well as the superlative beauty and splendor of character by which they outshine all other intelligent creatures, and not improbably, an intimation of their office as the harbingers of the Sun of Righteousness. Under this head it may be as well to remark, that the term of *Sons of God* has been applied to believers under the Old and New Testament dispensations, as in the 6th chapter of Genesis and the 2d verse;*

* Mr. Moore's luscious poem entitled *Loves of the Angels*, is founded on a misapprehension as well as misapplication of this text, "That the sons of

and also Hosea i. 10; John i. 13; Romans vii. 14, 19; Phil. 2; 1 John iii. 1, 2. A prophetic dream or vision, the pillar of fire that went before the Israelites in the journeyings of the wilderness, winds, flame of fire, specials providences, the elements, &c., as the angel over the waters, Rev. xvi. 5; angel over the fire, Rev. xiv. 18, as well as judgments, are called in the Scriptures angels of God's providential dispensations and gracious purposes.

ANGELS OF THE CHURCHES* are frequently alluded to

God saw the daughters of men that they were fair; and took them wives of all they chose." Some understood by the *sons of God*, the great men, nobles, rulers and judges, who being captivated with the "beauty of the daughters of men," that is of the meaner sort, took by force and violence as many as they pleased. (May not the classic fable of the Romans carrying away the Sabine women, have originated from a tradition of this misunderstood text of Holy Writ ?) But other ancient interpreters, together with those of modern times, by the "Sons of God," understand the posterity of Seth, who were worshippers of the true God, (chap. iv. 26,) and who now saw and conversed with "the daughters of men," that is, the daughters of the ungodly race of Cain.

* Ephesus was the chief of the Seven Asiatic churches, the metropolis of Proconsular Asia, and principal residence of St. John; for which reason, his first epistle was addressed to this particular church, over which, as well as the others, he appointed bishops, in the ecclesiastical capacity of their metropolitan.

According to Strabo, Ephesus was one of the best and most glorious of cities, and the emporium of this part of Asia. It was called by Pliny, one of the eyes of Asia, Smyrna being the other, but recent travellers who have visited it relate, that it has nothing venerable remaining excepting the ruins of palaces, temples, and amphitheatres. It is spoken of by the Turks, by a name which signifies the temple of the moon, from the magnificent structure anciently dedicated to the goddess Diana. The church of St. Paul is wholly destroyed. The little which remains of the church of St. Mark is a complete ruin. The only church remaining is that dedicated to St. John, which is now converted into a Turkish mosque. The whole town is nothing but a habitation of herdsmen and farmers, living in low and humble mud cottages, sheltered from the inclemency of the weather by mighty masses of ruinous walls. The pride and ostentation of former days, by St. John, in the Revelation, as designative of the Pastors of the seven churches of Asia, to whom he wrote epistles of warning, admonition, and condemnation. Prideaux observes, that the minister of the Synagogue, who officiated in offering the public prayers, being the mouth of the congregation, delegated by them as their representative, messenger or angel to address God in prayer for them, was in Hebrew named *Sheliack-Zibbor*, that is, the angel of the church; and that from hence the chief of the ministers of the seven churches in Asia, in the apocalypse are, by a title borrowed from the Synagogue, called the angels of the churches.

WATCHERS, is also a title by which the angels are denominated in the prophecy of Daniel, iv. 13: "and behold a watcher, and an holy one came down from heaven;" and at verse 17: "The matter is by the decree of the watcher," who, in the divinely admonitory dream of Nebuchadnezzar, forewarned him of his doom. The Hebrew root signifies one that watches, or is waking, or one that wakeneth and stirreth up others. In Malachi ii. 12, it is rendered Master.—"The Lord shall cut off the man that doeth this; the master and the scholar." It was a proverbial expression descriptive of an instructor, or one that "wakeneth the ear" of his disciple. The Septuagint or Greek version, use the word Ειρ, from which, as some think, the Greeks derive their *Iris*, or messenger of their Gods. They are called watchers or wakers, either in respect of their spiritual and incorporeal nature not needing sleep, or in respect of their

and the emblem, in these of the frailty of the world, and the transient vanity of human glory. All the inhabitants of this once famous city amount not now to more than forty or fifty families of Turks, without one Christian family among them. So strikingly has the denunciation been fulfilled, that *their candlestick should be moved out of its place.—D' Oyly and Mant.*

watchful office, being always ready to do the will of God; and from their constant care and vigilant guard of God's people, are emphatically called *Watchers*. Bishop Horsley contends that angels are not intended by the "watchers." He says, "amongst those who understand the titles of 'Watchers' and 'Holy Ones' of angelic beings, it is not quite agreed whether they are angels of the cabinet or the provincial governors—the tutelar angels to whom these appellations belong. The majority, I think, are for the former. But it is agreed by all, that they must be principal angels —angels of the highest order. Of how high an order, indeed, must these 'Watchers' and 'Holy Ones' have been on whose decrees the judgments of God himself are founded, and by whom the warrant for the execution is finally issued! It is surprising that such men as Calvin among the Protestants of the Continent,—such as Wells and the elder Lowth in our own church,—and such as Calmet in the Church of Rome, should not have their eyes open to the error and impiety, indeed, of such an exposition as this, which makes them angels. The plain truth is, that some learned men, though but few, have seen it, that these appellations, 'Watchers' and 'Holy Ones,' denote the Persons in the Godhead; the first, describing them by the vigilance of their universal providence,—the second, by the transcendant sanctity of their nature."

In this view of the subject, few expositors coincide with the Bishop, whilst the title appropriately portrays the attributes and characteristics of angels; for their sleepless diligence in executing the appointed services of their Almighty Sovereign, and their watchful attendance, protection and assistance to the faithful people of God during all the toils, and trials and temptations of their earthly pilgrimage; and well, therefore, might the inspired psalmist invoke them: "Bless the LORD, ye his angels that excel in strength, that do his commandments, hearkening unto the voice of his word." —Psalm ciii. 20.

THRONES (θρονοι), DOMINIONS (κυριοτητες), PRINCIPALITIES, (αρχαι), POWERS (εξουσιας), are titles given to the angels by St. Paul, in his epistle to the Colossians i. 16, and denote metonymically that they "sit on thrones, exercise dominion, hold authority, preside in governments, and are invested with the powers necessary for these great purposes."* "They are also styled *Chief Princes*, to intimate that they are the first order of rulers in the universe, under Him *who has prepared his throne in the heavens, and whose kingdom ruleth over all.* They are called the *Sons of God*, to teach us that they are beings related to God in character, favor, place, and authority. They are called *Morning Stars*, implying the splendor and glory by which they surpass all other intellectual beings. They are called *Cherubim* and *Seraphim*, to inform us that they are beings furnished with superior knowledge to discern, and with superior holiness to pursue whatever is good and right, honorable to the Creator, and useful to his creatures.

From the preceding scriptural nomenclature, descriptive of the qualifications and attributes of Holy Angels, we are confirmed in the belief of the transcendent nature which they possess, the supereminent station which they sustain amongst created intelligences, and the permanent dignity by which they are adorned and distinguished, as the royal attendants around the throne of the Most High; nor can we worthily honor the "living oracles" of God as regards the information which they supply respecting them, justify our profession of faith, based on the testimony of Inspiration, neither realize the full extent of that consolation, support

* President Dwight.—System of Theology.

and felicity which the biblical doctrine of their real existence and varied ministrations is intended to impart, unless we sincerely apply our understandings and hearts to a sober and serious investigation of a subject so sublime and glorious, delightful and edifying; whilst for the constant, though invisible protection, assistance, and guidance of these benevolent, illustrious, and immortal spirits, it behooves us to render the acknowledgments of grateful praise to the Maker of heaven and of earth—the Lord of angels, who sends them forth with embassies of favor and grace, to "*minister especially for them who shall be the heirs of salvation.*"

TRADITIONARY AND SPECULATIVE.

Jewish traditions, with their characteristic extravagance and variety, abound with allusions to the celestial hierarchy, which they have described as containing four orders or companies, each presided over by its particular archangel; the *first order* is under the gubernatorial superintendence of Michael; the *second*, under the government of Gabriel; the *third*, under the dominion of Uriel; and the *fourth*, belongs to the jurisdiction of Raphael. Others multiply the number to ten orders, and others again, greatly increase their ranks, having numerous associations of bright spirits under their immediate direction and control, within the circuit of the seven celestial regions; whilst the various speculations of the Christian fathers, and ecclesiastical writers, in general, include nine orders, comprehending *three* hierarchies, founded on that passage in Colossians i. 16: *For by him were all things created, that are in heaven, and that are in earth, visible and invisible, whether they be thrones, or dominions, or principalities, or powers: all things were created by him and for him.*

The Jews supposed the angelical world to be organized under

ten denominations, to which they have given the following names: Chaioth-Hakkodesh, Ophanim, Erellim, Chasmalim, Seraphim, Melachim, Elohim, Ben-Elohim, Cherubim, Islim. In the hierarchy of the heavenly host, the Rabbins single out as the most illustrious, *Metraton*, respecting whom the following particulars are related in the collection of cabalistical doctrines, called the book of Zohar, or *The Book of Light.* This mysterious person the Zohar styles the angel of the Lord, which denotes the Shechinah referred to in Exodus iii. 2, "It is he who liveth forever and ever, who is arrayed with the name (Metraton) Mediator." The Mediator is the servant of the Lord, the Elder of his house, who is head of the creation of the Lord, exercising dominion over all things that are his; for the Holy and Blessed God hath given him dominion over all.

Buxtorf and Witsius have also collected some singular traditions concerning Metraton, an appellative probably derived from the latin Metator, and subsequently employed in the sense of Mediator. "The Targum of Jonathan gave the same appellation to Enoch after his translation. In subsequent times, it was differently understood; and the doctrine arose of an inferior Metraton, Enoch, and a superior, who is called Zohar. The very Shechinah himself,—the Crown of the ten Perfections,—the Pillar of the Metraton,—in whom the Holy and the Blessed God appears in his Shechinah."*

Dr. Owen, in alluding to this angel, whom the Talmudists call Metraton, speaks of the title as a tradition of the glorious name of Messiah; of which even since their utter rejection, the Jews retain some obscure remembrance, and by which they obviously intend any uncreated angel; and the Cabalists say, *Metraton* was the master *or teacher of Moses himself;* the Talmudist adding, that he hath power to blot out the sins of Israel; whence they call him the *Chancellor of Heaven;* but Bechai, a famous master amongst them, affirms, that his name sig-

* Vide Dr. J. P. Smith. *Testimony to the Messiah.*

nifies both a Lord, a Messenger, and Keeper. A Lord, because he ruleth all; a Messenger, because he standeth always before God to do his will; and a Keeper, because he keepeth Israel.*

From amongst the puerilities and degrading superstitions which becloud the understanding of the Messiah-rejecting Israel, the following traditions appear. The angel Metraton is the king of. angels. Metraton distributes among all princes or angels of the nations their necessaries. He gathers all songs that are made in the universe, weaving the prayers and songs of the Israelites into garlands, because he is set over the songs of sinners to bring them into the innermost. He ascends up to the throne of glory above nine hundred firmaments, to carry up the prayers of the Israelites. Metraton, by some of the Rabbins, is considered as the great personage mentioned in the Old Testament, under the term of "The angel of the Lord," or "The Angel-Jehovah." "The Messenger of the Covenant," specified in Malachi, chap. iii. 1. Another Rabbi declares, "There is a man that is an angel, and this is Metraton. And there is a man in the image of God, who is an emanation from him, and this is Jehovah; of whom can be affirmed neither creation, nor formation, nor fabrication, but only emanation." One authority insists, "Behold, out of the bodies of Enoch and Elijah, are made angelical forms; for out of Enoch is made Metraton, but out of the body of Elijah, Sandalphon." The following is a specimen of absurd extravagance: "While Enoch, *alias* Metraton, was in the course of his ascension to the celestial regions, the various orders of angels smelled the scent of him five thousand three hundred and eighty miles off, and were somewhat displeased at the introduction of a being of the human race into their superior world, till God pacified them by explaining the cause of his translation." To complete the ludicrous contrast of meanness with magnificence, it is fur-

* Dr. Owen, *on the Hebrews.*

ther asserted, that " Metraton was a cobbler, and was intent on every stitch, and he spake of God. The name of the glory of his kingdom be blessed forever."*

Some of the Jewish writers have endeavored to prove, that all the angels have their proper names; and the Cabalists contend that the names of all the angels are contained in the Scriptures mysteriously.

The Mussulmen say of Gabriel, that he descended, in one hour, from heaven, overturning a mountain with a single feather of his wing.

Dionysius enumerates nine orders of angels, corresponding to the number specified in the Scriptures, and describes their several distinctions in the following manner:—The first three orders are for immediate attendance upon the Almighty; the next three, for the general government of his creatures; the last three, for the particular good of God's elect: that the archangels surpass the beauty of angels, ten times; principalities exceed the archangels, twenty times; powers excel the principalities, forty times, &c. The learned Mede, in his diatribe on the angels, speaks of seven principal angels which stand before the throne of God, and also represents them as the seven eyes of Jehovah, which run to and fro through the whole earth, being the seven spirits mentioned by St. John. The erudite prelate further remarks—that these titles which they attach to the respective class of angels are characteristic either of the qualities in which they excel, or of the offices assigned to them by God. Thus they choose to call those *Cherubim* which excel in the splendor of knowledge; *Seraphim*, those which are most ardent in divine love; *Thrones*, those which contemplate the glory and equity of the Divine judgments. The *Cherubim*, they say, enlighten others with wisdom; the *Seraphim* inspire them with love; the *Thrones* teach to rule with judgment. Those of the first class they suppose never to be sent forth to discharge any office, but wait upon God continually. In the middle class they

* Allen, *Modern Judaism—passim.*

place the *Dominions*, as they suppose, to regulate the duties of the *Angels*; the *Principalities* preside over the people and the provinces; the *Powers* are a check upon evil spirits. In the last class, they put the virtues, as having the power of working miracles assigned to them; the *Archangels* are sent as messengers on matters of importance; *Angels*, on those of less consequence. St. Augustine intimates his belief in these distinctions, but confesses his inability to define them with precision, and challenges any one else who can.

"It is the opinion of that great doctor and prince of divines, St. Thomas Aquinas, that the angels are so different in nature and perfection, that there is not two of one sort and kind (as there are of men and other creatures), but that every one is distinguished in nature and office from every one, even from the highest to the lowest. Which his opinion is generally received of all Thomists, who for their numbers and learning bear no little sway in the schools, and are no little esteemed in the church of God. The same doctor is also of opinion that the angels are far more in number than are all the species or kinds of all corporeal creatures in the world, that is, more than the celestial bodies, than the simple bodies which we call the four elements, yea, than all the mixed bodies composing them, be they animate or inanimate, living or not living, as beasts, plants, herbs, metals, and the like, which is the opinion of all his followers, do embrace as constantly as they do the former."
—MATHEW KELLISON, *from Southey's Common Place Book.*

Plato's Theology classified his gods, demons or spirits into three kinds,—superior, inferior, and intermediate. The superior reside in the heavens, and by the excellency of their nature, are so far above mortals, that except by the intervention of the intermediate gods, who inhabit the air, mankind can hold no intercourse with them, and whom they commission as ministers to the human race, carrying the behests of the Supreme to men, and returning with the offerings and vows of mortals to the gods, according to the appointment of each, in his respective department of the government of the world, and who preside over oracles, and divinations, in all their variety; are the authors of all miracles which are performed, and those prodigies which happen. The third class he places over rivers, and also assigns them the influence of instilling dreams as well as the performance of wonders, similar to the power of the intermediate, who, fill all parts of the universe, appearing to, and vanishing from mortal vision constantly. It is most probable that the sentiments of Plato originated from the sylphs, salamanders, the elves and gnomes of the Cabbala.

Plato also inculcated the opinion, that the demon or angel which attends us at our birth, conducts the soul after death, to the place of judgment. Those who are considered to have led neither an entirely criminal, nor yet an absolutely innocent life, are transported by Acheron's boat to the Acherusian lake, where they dwell and suffer punishment proportionate to their vices, and remain, till after having undergone a sort of purgatorial abstersion from their sins, they are set at liberty and obtain the recompense of their good actions. Those whose wickedness is deemed incorrigible, who have been guilty of sacrilege and murder, or other offences of equal depravity, are by a just and fatal destiny thrown into Tartarus, where they are incarcerated forever. But those under the imputation of curable delinquencies, though considerable ones, such as homicide, are conveyed into the waters of Cocylus; parricides being cast into Phlegeton, which ultimately draws them into the Acherusian lake.

The following arrangement of angels, according to the signs of the Zodiac, will explain the pictorial representation of the *Frontispiece*. The ancients divided the Zodiac into twelve signs, or compartments, or houses. The first house, is the house of life; the second, of riches; the third, of brothers; the fourth, of parents; the fifth, of children; the sixth, of wealth; the seventh, of marriage;

the eighth, of death: the ninth, of religion; the tenth, of dignities; the eleventh, of friends; the twelfth, of enemies. Each house had one of the heavenly bodies as its peculiar and presiding lord.

For further particulars of the singular work, from which the subjoined extracts are taken see *Mesmerism* in the Parterre, at the end.

——The Rabbins they,
And Cabalists, further proceed and say,
(How warranted I know not). That there be,
Twelve potents of this Divine faculty;
Three oriental, and three occidental,
Three septentrional and three meridional.
Chaoz, the first great eastern power they call,
Whose prince *Mathidielis*, and he sways all
That doth belong to *Aries;* the next place
Corona hath; and *Vaschiel* hath the grace,
Of that to be the chief regent; *Leo* he,
Hath subject in his second Empyree;
Hermaus the third; *Adnachiel* dost carry
That potence, and rules the Saggitary.
The first of the occidental, *Gelphor*, and
Ambriel the prince, the Gemini they stand,
Beneath his sway, Bleor next; his lord
Zaniel, who guides the sceptre and the sword,
Caphet the last; Gabriel the president
And o'er *Aquarius* hath the government.
The first Septentrional, *Bethzan*, *Manuel* prince,
And he the sign of *Cancer* doth convince.
The next *Zonocharel* by name they know,
Barchiel the chief, and rules o'er *Scorpio*,
Over the third, *Elizan*, *Varchiel* reigns,
He *Pisces* in his principate contains.
The first power Austral, they *Pantheon* style
Asmodes prince, in that doth reconcile
The sign called *Taurus;* and the second *Tim*,
Hamabiel is the prince and governs him.
In the sign *Virgo*, *Haim*, is the third born,
Hannuel, the prince, and governs *Capricorn*.

Ancient names corrresponding with the Scripture titles of the nine orders of the celestial hierarchy.

URIEL—SERAPHIM.

The blessed Seraph doth imply,
The love we owe to the Most High.
Amant Sapientes capiunt cæteri.

ZOPHIEL—CHERUBIM.

God's knowledge treats the Cherubim,
He nothing knows, that knows not God.
Nil scit qui Deus nescit.

ZAPHKIEL—THRONES.

All glory to the Holy One,
Even Him that sits upon the Throne.
Gloria sendentia super.

ZADKIEL—DOMINIONS.

There is no power, no domination,
But from the Lord of our Salvation.
Omnis dominatio a domino.

HANIEL—VIRTUES.

We aim at the celestial glory,
Below the moon all's transitory.
Sancti vulnere vivescunt.

RAPHAEL—POWERS.

The mighty power of God was shown,
When the great Dragon was o'erthrown.
Puros creavit, perdite ceciderunt.

CHAMIEL—PRINCIPALITIES.

In heaven, in earth, in hell some sway,
Others again are taught to obey.
Protago, Protero.

MICHAEL—ARCHANGEL.

Michael whom Satan durst oppose,
Can guard us from inferior foes.
Vincit qui patitur.

GABRIEL—ANGEL.

The angel unto man known best,
As last of nine, concludes the rest.
Missus ad missos.

The *Cherubims* with wings far stretched, again
As Moses (so the Scriptures tell us plain)
Ten curtains to the sacred machine made,
So in three parts of the world are said,
To be no less than ten distinct decrees.
And first of the supercelestial; these,
Th' *Angels*, *Archangels*, and the *Principates*,
Thrones, *Dominations*, *Virtues*, *Potentates*,
The *Cherubims* and *Seraphims;* then He,
(Above all the rest) the Supreme *Deity*.

Some write that over every heaven and sphere
Are several angels plac'd and governs there.
The sophist those *Intelligences* call;
The Hebrews *Cherubims;* whose lot thus fall;
Metraton doth the *Primum Mobile* guide;
Ophaniel, in the starry heaven reside;
The *Sun's* sphere, *Varcan;* the moon's lower ray
Arcan disposeth: *Mars*, (his) *Satan* sways.
Mercury's, *Madan; Jove's Guth:* Venus star
Jurabates: and *Saturn's* seen from far;
Maion. And all these in the height they enjoy,
Have power inferior spirits to employ.

Seven angels (as the Scriptures witness) stand
Before the Almighty, first at his command;
And these by his divine infusion know
How to dispose of all things here below;
As those celestials; who doth institute
Those *Seven*, his divine will execute.
Years, days, and hours amongst them they divide,
The planets and the stars they likewise guide.
The precedent of *Sol* is *Raphael*,
The guardian of the Moon, called *Gabriel*,
Chamuel the third, *Mars* his bright star protects,
Michael the sphere of *Mercury* directs.
Adabiel, o'er *Jove* hath domination,
And *Haniel* of *Venus* gubernation.
Zaphiel is Saturn's prince and of spirits seven
Saint *John* makes mention with their place in heaven.

The Angels who control the elements:—

Which from th' Evangelist have doctors ground,
Because it is in the *Apocaylps* thus found;
On the four angles of the Earth I saw,
Standing four angels, those that kept in awe,
The four great winds restraining them from blowing
On earth, on sea, or on any tree growing.

Four angels, as four viceroys, are exprest,
To sway the four winds placed above the rest;
All princes, and with mighty power endued,
Remarkable for their celsitude.
The *East*, whence *Eurus* blows, sways *Michael*,
The *West*, whence *Zephyr* breathes, guide *Raphael*,
The *North*, whence *Boreas* blusters, *Gabriel;*
The *South*, whence *Auster* comes, rules *Uriel.*

Others there be that doth not doubt to say,
That the four elements are forc'd t' obey
Four several angels; *Seraph* reigns o'er fire,
Cherub, the air; and *Thursus* doth aspire
Over the water, and the earth's great lord,
Ariel, the Hebrew Rabbins thus accord.

Nine orders of Devils, corresponding with the nine orders of Angels, incorporated with those singled out by *Burton :*

BEELZEBUB.—Prince of devils, and presides over oracles, &c.

PYTHON.—Author of lies, equivocations, slanders, &c.

BELIAL.—Author of evils, and all iniquities, &c.

ASMODEUS.—Punisher of men for their depravities, &c.

SATAN.—The chief of magicians, author of witchcraft, &c.

MERESIN.—Author of storms, tempests, thunder, lightning, earthquakes, plagues, &c.

ABADDON.—Author of wars, discord, &c.

ASTAROTH, or DIABOLUS.—Author of false accusations, &c.

MAMMON.—Author of sinful temptations, frauds, &c.

Next touching the rare knowledge which insists
In them by nature; some Theologists
Affirm them pregnant in theologie,
Philosophy, Mathematics, Astrologie.
In Music they are skill'd, expert in Physicke,
In Grammar, Logicke and Arithmeticke.

We add the following eccentric poetical description of Satan's ubiquitous influence, knowledge, and attributes (using modern orthography).

In all materials he acquainted is,
From the earth's superficies, to the abyss;
He knows such virtues, as in stones abide,
Gems, minerals, creeping worms, and beasts (for hide
From him you nothing can) for he doth vaunt
Still in the marble, porphyry, adamant,
The coral, pumice, and the chrysolite,
The smaragd, topaz, and the margarite.
The onyx, carbuncle, gold, silver, lead,
Brass, iron, and sulphurs; He is likewise read
In the properties of creeping things,
Ants, toads, snails, serpents (all that the earth brings).
Of all the several fishes he hath notion,
Bred in fresh waters, or the briny ocean;
Of Beasts the sundry qualities he finds,
Sows, bears, tigers, camels, horses, hinds,
The elephant, the fox, ape, ass, mule, cat,
Sheep, wolf, hare, hedge-hog, with each other that
The earth produceth; So in herbs, and trees,
Plants, leaves, fruits, roots, seeds, juices, liquors, these
The artist hath like skill in. He can tell
The sev'ral qualities of fowls, and well
Distinguish them; as such and such belong
To the earth, air, or water. He is strong
In further knowledge of the elements,
As in their power, their nature, and extents.

He is further represented as the sovereign lord of every species of magicians, incantation, &c.

For most of this prognosticating tribe,
Metals unto each planet can ascribe;
Silver, unto the Moon, to the Sun was
Gold sacred, unto Jove copper and brass,
To Venus white lead, unto Saturn black,
Iron and steel to Mars; nor doth there lack
Amber to Mercury. To each of them
They likewise consecrate several gem,

Unto the sun, the carbuncle is due,
And hyacinth of color green and blue;
Th' adamant and crystal to the queen of night,
To Saturn the onyx, and the chrysolite,
The sapphire with the diamond to Jove,
The jasper and the magnet Mars doth love,
Smaragd and Sardis Venus doth not hate,
Nor Mercury topaz and agate.

ATTRIBUTES AND CHARACTERISTICS.

IN the present section of our inviting subject, the requisition devolves upon us, to examine a little more fully those wonderful attributes which have been manifested by angelic power and ministration, as well as portray those attractive lineaments which distinguish and adorn the disposition and character of the illustrious inhabitants of the celestial world—those constant, and innumerable, and fascinating courtiers which surround the resplendent Majesty of heaven, as confirmed and illustrated by a variety of declarative facts and striking circumstances recorded in the scriptures of the Old and New Testament.

Under this head it may not be inexpedient to premise and interpose the expostulation,—that the visions, which to the experience of the patriarchs, the prophets, the apostles, the evangelists, and the primitive disciples of Christianity which have preceded or attended the instrumentality of angelic operations, must be received by the mind, unencumbered by sinister reservations or suppositions, referring them to fictitious representations, as opposed to positive and veritable realities; for many unestablished, in the biblical reception of divine and revealed truth, by reason of the superficiality of their faith, are apt to consider that those marvellous exhibitions of omnipotent purpose, and prophecies of gracious promise performed by angelic agency, of which they read in the Bible, are to be regarded as the mere imagery, the gorgeous drapery of a dream, the shadowy apparitions of optical illusion, because, forsooth, of the difficulty with which they realise to themselves the actual existence of incorporeal or spiritual beings; usually applying the term *vision*, in a sense and manner contrary to its scriptural and intended import—virtually interpreting the epithet as something intangible or not seen—a mental phantasmagoria, unreal, and easily produced by a disordered state of the bodily functions, affecting with a sympathetic morbidity, the workings of a distempered brain. Such an anti-christian conclusion no sincere believer in the declarations of an unimpeachable Inspiration can, for an instant, admit or venture upon; though many are inclined to suppose that what the inspired writers have described of what they have beheld and witnessed of angelic beings and their miraculous interpositions, must be understood as a sort of allegorical representation—a vehicle for conveying to the mental perceptions of mortals, the designs and purposes of the Divine will. With these phantomising interpretations we entertain no sympathy, and therefore believe on the sacred authority of immutable and eternal truth, that Daniel really saw with his bodily eyes the angels of God, as also the stationed keepers at our Lord's sepulchre, and the inquiring disciples after the resurrection of Christ from the entombment of the grave, as in like manner we shall all behold them when they attend the Redeemer's second advent to earth, as He comes in "the glory of his Father," surrounded by the splendid retinue of "holy angels," amidst the inconceivable agitations and awful solemnities of the judgment-day, at the assize of an assembled universe!

That God, if he please, can hold intercourse with his chosen servants without the intermediate agency of angelic interference, is proved by several instances interspersed throughout the Scriptures, but in some cases it has been His pleasure to employ one or more of the heavenly hosts in his communications with sinful humanity, and who has also commanded his witnesses to record such supernatural and superhuman interpositions for man's instruction and hope, encouragement and comfort. And assuredly we owe it to our Divine Teacher, to receive with the gratitude of reverential humility and undoubting credence, what Deity has vouchsafed to reveal to us of the disinterested cheerfulness with which benevolent angels are always ready to promote the spiritual welfare and temporal interests of those who put their trust in Jehovah, and repose implicit confidence in the assurances of divine promises; persuaded that not one thing contained in Holy Writ, dare we with impunity, presumptuously attempt to alter or impugn, *which has been given by the Inspiration of God, and most profitable for doctrine, for reproof, for correction, for instruction in righteousness*,—and that to receive such a book of divine origin, as a volume of riddles, enigmas or allegories, and not as a clear and comprehensive declaration of what we are to *believe*, as well as what we are *to do*, would be a palpable violation of the dictates of sober reason, as well as an egregious infringement of the precepts of an acquiescent faith. *For thus saith the Lord*,—is the solemn AMEN OF TRUTH IMMORTAL AND ETERNAL.*

* Could we better understand the angelical nature, properties, and perfection, and what converse and intercourse of these spirits is one with the other, and with God, how they love and praise him, and how He communicates himself to them, we should have more worthy and awful thoughts of God, the Maker and Lord of them,—we should have more worthy thoughts of His power, wisdom, and greatness. Nor should we so easily question his goodness, as now we do. When we hear of God's severity declared against ungodly ones, we are ready to say, Where is the goodness of God if he will send the greatest part of men to hell, to be eternally torment-

Consistently with our previous intimation, our intention is, to adhere closely to the evidence presented to, and enforced upon, our consideration, by the several descriptive statements furnished in the Bible, respecting the astonishing and surpassing qualifications, and those noble and intellectual faculties with which the holy angels are endowed, and by which they are empowered to accomplish the behests of Jehovah, according to those special purposes of providence and grace, for the execution of which they have been delegated. In Genesis iii. 24, where angels are first mentioned under the title of cherubim, we learn they were dispatched, and divinely appointed to keep watch and guard at the passage of the garden of Eden, to prevent any endeavor, by the disobedient and fallen parents of mankind, of making the attempt for a re-entrance, being armed with the majesty of a most terrific splendor, and the dreadful appearance of the glittering brandishings of a sword of flaming fire; reflecting a glory, which, according to ancient Jewish interpretation, probably furnished the archetype of the Shechinah, first, in the tabernacle in the wilderness, and afterwards in Solomon's magnificent temple. With this characteristic grandeur and awfulness, have angels frequently appeared to, and disappeared from, mortal vision. The angel that descended to roll away the stone (a large fragment of rock), placed at the entrance of our Saviour's supulchre, presented the personal spectacle of such a superhuman and ethereal appearance, as to overpower with affrighted terror, the Roman guard, who trembled and became as dead men:—"*for his countenance was like lightning, and his raiment*

ed? Alas! God has myriads of creatures to glorify his goodness on, beside those few mortals whose dwelling is on earth. There is a world of angels as well as of men. Oh! glorify the God of angels, magnify Him.

Pneumatologia, 1701.

white as snow; and for fear of him the keepers became as dead men." "*And I saw*," declares St. John, "*another mighty angel come down from heaven, clothed with a cloud, and a rainbow was upon his head, and his face was as it were the sun, and his feet as pillars of fire.*" Angels, beside the splendor of their appearance, are also endowed with amazing power, forcibly indicated by the names of *might and power*, which, in several places of the Scriptures, are ascribed to them, and further established by the corroborative testimony of the Psalmist, where King David, inviting the choral celebration of heaven and earth, bursts forth into the jubilant exclamation: *Bless the Lord ye his angels that excel in strength!* A *strong angel*, and a *mighty angel*, in the Apocalypse, are expressive and evidential of the same truth. Their great power is still further manifested by reference to those extraordinary achievements which they have performed in the execution of the Divine commission. The destruction of the first-born of Egypt was the work of an angel. Two angels overthrew the abandoned cities of the plain—Sodom and Gomorrah, smiting its guilty and profligate inhabitants with instantaneous blindness. An angel destroyed, in three days, three score and ten thousand persons out of Judah and Israel, in consequence of the sin of David in numbering the people. An angel slew, in a single night, of the army of Sennacherib, an hundred four score and five thousand men. In the Revelation of St. John, the irresistible potency of angels is represented by their holding and restraining the four winds of heaven; and as executing, in a long series, the successive judgments of God upon this evil world. In the twentieth chapter of the Apocalypse, a single angel is represented as binding that fierce, strong, and malignant spirit *the dragon, that old serpent, the Devil, the prince of the power of the air*, who has so extensively and dreadfully distressed this sinful and unhappy world, *as casting him into the bottomless pit, and setting a seal upon him, binding him with a chain, that he should deceive the nations no more, until the thousand years should be fulfilled.* Instances and exemplifications these, of the *strength* and *might* belonging to no other intelligent creatures, and of which humanity can only form very inadequate conceptions.

In 1 Chronicles xxi., what a splendid vision is there presented to us.—A spiritual warrior with a drawn sword and outstretched arm, of surpassing strength, glorious brightness, and probably of prodigious magnitude, standing in mid-air, extended over the holy city of Jerusalem, which lay in beauty and repose beneath an evening sky. This is one of the glimpses afforded us of what is perpetually passing around us, but which our eyes are holden from seeing. We speak of casualties, of epidemics, of contagious disorders, but we regard not the hand that with unerring fidelity deals forth each mysterious dispensation, directed by the appointment of the Almighty Lord and Maker of heaven and earth. The same absurd and presumptuous disregard to the delineations of the Bible has clothed evil spirits with fantastically frightful grimaces and grotesque figures, and also invested the holy angels with a puerile childishness of appearance, wholly at variance with every scriptural representation. Baby faces between a pair of bird's wings, destitute of bodies; slender girls with long and flowing ringlets, and the appendage of pinions well feathered with silvery plumes,—these are the imaginary and inconsistent similitudes of things in heaven, which we are interdicted and warned from representing in such material shapes and fanciful apparitions to our minds, so palpably destitute of that terrible grandeur and ethereal glory with which God has invested those illustrious and beautiful ambassadors of his rainbow throne and imperial sovereignty.

Our conceptions respecting the potential attributes of angelic beings may be yet further greatly assisted by a reference to those illustrative and surprising objects, selected from the natural history of the Scriptures, as described with such superlative sublimity in the Book of Job, where God, when answering the humbled patriarch out of the whirlwind, sets before him a few of the representatives of his Omnipotence, illustrated in the creatures of his workmanship. " The *ocean*, with its proud waves, and secret springs, its garment of clouds and swaddling band of thick darkness ; the *war-horse*, with his neck clothed in thunder, pawing in the valley and rejoicing in his strength, mocking at fear, and swallowing the ground with fierceness and rage; *Behemoth*, drinking up a river, and trusting that he can draw up Jordan into his mouth, whose bones are like brass and iron; *Leviathan*, making the deep to boil like a pot ;" —these are the handiworks of the Almighty, on which He bids the patriarch to meditate, as exhibitions of His majesty and glory; nor can it admit of a sober doubt that Jehovah invests his celestial hosts with still more stupendous powers, whilst waging constant battle with the myriads of apostate spirits which environ and besiege the redeemed children of faith and obedience—*the heirs of salvation.*

Another distinguishing attribute of the angelic nature is their astonishing *activity*, referred to by the Psalmist, civ. 4, and cited by the apostle in Hebrews i. 7 : *Who maketh his angels spirits, and his ministers a flame of fire.* The word in this passage rendered *spirits*, usually signifies *winds.* In either sense the phraseology forcibly implies the remarkable velocity of the beings described by it, who are represented as moving with the swiftness of the winds, and operating with the irresistible energy of fire. The same doctrine is emphatically inculcated in the frequent attribution of many wings to the *cherubim* and *seraphim*, and other orders of angels; and although the language is symbolical, yet its intention is very apparent, as significant of the celerity, and the alacrity with which they fulfil the missions of divine command. The following narrative in the prophet Daniel, exhibits this position with peculiar and unrivalled force. Chapter ix. verse 3 and 20–23—*And I set my face unto the Lord God, to seek by prayer and supplication, with fasting, and sackcloth and ashes. And while I was speaking, and praying, and confessing my sin, and the sins of my people Israel, and presenting my supplication before the Lord my God, for the holy mountain of my God; Yea while I was yet speaking in prayer, even the man Gabriel, whom I had seen in the vision at the beginning, being caused to fly swiftly, touched me about the time of the evening oblation. And he informed me, and talked with me, and said, O Daniel, I am now come forth to give thee skill and understanding. At the beginning of thy supplication, the commandment came forth; and I am come to show thee; for thou art greatly beloved; therefore understand the matter and consider the vision.* From this remarkable story, we learn that some time in the day, *Daniel set himself to seek the Lord in fasting and prayer;* that after his prayer was begun, the *commandment* was given *to Gabriel*, to explain to him the vision and the prophecy. In verses 20 and 21, we are told, that *Gabriel* came to him, while he was speaking; that this was his evening prayer; and that during the time, in which he was employed in uttering his prayer, *Gabriel* came from the supreme heaven to this world. This is a rapidity exceeding all the comprehension of the most active imagination, surpassing beyond comparison, the amazing swiftness of light. Light, we know, is several years in coming from such fixed stars, as are visible to the eye of mortals. But there is reason to believe, that the Heaven of Heavens is at a much greater distance than those stars; so as, not improbably, to be a Heaven to them, as the starry firmament is to us. The poet, therefore, is justified by this wonderful fact in that cogent expression :—

"The speed of Gods (angels) time counts not."

No stronger exhibition can be required or presented, of the rapidity of these celestial beings.*

Another peculiar and distinguishing attribute with which angels are endued, is their *unfading and immortal youth.* This peculiarity is beautifully pointed out by the name *ζωα*, *living ones*, applied to them by St. John, in the Apocalypse, and by Ezekiel in his first chapter, as well as in several parts of his prophecy. By this appellation we are instructed, that life is a pre-eminent and glorious constituent of their nature—life as a peculiar property, and in a most distinguishing degree; the most perfect manifestation of that quickening energy which Christ ascribes to the Father, and challenges to himself, as an exclusive, appropriate, and wonderful attribute of the Godhead.

The truth of the immortality of the angels is also beautifully exemplified and confirmed by the adolescent appearance

* Yet, notwithstanding the incogitable force and dexterity of spirits, the theologists are of opinion that they are not of power to destroy any one element, or to pervert that constant order by which the fabric of the world is guided and governed. Yet of their incredible celerity and strength, histories are very frequent, both in the sacred Scriptures and elsewhere. We read that the angel of the Lord took the prophet Habakkuk (as he was carrying meat unto the reapers) by the hair of his head, and in the strength of the spirit, in an instant, transported him from India to Babylon.—HEYWOOD'S *Hierarchie.*

of those which were seen by *Mary*, in the tomb of Christ. These illustrious individuals were then, at least, four thousand years old; still they had the appearance of young men; and in all that long succession of ages, had not undergone the slightest indications of decay. Their youth, a bright and beautiful blossom, still shone with all its lustre and fragrance; and directly indicated that it was superior both to accident and time; and would, after many such flights of years, survive in all its undiminished vigor. Even this representation may probably, after all, be only an imperfect adumbration. The youth of angels, like their other attributes, is destined to refine, improve, and brighten forever.

This distinguishing and exalting feature of the angelical nature—*their immortality*,—was strikingly pointed out, by the Great Teacher, during his sojourn upon the earth, whilst he "tabernacled in the flesh;" when He disconcerted, by the divinity of his answer,—as the Creator and Lord of angels,—the captious inquiry and curious question propounded by the infidel Sadducees, respecting the hypothetical marriage of a woman with seven husbands,—"*whose wife she should be in the resurrection?*" to which our Savior replied, that those who should be counted worthy to obtain admission into heaven, *would neither marry nor be given in marriage; neither can they die any more; for they would be equal to the angels, and are the children of God, being the children of the resurrection*, subject to none of the changes, and decays, and vicissitudes incidental to this mortal state, where death reigns, and marriages are requisite to supply the vacancies arising from the ravages of mortality—and therefore necessary to prevent the entire extinction and extirpation of the human family; but in the celestial kingdom, the redeemed of mankind will resemble the angels of God, glorious, unchangeable, and immortal,—resplendent in the presence of Jehovah, and beatified in the eternal enjoyment of an unalterable felicity and unfading glory.

Another prominent, most distinguishing and superlatively attractive attribute of the angelical constitution is the surprising and inconceivable extent of their *knowledge and intelligence*, arising from their proximity to the overflowing and inexhaustible fountain of Divine wisdom and benevolence,—their closer and concomitant insight into the plans and purposes of Jehovah, as connected with the sovereign dispensations of his providence and the mysterious economy of redeeming grace.

Doubtless, too, they have a great familiarity with our thoughts and desires, circumstances and moral necessities, and are delegated from the up-lifted throne of the Most High, to render us important and needful aid in the services and excursions of our faith, the prayers and aspirations of penitential supplication, and the retired meditations of a contemplative devotion,* being also well acquainted with the favorites of heaven, as evidenced in the prophet Daniel, *the greatly beloved*, on whose behalf they restrained the ferocity of the ravenous lions into whose den the prophet had been cast, by the impious and irrevocable decree of King Darius.†

Amongst the ancient Jews, whose religious belief earnestly embraced and vindicated the doctrine of the existence

* How gentle are the footsteps of angels! How tender their touch! How soft their whispers! How courteous their hints to dull and weary pilgrims in the wilderness!—AMBROSE. *Communion and Ministry of Angels*, 1664.

† He had other company than the ravenous beasts, who were thus chained back into the innocuous character they sustained in the garden of Eden, and to which they shall again be restored, when the conqueror of death and sin comes to reign over a renovated earth.—CHARLOTTE ELIZABETH. *Principalities and Powers.*

and ministry of angels, the high estimation with which they regarded the exalted and intellectual prerogatives of these magisterial and celestial beings, is clearly indicated by the proverbial expressions and sayings which were in general use amongst them; illustrated in the stratagem and flattery of the *wise women of Tekoah to King David. For as an angel of God, so is my lord the king, to discover good and bad; and my lord is wise, according to the wisdom of an angel of God, to know all things that are upon the earth.*—2 Sam. xix. 17–20. Nevertheless, our knowledge, even with the aid afforded us, by the partial disclosures of Revelation, are very limited respecting the vast knowledge, sinless purity, and expansive benevolence, of these affable and amiable Immortals, either in relation to each other, or to beings in the far off regions, and distant empires of the universe. The ennobling superiority of sagacity and wisdom possessed by angels has been duly noticed and largely expatiated upon in the *exegesis* of theologians, the disquisitions of the philosopher, the breathing thoughts and burning words of profane and sacred Poesy. The learned and eminent expositor, Greenhill, *in his Commentary on Ezekiel,* observes, "That the prophet was guided by the spirit, and his cherubim hold forth the same parties to us, that Isaiah's seraphim did to him. *They had the likeness of a man,* verse 5. By their likeness to a man, is laid before us, the rationality, knowledge, and understanding of angels. They are the most understanding creatures in heaven and earth. They have prophetical knowledge in them, and a treasury of things that are past and done long since. There is mention, Rev. iv. 6, 8, of four living creatures, the same with those of Ezekiel, *full of eyes before and behind,* because they see and know what is past, and what is before them; their natural knowledge is great, being such excellent spirits. But besides that, they have much revealed to them concerning God, Christ, the church, and things contingent. Hence it is said, 1 Peter i. 2, *which things the angels desire to look into*. They understand partly by their essence, and partly by special communications to their understanding, as to ours. Angels are good philosophers; they know the principles, causes, effects, life, motion, death of natural things.—Rev. vii. 1, 2. They are great statists, and know the affairs of kingdoms.—Dan. x. 13. Gabriel saith: *I remained with the kings of Persia;* he became a courtier, and acquainted himself with the affairs of Persia.

In his truly eloquent and thrilling discourses on this interesting and engaging subject, Dr. Dwight admirably represents the high intelligence of angels as one of the most distinguishing features which adorn the character of these bright, and noble, and heavenly beings, observing that "*Angels are endowed with the greatest intellectual faculties, and of course are possessed of knowledge superior to that of any other created beings*. This character is represented to us in the Scriptures in many forms. The Living ones mentioned by the apostle John, in the Book of Revelations, are declared to have been *full of eyes within;* that is, to have been all sense, all intellect, all consciousness, turning their attention every way, beholding all at once all things within the reach of their understandings, and discerning them with a clearness of perception which is the most perfect created semblance of the intuitive and boundless views of the Omniscient Mind.

" The *face* also *of a man*, attributed to one of these illustrious beings by St. John, and to all those which appeared to Ezekiel by that prophet, is another ascription of this character to angels. The face of a man was amongst the Jews and other eastern nations, the standing symbol of *Intelligence*, and denotes here the superior possession of this attribute by those to whom it is ascribed.

" Angels were originally formed with an entire freedom from sin, the only source of prejudice, and the chief source of errors. Their faculties were at first such as became *the morning stars* of the highest heavens,—the sons of God intended to surround the throne of JEHOVAH, and to hold the chief places of power, distinction, and glory, in his eternal kingdom. They were such as to become those to whom, in the beginning, was given by God himself, the name of *Cherub*, or *fulness of knowledge*.

" They were such, in a word, as to become their other transcendent attributes of power, youth, activity, and the exalted station which they were destined to fill forever. With the nature and extent of their faculties, has the place of their residence exactly accorded. They have ever dwelt in the world where truth reigns without opposition—where knowledge is the universal state and character—where all mysteries are continually disclosed—and where the nature and propriety of both the means and the ends of Providence are, more than in any other part of the universe, unfolded. There, day and night, for six thousand years, they have been unceasingly employed in studying the works of God. Weariness and decay they know not. Strength of understanding in them is incapable of being impaired. Every object of investigation is to them delightful, and every faculty by its nature susceptible of improvement. What then must be the extent of their attainments at the present time?

" Beyond this, the favor of God is extended to them in a degree incomprehensible by such minds as ours. To communicate just and extensive views of his works to these glorious beings, is declared to be Jehovah's especial intent in the creation of things by Jesus Christ (Eph. iii. 9, 10), and peculiarly his manifold wisdom in his dispensations to the church. No communication on his part, and no attainments on theirs, can be imagined too great for this divine purpose, or the goodness by which it was formed. In Matt. xxiv. 36, our Savior declares that *of that day*, not the day of his coming to the destruction of Jerusalem, *knoweth no one, not even the angels in heaven.* This appeal, if we understand the passage in the common acceptation, can have force and pertinency, only on the supposition that nothing which is known of the works and ways of God is hidden from angels, and is, therefore, a complete proof of the entire superiority of their intellectual nature and attainments to those of any other created being."

Various writers, differing in the calibre and dimensions of their minds, or ascending in the loftier flights of their imaginations, have been attracted into animated descriptions of this ennobling and surpassing distinction of the angelical nature. The Rev. John Wesley with admirable point suggests, "What an inconceivable degree of *wisdom* must they have acquired, by the use of their amazing faculties, over and above that with which they were originally endued, in the course of more than six thousand years!" That they have existed so long we are assured; for they "sang together when the foundations of the earth were laid." How immensely must their wisdom have increased during so long a period, not only by surveying the hearts and ways of men in their successive generations, but by observing the works of God,—his works of creation, his works of providence, his works of grace! and above all, by continually beholding the face of their Father who is in heaven.

The actual possession and abundant advantages of such means for advancing their intellectual acquisitions, is thus presented by Dr. Chalmers in his "*Astronomical Discourses*: "God walked with our first parents in the garden of Paradise, and there did the angels hold their habitual converse;* and should unblotted innocence, which charmed and attracted these superior beings to the haunts of Eden, be perpetuated in every planet but our own, then might each of them be the scene of high and heavenly communications, and an open way for the messengers of God be kept up with them all, and their inhabitants be admitted to a share in the themes and contemplations of angels, and have their spirits exercised on those things of which we are told that the angels desire to look into them; and thus, as we talk of the public mind of a city, or the public mind of an empire—by the well-frequented avenues of a free and ready circulation, a public mind might be formed throughout the whole extent of God's sinless and intelligent creation—and just as we read of the eyes of all Europe being turned to one spot where some affair of eventful importance is going on, there might be the eyes of a whole universe turned to the one world, where rebellion against the Majesty of Heaven had planted its standard; and for the re-admission of which, within the circle of his fellowship, God, whose justice was inflexible, but whose mercy he had, by some plan of mysterious wisdom, made to rejoice over it, was putting forth all the might, and travelling in all the greatness of the attributes which belonged to him."

In the overtures of Divine compassion and the provisions of Almighty grace, holy angels are invariably represented as exercising a most deep and ardent solicitude, as connected with the salvation of mankind, wrought out in the

* Lord King, in his *Morsels of Criticisms*, expresses the idea, that some period will arrive, when the communications of earth and heaven will be visible, and the angels of God descend and ascend to converse with men.

Redemption effected by the Cross of Christ. The Scotch divine further observes, " It is an impressive circumstance, that when Moses and Elias made a visit to our Savior on the Mount of Transfiguration, and appeared in glory from Heaven, the topic they brought along with them, and with which they were fraught, was the decease he was going to accomplish at Jerusalem. And however insipid the things of our salvation may be to an earthly understanding, we are made to know, that in the sufferings of Christ and the glory which should follow, there is matter to attract the notice of celestial spirits ; for these are the very "things," says the Bible, "which the angels desire to look into." And however listless we, the dull and grovelling children of an exiled family, may feel about the perfections of the Godhead, and the display of those perfections in the economy of the gospel ; it is intimated to us in the book of God's message, that the creation has its districts and its provinces ; and we accordingly read of " thrones, and dominions, and principalities, and powers ;" and whether the terms denote separate regions of government, or the beings who, by a commission granted from the sanctuary of heaven, sit in delegated authority over them,—even in their eyes the mystery of Christ stands arrayed in all the splendor of unsearchable riches ; for we are told that this mystery was revealed for the very intent " that unto the principalities and powers in heavenly places, might be made known, by the church, the manifold wisdom of God."

As a minor, yet additional confirmation of the exalted and transcendent *intelligence* of angels, we produce the apposite allusions of apostolic averment respecting the utter inutility of the most splendid mental endowments, as well as the denounced inefficiency of the penetrative sagacity of an intellectual philosophy, or the oratorial eloquence of a persuasive rhetoric, in lieu of the enlightened apprehensions of an evangelical faith to understand the economy of grace in the realized blessings of Redemption :—*Though I speak with the tongues of men and of* ANGELS, *and have not charity, I am become as sounding brass or a tinkling symbol. And though I have the gift of prophecy, and understand all mysteries and all knowledge, and have not charity, I am nothing.*—1 Cor. xiii. 1, 2. *But though we, or an* ANGEL *from heaven, preach any other Gospel unto you than we have preached unto you, let him be accursed.* Gal. i. 8.

With augmented attractiveness, our subject now invites us to consider—though within too circumscribed a limit—the ennobling and radiant *characteristics* which adorn and magnify the angelical nature. And as the firm foundation, surest safeguard, and impregnable citadel of the unfading and immortal excellencies of the angelical character we present to prominent view, their confirmed and consummate *holiness*. Throughout the Scriptures, instances are multiform. and the evidence is abundant confirmatory of this delightful and exalting truth. Holiness is the well-spring from whence unceasingly flow the crystal streams of their beauty, their morality, their sensibilities, and their unalloyed pleasures. These elements and attributes of moral excellence and celestial happiness are derived from *this* virtue which constitutes the imperishable beauty of the mind, and is as superior to the exterior grace of the body as the spirituality of the soul is superior to the earthy tabernacle in which she resides. Virtue is the essential beauty and unfailing felicity of the heavenly world; and while it engrosses the attachment and the homage of angels themselves, is regarded with entire complacency by its divine author. In virtue, according to the decision of mankind, sinful as they are, is placed the moral grandeur and loveliness of intelligent beings,—that which unbiassed reason approves; which is always excellent; which is uniformly the object of delight; which will never change; and which will never cease to be desired. This peculiar and distinguishing feature in the angelical character will be better understood and enhanced in its glory by the contrasted effects of its opposite principle, which occasioned the apostacy of the fallen angels, revealed and described in the apocalypse by St. John: *And there was war in heaven: Michael and his angels fought against the dragon; and the dragon fought and his angels.*

"FALLEN ANGELS were once possessed of this illustrious attribute, and held the exalted station, which is now exclusively enjoyed by their fellows. Fallen angels are still possessed, in an eminent degree, of power, life, activity and knowledge; but they yielded up their holiness, when they revolted from their Maker; and changed forever their character and their destiny, by sinning against God. Sin converted them into fiends, and made hell their habitation. From sin, that dark and dreadful world derives all its gloom, sorrow, and despair. Sin ushered it into being; raised its prison walls; barred its iron gates; shrouded its desolate regions in the blackness of darkness; kindled the fires by which it is gloomily enlightened, and awakened all the cries, and groans, and curses, and blasphemies, which echo through its regions of sorrow. Sin changed angels, once surrounding the throne, and harmonizing in the praise of God, into liars, accusers, calumniators, adversaries, and destroyers. How amazing and dreadful the change! How loathsome, how detestable, the spirit by which it was accomplished!"

"The mighty difference between Heaven and earth, angels and men, lies in holiness and sin.* Angels are holy;

* Sin made a sad and lamentable breach, both between God and men, and

we are sinful: their residence is happy; ours, in many respects, wretched. This world was originally formed to be a delightful habitation; and at the close of creation, was by God himself pronounced to be very good. Man was once immortal and happy; because he was just, kind, sincere, humble and pious. What has the world, what has man, gained by the change? The afflicting answer may be summed up in a word. God made the earth a beautiful image of heaven; man, by his apostacy, has changed it into no obscure resemblance of hell. God made man *a little lower than the angels, and crowned him with glory and honor. Man, being in honor, abode not, but became like the beasts that perish.*"*

As a glorious manifestation of this principle in the constitution of the angelical character, *obedience*, is a conspicuous virtue, whereby they fulfil, with an alacrity, represented in the expressive imagery of a *flash of lightning*, the gracious purposes, as well as punitive procedures of the Divine Will.

"Some may think it needs be to the angels loss to leave heaven and God's presence there, to follow business in this lower world and wait upon man; but no such matter. They count it no loss to follow their master's work wherever it lie.† Neither is there an instance throughout the Bible, where an angel appears to have acted independently

between men and angels too, yea, and between them and all creatures.—*Pneumatologia.*

* Dr. Dwight, (late President of Yale College, New Haven, Connecticut, U. S.) from whose masterly and eloquent discourses *in his System of Theology*, on this superlatively beautiful subject, I acknowledge, once for all, that I have freely borrowed; and no writer that I have had the opportunity to consult equals him, either in the felicity of his diction, the force of his ratiocination, or the fertility of his chastened imagination. G. C.

† Pneumatologia.

of the divine command. Perfect submission to the authority, and cheerful performance of the behests of Jehovah, is the unvaried and exemplary character of the heavenly hosts. *Thy will be done on earth as it is in heaven*, in our Savior's comprehensive formula of prayer, is declarative of the joyous subordination which reigns with supreme harmony in the kingdom of heaven, and that encircles the throne of Deity. *Bless the Lord, ye his angels, that do his commandments, hearkening unto the voice of his word, ye ministers of his that do his pleasure*, exclaims the devout Psalmist, with the admiring emotions of expostulatory praise.

Another most attractive feature in the formation of the angelical character is their profound *humility** and instructive *meekness.* In these great and ennobling virtues, how affecting the contrast between sinful man and unfallen angels; for though greatly exalted above mortals, the illustrious inhabitants of the celestial world are unspotted by pride, and vanity, the *root* of sin, and the *stem* of bitterness. Haughtiness or vanity would instantly disrobe of all their comeliness and glory the blessed spirits of the upper sanctuary, and cause them to resemble the worst and most odious of all the creatures of God!

Who would not rather aspire to be clothed with the stainless, spiritual, and never-fading robe of humility and righteousness;—that faith, repentance, and love of the Gospel, which compose the embroidered garment, *the fine linen of*

* Indeed there shines in them such a brightness of the majesty of God, that there is nothing in which men might be more easily drawn, than with a certain admiration, to fall down in worshipping them. This very thing, St. John, in the Revelation, confesseth of himself, but he added withal, that he received this answer, "See thou do it not, for I am thy fellow-servant, and of thy brethren that have the testimony of Jesus: worship God."—AMBROSE, *Communion and Ministry of Angels.*

the saints, wrought and made white in the heavens ;—that best and beautiful robe with which, in his father's house every repenting and returning prodigal will be appareled and adorned.

How beautifully are the humility and meekness, and obedience of angels exemplified in the thrilling parable of Dives and Lazarus, "presenting to our view a choir of these illustrious and sympathising beings leaving the glory of Heaven, and directing their flight to this forlorn and sinful earth, to accompany and escort the departing spirit of poor, despised, forgotten *Lazarus*, to the world of happiness and love ; to point the way to that delightful region ; and to aid his trembling wing to the house and presence of his Father and his God. What monarch, what noble, what gentleman, what plain man would, willingly, have even attended his funeral ? Who would have received him, when alive, into his house, powerfully as his sufferings pleaded for relief ? Who, much more, would have consented to become his companion ? Who, still more, would have acknowledged himself his friend ? Yet all this, angels did not disdain.

Let us take to ourselves shame and confusion of face at the remembrance of our pride of feeling and haughtiness of heart. How often do we despise, neglect, insult, and trample under foot the disciples of Christ,—those who, in the sight of God, are far better than ourselves ! For what do we despise them ? Because, perhaps, their houses, their persons, their dress, their wealth, or their talents are inferior to our own. We might, indeed, sometimes pity them for these reasons, and be justified. But where shall we find an excuse for despising them ?"*

But the most fascinating and radiant lineament in the

* Dr. Dwight.

portraiture of the angelical character, is, their unbounded and affectionate *benevolence*;—LOVE, an essential adjunct of their nature,—the atmosphere of their existence,—their nearest approach to the most glorious of the attributes of that Supreme Being denominated the *God of Love*—the essence of Redemption—the especial provision in the novel and valedictory commandment of the Great Teacher, during the days of His humiliation, when He tabernacled "in the flesh for us men and our salvation," to his persecuted and disconsolate disciples recorded by St. John in his gospel, chap. xiii. 34, emphatically the apostle of love,—the inexhaustible fountain of terrestrial happiness and celestial felicity. The very foundation of meetness for the beatitude of heaven, must be laid in the principle of love, productive of a complete renovation in the moral faculties and sensibilities of humanity.

The grand object which love proposes to accomplish, is the communication of happiness. There is not a more amiable, attractive, or comprehensive idea of the Divine Being any where to be found than that which is exhibited by the apostle in three monosyllables—*God is Love*. He is the uncreated and eternal source of all felicity, from which flow the varied streams of joy which gladden the heart of angels and archangels, cherubim and seraphim. To manifest the exuberance of His benignity, the Almighty Creator willed into existence the material universe to serve as an immense theatre upon which to display to countless orders of sensitive and intellectual creatures, for their delight and comfort, the diversified blessings of His unlimited and spontaneous beneficence.

The excellence of love, as a principle in the moral and intelligent system, bears a striking analogy to the law of attraction in physical nature. It draws into intimate fellowship and hallowed union all holy intelligences wherever dispersed, throughout the amplitudes of creation. It assimilates and unites man to God, to the angels and archangels—those glittering courtiers of heaven, the beautiful and beatified companions of our adorable Redeemer, Jesus Christ!

Of this distinguished and attractive loveliness of character angels are supremely possessed. "Angels are sincere, gentle, meek, kind, compassionate, and perfectly conformed to that great moral principle communicated in *the word of our Lord, which he said: It is more blessed to give than to receive.* This sublime excellence, incomparably *more precious than gold which perishes,* has in them been, from the beginning, debased with no alloy, tarnished with no spot, impaired by no length of years, and changed by no weakness or imperfection. Free from every defect, and every mixture, it has varied with length of years, merely towards higher and higher perfection, and shone not only with undiminished, but with increased beauty and lustre. There is no good which it is proper for angels to do, which they are not habitually prepared to do. There is no kindness capable of being suitably exercised by them which they do not in fact exercise. The more their faculties are enlarged, and the more their knowledge is increased, the more their means of usefulness is multiplied; the more exalted is their excellence, the more disinterested and noble their dispositions; the more intense their benevolence, and the more lovely and beautiful their character; the good which they have already done, has only prepared them to do more and greater good; and the disposition with which it was done has only become stronger by every preceding exertion."

Associated with this elevating and bland distinction, angels combine in their character those magnanimous and sublimer virtues which constitute personal dignity and glory, tempered and refined by consummate humility, as connected with their intense love and undeviating apprehensions of divine truth. *Truth*, which consists in an account of the character and works of God,—subjects elevated above all height, and extended above all limits ; possessed of inherent grandeur and sublimity literally infinite ; fitted to awaken in every mind formed with an understanding to perceive, and a taste to relish them, great ideas and exalted conceptions ; and calculated to inspire habits of thinking and feeling, of the most dignified nature. To these subjects angels have already devoted themselves throughout a vast period of time, with burning intensity and fervor. Their views have all been formed without error, decay, or weariness ; and their relish for the objects of their knowledge has only been strengthened by indulgence. Of course their progress in understanding has been rapid, and their attainments have been very great. Of course, also, their minds have been continually expanded and ennobled by all the conceptions which they have entertained concerning these wonderful subjects.

With all the accumulated knowledge of their vast capacities and early history, angels supremely rejoiced when they announced to our fallen, and sinful, and ruined race, the incarnation of Christ—the mystery of godliness—redemption for a lost world ; for on that wondrous and nation-desired event, a multitude of the heavenly host sang *Glory to God in the highest, and on earth peace, good-will to men*, Luke ii. 14 ; whilst our blessed Savior's declaration represents their delight on the recovery of a penitent from his way of sin and misery. " The conversion of sinners is the jubilation of angels—heaven rings with the joy, and this plain sense or meaning of Christ's words, that when they see the ranks and files of lapsed angels filled with new recruits of men and women, penitent for their sins, this is matter of joy, of ecstatical joy to the holy angels of God. *For there is joy in the presence of the angels of God over one sinner that repenteth ;* Luke xv. 10, as if every convert was an addition to their happiness. Whilst they praise God for such an instance of his goodness, they exult in the victory obtained over the powers of darkness, and in the enlargement of the Redeemer's kingdom. They receive the young believer under their care, being commissioned to watch over him for his protection and comfort.*

"Angels have kind propensions towards men, especially good men, in this world, knowing these are of the same society and church with them; though the Divine Wisdom hath not judged it suitable to our present state of probation there should be an open and common intercourse between them and us. It is, however, a great incongruity that we should have strange, uncouth, shy, frightful or unfrequent thoughts of them in the mean time. We should bear our part in the joys of heaven; and when we are told there is joy there, among the angels of God, for the conversion of such, who are thereby but prepared to come to their assembly, we may conclude there is much for their glorification.†

It is their de light to attend upon the saints. They know one day that they shall live together, and sing together, and rejoice together; they know that the saints shall supply the room of the fallen angels, and when they meet, Oh! the joy that will be betwixt them, knowing what Christ hath done and suffered for them. The mystery of godliness is seen of angels, yea, they are ravished in the very beholding of it, as a new and strange object; *they look into*, saith Peter,—their whole spirits are taken up with it, as if it were the blessedest sight they could behold, and they are also ravished at the work of our Redemption; how should they but with delight attend the redeemed ones of Jesus Christ.—AMBROSE.

* ROBINSON—*Scripture Characters.*

† Rev. John Howe.

"God is love, and he that dwelleth in love, dwelleth in God, and God in him."—1 John iv. 16. Such is the testimony of the apostle regarding fallen men; but it is at least equally true of the holy angels. "It doth not yet appear what we shall be," the same apostle states, "but we know that when he shall appear, we shall be like him, for we shall see him as he is."—iii. 2. The vision of God transforms the character; and what an influence must that vision have upon unfallen angels? It is the present lot of the angels, that they behold the face of our Father in heaven, and it would seem as if the effect of this was to form and perpetuate in them the moral likeness of himself; and that thus a diffused resemblance to the Godhead is kept up amongst all those adoring worshippers, who live in the near and rejoicing contemplation of the Godhead. Mark then, how that peculiar and endearing feature in the goodness of the Deity, how beauteously it is reflected downwards upon us in the revealed attitude of angels! From the high eminences of heaven are they bending a wakeful regard over the men of this sinful world, and the repentance of every one of them spreads a joy and a high gratulation throughout all its dwelling-places. Put this trait of the angelic character into contrast with the dark and lowering spirit of an infidel.

"The infidel, with his mind afloat among suns and systems, can find no place in his already-occupied regards for that humble planet which lodges and accommodates our species; the angels, standing on a loftier summit, and with a mightier prospect of creation before them, are yet represented as looking down on this single world, and attentively marking the every feeling, and the every demand of all its families. The infidel, by sinking us down to an unnoticeable minuteness, would lose sight of our dwelling-place altogether, and spread a darkening shroud of oblivion over all the concerns and all the interests of men; but angels will not so abandon us; and, undazzled by the whole surpassing grandeur of that scenery which is around them, are they revealed as directing all the fulness of their regard to this our habitation, and casting a longing and benignant eye on ourselves and on our children. The infidel will tell us of those worlds which roll afar, and the number of which outstrips the arithmetic of the human understanding—and then, with the hardness of an unfeeling calculation, he will consign the one we occupy, with all its guilty generations, to despair. But he who counts the number of the stars, is set forth to us as looking at every inhabitant among the millions of our species, and the word of the Gospel beckoning to him with the hand of invitation, and on the very first of his return is moving towards him with all the eagerness of the prodigal's father, to receive him back again into that presence from which he had wandered. And as to this world, in favor of which the scowling infidel will not permit one solitary movement, all heaven is represented as astir about its restoration; and there cannot a single son, or a single daughter, be recalled from sin unto righteousness, without an acclamation of joy among the hosts of Paradise.

The expansive range of angelic benevolence extends far beyond the boundaries of human capacity and comprehension. Angels have indeed a mighter reach of contemplation than can be comprehended by mortal ken. "Angels can look down upon this world and all it inherits, as the part of a large family. Angels were in the full exercise of their powers, even at the first infancy of our species, and shared in the gratulations of that period, when at the birth of humanity, all intelligent nature gave a gladdening response, and the morning stars sang together for joy. They loved us with the love which a family on earth bears to a younger sister; and the very childhood of our tinier faculties did only serve the more to endear us to them; and though born at a later hour in the history of creation, did they regard us heirs of the same destiny with themselves, to rise along with them in the scale of moral elevation, to bow at the same footstool, and to partake in those high dispensations of a parent's kindness, and a parent's care, which are ever emanating from the throne of the Eternal on all the members of a duteous and affectionate family. Take the reach of an angel's mind, but, at the same time, take the seraphic fervor of an angel's benevolence along with it, how, from the eminence on which he stands, he may have an eye upon many worlds, and a remembrance upon the origin and successive concerns of every one of them; how he may feel the full flow of a most affecting relationship with the inhabitants of each, as the offspring of our common Father; and though it be both the effect and the evidence of our depravity, that we cannot sympathise with these pure and generous ardors of a celestial spirit; how it may consist with the lofty comprehension, and the sweet breathing love of an angel, that he can both shoot his benevolence abroad over a mighty expanse of planets and of systems, and lavish a flood of tenderness on each individual of their teeming population."*

Oh! ye blessed spirits, by virtue of the untarnished perceptions of your cherubic knowledge, and the sympathy of your seraphic benignity; full well ye understand, that *affection*, is no pretender; *grief*, no sophist; *death*, no solemn fallacy; the *Bible* no romance of cunningly-devised fables;—the warnings of perdition, and the overtures of salvation, no superstitious delusions. Full well ye know that

* DR. CHALMERS, *Astronomical Discourses.*

ye have now struck, though with the gentlest touch, an Æolian string in that Harp of Sorrow, which ye found suspended on the weeping willow of afflictive bereavement! That beloved *one*, the apparition of whose saintly form, oft I see, when entranced in the reveries of my day-dreams, and during the sleepless vigils of nocturnal vision, resembled ye in the adorning traits of your virtuous dispositions. Blessed spirits! ye were no indifferent observers of the sacredness of that parting hour, when after taking a farewell embrace of the darling object of her maternal solicitude,—the expressive type, and fragrant blossom of the rosy freshness of her unvarying love, prophesying from the loveliness of his infantile character, that he would not be long absent from her bosom —she softly wrapped around me the pure and radiant mantle of her ardent affection, whilst ye hovered around her dying couch and whispered* to her believing spirit, preparing for its anxious flight, the assurance of divine favor, "*Fear not*, I *am with thee*,"—awaiting the summons of her Savior, to waft her soul, upon the downy chariots of your swift and golden wings, to the unfading inheritance of the upper skies, as she ascended in *faith*, bright as the morning star; in *hope*, serene as a summer's eve; in *charity*, joyous as the bliss, and seraphic as the love of heaven; singing in strains which, to the sanctified ear of a scriptural anticipation, are more ethereal, harmonious, and enrapturing than were ever warbled by the fabled and expiring melody of the classic and celestial Swan.

* If the notes of distant music wafted on the air to the ear can reach and melt the heart and lift it from earth to heaven, as they often do, why cannot angelic whispers do the same? If the sighing of every evening zephyr can move the strings of the heart, and produce a concord of the tenderest and loveliest feeling, why cannot unseen angelic influences do what is thus done by "the viewless spirit of a lovely sound?"—SLACK, *Ministry of the Beautiful.*

THE ESCORT OF ANGELS.

"*Now*, Saviour, *now*, my soul receive,
Transported from this vale, to live
And reign with thee above;
Where *faith* is sweetly lost in sight,
And *hope* in full supreme delight,
And everlasting *love*."

Beholding, through the medium of the bright mirror of faith, and as reflected in the revealing glass of Inspiration, the resplendent halo of those moral excellencies which encircle the celestial worshippers of the upper sanctuary—those shining ministers of state which surround the sapphire throne of the Majesty on High; well does it behoove us in viewing the contrast of our disobedience, depravity, demerit and degradation, humbly to adopt, in the prostration of admiring devotion, the impulsive exclamation of the Royal Penitent: *O Lord, our Lord, how excellent is thy name in all the earth! What is man that thou art mindful of him? and the son of man that thou visitest him? For thou hast made him a little lower than the angels, and hast crowned him with glory and honor.** Psalm viii. 1, 4, 5.

* The present note comprises the general opinion of the most able commentators and divines respecting the literal and spiritual meaning of the fifth verse of this Psalm. He is made but a little lower than the angels;—lower, indeed, because by his body he is allied to the earth, and to the beasts that perish,—yet by his soul, which is spiritual and immortal, he may be truly said to be but a little lower than they. He is but for a little while lower than the angels; for the children of the resurrection shall be no longer lower than they. Luke xx. 36. He is endued with noble faculties and capacities. God gave him his beings—has distinguished and qualified him for dominion over the inferior creatures. Man's reason is his crown of glory; let him not profane that crown by disturbing the use of it, nor forfeit that crown by acting contrary to its dictates. He is invested with sovereign dominion over the inferior creatures, under God, and is constituted their lord. This is such a display of the Divine love to us, vile sinners, as cannot be expressed or comprehended, but should be humbly admired and adored. Every time we partake of them, we realize this dominion which man has over the

REMARKS AND STRICTURES.

To hear *marriage* spoken of by those who have assumed the Christian profession, (for in this matter, we renounce all intercourse with infidels, profligates, and socialists,) as a LOTTERY is an awful outrage upon our natural instincts, a deliberate violence committed upon our reason, and an impious impeachment of the wisdom and benevolence of God, who has circumvallated and garrisoned the domestic constitution by the most efficient provisions of our physical organization and the exquisite mental and moral sensibilities of our nature;—whilst all the discord, and concomitant infelicities which occur in this sacred enclosure have, unquestionably, arisen from those who have gained admission therein, by the imbecility or stratagems of an odious treachery. In the apostolic injunction, *Be not unequally yoked*, where can be discovered the *necessity* of the chance or fatalism of a pretended or affirmed *sortilege?* If through the fatal influence of family pride, the unhallowed lust of passion, the sordid love of money, an immoral compliance with the artificial requisitions of fashionable life, or an unauthorized submission to the urgency of parental pertinacity, (for of all oppressions the most insidious and contemptible is domestic tyranny,) an ill-starred marriage

works of God's hands; and it is a reason for our subjection to God, our chief Lord, and his dominion over us."

The text, also, has a particular reference to Jesus Christ, as expounded and illustrated by St. Paul, in Hebrews ii. 6–8, where, to prove the sovereign dominion of Christ, both in heaven and in earth, the apostle shows that he is that Man, here spoken of, whom God has crowned with glory and honor, and made to have dominion over the works of his hand. The greatest favor ever manifested to the human race, and the greatest honor ever put upon human nature, were exemplified in the incarnation and exaltation of the Lord Jesus; these far exceed the favors and honors done us by creation and Providence, though they also are great, and far more than we deserve. In this, every other instance of Divine condescension is eclipsed,—all our thoughts are swallowed up, and our contemplations must issue in wonder, love, and praise."

is effected, all the unhappiness and vicious consequences accruing therefrom,—like the unalterable law of cause and effect,—is exclusively attributable to the gross prostitution of that divine ordinance instituted by Jehovah himself, in the garden of Eden, when unpolluted by the stain and crime of man's disobedience, involving all the disastrous results which have flowed therefrom.

"Sacred wedlock! law of heaven,
By wisdom framed, in mercy given;
The spring, whence all the kindred ties
Of parents, children, brethren rise!

Curs'd be the lusts that violate
The honors of the married state;
The Lord himself in wrath severe
Will judge the vile adulterer."

The spirit of the apostolic injunction, likewise, clearly denounces the unnatural and indecorous affinity of blooming womanhood with decrepid senility, originating either in the promptings of mercenary motives, or the unseemly indulgence of amorous propensities. Equally abominable in the sight of a holy God, must be the intentions and conduct of those who think to assume the momentous responsibilities of the ministerial office, with the ostensible or avowed design of converting the pulpit into a stepping-stone for personal aggrandizement and social elevation, through the medium of an advantageous, though insincere, matrimonial alliance; while some have even gone so far as to desecrate the solemn sacrament of the Eucharist for the accomplishment of a similar purpose; neither are those clergymen free from reprehension, who, apparently unimpaired in physical strength and mental faculties, retire to the fashionable residences of watering places and summer resort, from the stated performance of ministerial labors; as soon as they have secured the *otium cum dignitate* of a *petticoat pension.*

8

What an offensive spectacle in the sight of God, Angels, and Christians, is the frequent exhibition of ecclesiastical coxcombs, whether in the adolescence, maturity, or decline, of their ministerial functions, that when they should be wooing a soul, they are evidently more anxious to court the admiration of their persons, manifested in the bestarched cravat, the becurled periwig, preparatory attitudinizing, the studied display of the perfumed cambric, dangling from the trimmed digits of the bejewelled fingers of a bepoulticed hand. The subtilty and malignity of Satan, the magnitude and grievous effects of sin, the priceless boon of Inspiration, the blood-bought gift of Redemption, and the sacred influences of the Holy Ghost cannot tolerate such solemn mockeries!

If, in the foregoing remarks, the writer is considered to have indulged in observations too severe and *outre*, he would recommend his censurers to consult the sentiments and strictures of that extraordinary theologian, the late Robert Hall, who invariably placed in juxtaposition—side by side—with vulgarity, affectation, buffoonery, pride, vanity, and pharisaism in the sacred desk—Satan, his angels and allies.

The extravagant expense for the ostentation of personal pride and social importance displayed in the fitting up, and *auctioneering*, for the most fashionable pews, in professing Christian churches, are also very serious abominations, converting the House of God—*the house of prayer.* into a house of merchandise,—*a den of thieves.*—Matt. xxi. 12, 13.

Description of the Plate.—The plate represents the escort of a departed believer to the gate of heaven. The conducting angel, being preceded by the announcing angel, on the banner of whose trumpet are given those passages which constitute the credentials or passport of Faith, and which, upon being presented to the receiving angel, the portals of the city of the heavenly Jerusalem are instantly thrown open for the admission of their charge. Lower down, is a guardian angel, surrounded by happy cherubs, conveying the son of the departed to the Paradise above; upon the drapery of whose ethereal vestment is inscribed that passage upon which is founded the doctrine of infant salvation, for the reception of such juvenile inhabitants amongst the angels of God.

RESIDENCE AND SOCIETY.

In the unwearied and exhilarating progress of our advancing and animating inquiries respecting the spiritual nature, exalted rank, amazing attributes, and beautiful characteristics of celestial intelligences, we have now arrived at an important point of our elevating and delightful theme, requiring the sober and serious consideration of the local or constituted residence of angels, usually denominated Heaven; and which is variously represented in Scripture—as the city of the living God,—the resplendent habitation of the innumerable company of angels,—the magnificent palace of the celestial Jerusalem,—the bright mansions of the incorruptible, unfading, and eternal inheritance of the saints in light,—the holy and glorified throne of Redemption and the Godhead,—the sacred Mount Zion and upper sanctuary of the Christian church, resounding with the triumphant hallelujahs of the ransomed inhabitants, victorious over Satan, sin, and mortality,—THE AUGUST AND EFFULGENT SHECHINAH OF ETERNITY.

Various and momentous as are all the revealed communications of the Bible, it is a striking circumstance, eliciting admonitory reflections, that scarcely anything is taught us in Holy Writ concerning any of the worlds included under the general name of *Heavens*, except the *Supreme* Heaven.

The reason for which, it is not difficult to ascertain, being found in the truthful conviction that whatever information might have been given or knowledge attained respecting them, would, after all, be the mere gratification of curiosity, incapable of being directed to any valuable end, as connected with our advancing holiness, or promotive of our spiritual edification; for, under the fluctuating and deceptive influence of this powerful principle, in all probability we should have been diverted by such communications, if they had been made, from the thoughtful reception of those solemn and glorious verities which ought to occupy our thoughts, as more needful in the attainment of those things which accompany salvation. Few affections of the human mind exert a stronger influence over its conduct than curiosity. Well-directed, and cautiously kept within proper bounds, it is eminently profitable to man, by prompting him unceasingly to useful inquiries, improvements in knowledge, and discoveries in science; but when suffered to wander without restraint, it conducts to mere gratification, hazardous to the real interests and eternal welfare of the soul.

But with the *Heaven of Heavens* we have a continual and most important concern. This glorious and delightful world is the place to which all our ultimate views are urgently directed by our Maker, God, and Saviour,—the blissful home to which a merciful and gracious Jehovah invites us to look, as our final rest and rescue from trouble and temptation; and the final seat of all the enjoyment which we are capable of attaining. With its illustrious and benevolent inhabitants, we shall, if we are wise, become familiarly acquainted and intimately united, and shall live in the midst of them, through ages which cannot end. Of this world, therefore, and of those happy and dignified beings who dwell therein, it has pleased an All-wise God, in the infinite condescension of his loving-kindness, to furnish us with information beneficial, various, and extensive, unfolding to our view the character of its noble inhabitants and attractive intercourse,—its sublime occupation, its gorgeous scenery, and inconceivable beautitude!

The word *heaven* is variously applied in different passages of the Bible. It is employed in reference to God, as in Daniel iv. 26. *Until thou know, that the heavens do rule.* To angels;—*The heavens are not clean in his sight*, Job xv. 15; in which passage, some commentators have supposed that an intimation is given of the fall of Lucifer. To the Christian church:—*There was war in heaven*, Rev. xii. 7,* implying the struggles and conflicts of the primitive saints and of Christianity. To a great height, *the cities are great and walled up to heaven*;†—to distin-

* By the *woman in heaven*, in the first verse of this chapter, some commentators understand the Christian church, and the *man child brought forth by her*, the first Christian emperor. The *war in heaven*, the persecutions which prevailed in the early history of Christianity. *Michael and his angels*, the confessors and champions of the gospel. *The dragon and his angels*, the idolatrous and bloody tyrants of Rome, pagan and papal, including every species of hostility against Christ and his disciples. *The casting out of this dragon*, was the overthrow of idolatry when the heathen lost the throne. *The accusations of the brethren*, those abominable, but altogether groundless, calumnies cast by the worshippers and slaves of the dragon upon the Christians and their religion. And *the wrath of the dragon or devil*, when thus subdued, exerted itself in the violence of some succeeding emperors, the heresies and discords sown among the members, and churches of Christ, and all the miseries consequent on the inundation of barbarous nations which tore in pieces the Roman empire itself. It is certain, also, that Christians, in the time of Constantine, thought the prophecy contained in this chapter was plainly fulfilled, by the great and baneful event of Constantine's advancement to the imperial throne of the Roman empire; the emperor's statue being set over his palace gate, representing him as trampling on a wounded dragon. Even Constantine himself, in his epistle to Eusebius, speaks of his conquest of Licinius, as the downfall of the dragon and the restoration of Christian liberty to all men.

† The people of the East anciently raised up the walls of their city so high, as not being liable to be scaled, they considered themselves perfectly secure from all external invasion. The same simple contrivance, is to this

guished glory. *How art thou fallen from heaven, O Lucifer, Son of the Morning,**—the firmament or expansion over our heads, in which are set the sun, moon, and stars;—the kingdom prepared before the foundation of the world;—the building not made with hands, eternal in the heavens;—the inheritance incorruptible, undefiled and that fadeth not away; the heavenly city which hath no need of a candle, nor the light of the sun or the moon to enlighten it, for God and the Lamb are the light thereof, and into which nothing that defileth can enter, being the blest abodes of purity, of knowledge, of triumph, where there are blessed companions and blest employ.

In the Scriptures the epithet *Paradise* is frequently applied to portray the distinguishing and superabundant felicity of heaven; and it is worthy of particular observation, that the word Eden, which imports extreme pleasure and delight, was often used by the inspired penmen of the Old

day, deemed a sufficient guard from the attack of the marauding Arabs. *Up to heaven*, was an oriental hyperbole or proverbial expression.

* Kings, princes, and rulers are sometimes represented by the heavenly hosts, and figuratively compared to the sun, moon, and stars. By Lucifer, in the above text, we are to understand, metaphorically, the king of Babylon, who outvied the other potentates of the East, as much as the morning star, by virtue of its peculiar brilliancy, outshines all other constellations in the firmament. The expression, also, doubtless alludes to the fall of Satan, the prince of the apostate angels, described by our Saviour, and recorded by the evangelist, Luke x. 18. *I beheld Satan, as lightning, fall from heaven.* The title of son of the morning, is common both to the morning star and to an angel; the angels being styled, in Job xxxviii. 7, *morning stars.* The fall of the apostate angels is not directly recorded in the Old Testament; but it is implied in the distinction which the inspired writers make between good and evil spirits, and is sometimes alluded to by the prophets, when they threaten destruction to proud and violent tyrants, who, in imitation of the pride of the devil, exalt themselves against God and his truth, and are the instruments of Satan in promoting idolatry and wickedness in the world.

Testament, to denote places which were either remarkably fruitful in their soil or enchantingly agreeable in their situation; in connection with the striking coincidences of divine Revelation, which opens and shuts with such corresponding and joyous subjects of contemplation. The Bible begins with the Mosaic description of the terrestrial Eden, and closes with the apocalyptic representation of the glories, magnificent grandeur, and exuberant happiness of the celestial Paradise.

Eden was remarkable for a river which issued from it; in like manner St. John describes, in the heavenly Eden, a pure river of the water of life proceeding from the throne of God and the Lamb. Each was adorned by a tree of Life, prolific with fruit, which grew in the midst thereof. These various analogies, as well as other similitudes, are evidently designed to teach us that Jehovah purposed, in the redemption of the second Adam, the Lord from heaven, to restore to his people a more perfect and enduring state of bliss than that which was forfeited by the sad and fatal disobedience of our first parents. In the closing chapters of Revelation St. John appears embarrassed and overpowered when he desired to exhibit the splendor and magnificence, the beatitude and glory of the holy and heavenly city;—its walls are jasper, high, deep, and wide;—its streets and dwelling-places of pure and pellucid gold, whose foundation and pavement are precious stones, with its twelve gates, each a pearl, watched and attended by angels.

In condescension to our limited faculties, and to aid our inadequate conceptions of invisible or spiritual things, St. John reiterates his splendid allusions to the heavenly metropolis, by reference to the holy city of Jerusalem, the pride of the Jews and the glory of the whole earth. And to express its perfect symmetry, excessive beauty, and the complete safety of its inhabitants, it is said to be four square, and to be surrounded by a wall, great and wide. It had three gates on every side, to intimate, that from all quarters of the globe there is a way opened to heaven for such who are suitably qualified to become its denizens, gathered from the east, and the west, the north, and the south, to dwell together, enfranchised with the privileges of the kingdom of God. On these gates were inscribed the names of the twelve tribes of Israel, to signify that none but the true Israel of God will be allowed admission within its sacred precincts; whilst on the twelve precious stones which composed the foundation of the city walls, were engraved the names of the apostles of the Lamb; implying that the church in heaven, like the church on earth, is built upon the foundation of the apostles and the prophets, Jesus Christ himself being the chief corner stone.

The word *Paradise* occurs three times in the Old Testament, where it is employed to express the high culture of beautiful gardens, fruitful orchards, and enchanting scenery; likewise in the New Testament, in relation to heaven, in the affecting spectacle of our Saviour, during the agonies and ignominy of the crucifixion, when he imparted the gracious promise to the penitent thief on the cross: *To-day shalt thou be with me in Paradise.* The ecstatic declaration of the apostle: *How that he was caught up into Paradise, and heard unspeakable words, which it was not lawful for a man to utter;*—the animating assurance afforded to the faithful warrior in the Christian warfare: *To him that overcometh will I give to eat of the tree of life, which is in the midst of the Paradise of God.*

Not only in Scripture terminology is this appellation employed, as a synonyme to convey the idea of the most exquisite pleasures and consummate beatitude which reign supremely in heaven, but the pagan world and ancient mythology attempted similar representations respecting the heaven of their gods, heroes, statesmen, philosophers, poets, and all those deemed worthy of an apotheosis, as a spot of peculiar and entrancing blessedness, which they situated in some far distant and lovely island, unvisited by mortals, or else their imagination placed it in the Hesperian gardens of their Elysian fields, which their fancy beautified with beds of odoriferous flowers, embowered walks, spicy groves, and shrubberies of aromatic sweetness, quiet valleys and crystal streams, sparkling fountains and unclouded skies, fanned by perfumed zephyrs, upon whose aereal wings floated, in unearthly melody, the harmonious chants of the matins and vespers of the blest.

But we eagerly return from this digressive reference to the dark superstitions of benighted heathenism, the classic philosophy of polished Greece, and the elaborate mythology of martial Rome, to some more appropriate reflections upon the spirituality of the heaven of Christianity ; and amongst the ineffable advantages which will attend our introduction into heaven, will be the inconceivable opportunities which will be offered to our renovated perceptions, of a more satisfactory knowledge and deeper insight into the inscrutible mysteries of Divine Providence, and the economy of all-mighty grace.

In heaven* our knowledge and attainments will brighten and expand in proportion, in glorious correspondency to the inconceivable and amazing advantages of the celestial state. Even in the present probationary and progressive steps of our fallen condition, aided by the astonishing discoveries of

* If the mind of an infant can expand, during the lapse of years, to the dimensions of a Newton's mind, notwithstanding all the unfavorable circumstances in which it is here placed, why may it not, during an eternal residence in heaven, with the omniscient, all-wise God for its teacher, expand so far as to embrace any finite circle whatever.—Dr. Payson, *Sermons.*

divulging science, what rapid advancement has recently been made in our apprehensions of the wonderful and hitherto hidden secrets—the sublime and surprising *arcana* of the natural world and physical nature. An acquaintance with the mineral kingdom has imparted to man the power of subduing the earth, and appropriating her productions for his use and comfort. From the science of astronomy, accompanied with an insight into the properties of the magnet, he has derived the ability to traverse the wide and tempestuous ocean, converting it from a separating barrier, into a connecting medium of brotherly intercourse, with the numerous families of the different nations dispersed over the surface of the terraqueous globe. A familiarity with the principles of aerostation, enables him to ascend and float in the subtle element of the circumambient air, and penetrate the clouds, until he becomes invisible in the distant regions of atmospheric space, enveloped in the variegated and elegant curtains of the starry firmament of the solar system ; so that, by the auxiliary information of analogy, drawn from the study of prying science, the rich and beauteous provinces of instructive nature, we are assured that when we dwell with celestial intelligences, our spiritualized perceptions will be rendered capable of reaching the loftiest attitudes of angelic sagacity and knowledge ; for says our Saviour : *The children of the resurrection—the children of God, will be equal to the angels,*—on the same equality with them in glory, honor, dignity, felicity, and immortal wisdom.

The noblest, more important, and by far the most attractive view of the angelical residence, is derived from the consideration of its being the especial dwelling-place of Jehovah, and which in the Scriptures is frequently styled the *Heaven of Heavens, the holy Mountain, the House of God,* the favorite habitation chosen by Deity, where God displays the manifestations of His glory and effulgence in a manner superior to any other place in the circle of the universe. It is also called by the pre-eminent distinction of the locality, *The throne of God*, the seat of universal and endless dominion, where the Divine authority is peculiarly exercised and made known, and the splendors of the Divine government exhibited with inconceivable lustre and grandeur.

It is likewise distinguished as being the blissful residence of his most favored creatures—the saints who are redeemed by the blood of his Son, and of the innumerable company of angels which *stand round about the throne*. As the centre of consummate holiness, radiating virtue, and Divine communications, it appears with transcendant beauty and glory; where the divine principle shines without alloy, and flourishes in immortal youth; where the finishings of Almighty workmanship and the endless diversities of omniscient skill are exhibited in the most exquisite forms, and in the last degrees of refinement and perfection; the ocean from which all the streams of infinite wisdom and goodness proceed, and into which they return, flowing with the unfathomable depth and inexhaustible fullness of joy everlasting, and pleasures for evermore!

The resplendent throne of God may further be considered as the capital of the universe.* "From this glorious centre

* There is an astronomical idea which may help us to form conceptions of *this glorious high throne*, which is the peculiar residence of the Eternal; it being highly probable, if not certain, from minute observations on the nature of the law of gravitation, and other circumstances, that all the systems of the universe revolve round one common centre, and that the centre may bear as great a proportion in point of magnitude, to the universal assemblages of systems, as the sun does to his surrounding planets; and since our sun is five hundred times larger than the earth, or all the other planets, and their satellites taken together, on the same scale, such a central body would be five

embassies may be occasionally dispatched to all surrounding worlds, in every region of space. Here, too, deputations from all the different provinces of creation may occasionally assemble, and the inhabitants of different worlds mingle with each other, and learn the grand outlines of those physical operations and moral transactions which have taken place in their respective spheres. Here may be exhibited to unnumbered multitudes, objects of sublimity and glory, which are no where else to be found within the wide extent of creation. Here intelligences of the highest order, who have attained the most sublime height of knowledge and virtue, may form the principal part of the population of this magnificent region. Here the glorified body of the Redeemer may have taken its principal station, as the head of all principalities and powers, and here likewise Enoch and Elias may reside, and according to the general tenor of Scripture, where God's throne is, where Christ in his glorified body is, in this royal city of the King of Kings, and there is also the home of the sainted dead.*

The residence of angels is also denominated, by way of eminent distinction, the *third heavens, the holiest of holies*,†

hundred times larger than all the systems and worlds in the universe. Here may be a vast universe in itself—an example of material creation exceeding all the rest in magnitude and splendor, and in which are blended the glories of every other system. If this is in reality the case, it may with most emphatic propriety be termed *the Throne of God*.—DR. DICK. *Philosophy of Religion.*

* DR. CHALMER'S *Astronomical Discourses.*

† The most exact representation of the heavenly world (considered as a place) that was ever given to men, was the ancient tabernacle, formed after the pattern given to Moses in the Mount. That magnificent and divine pavilion was the emblem and the type of heaven itself, and built by Moses partly to be a place of Jehovah's visible residence, as the King of Israel, and partly to be the centre and medium of that solemn worship which the Jewish people were required and enjoined to render to him. Within the

in which converge and are concentrated all the most glorious manifestations and displays of the divine Majesty; rendering the celestial scenery worthy of the infinite merit and purchase of the Son of God,—worthy of the most enlarged desires, anticipations and hopes of the redeemed,—the amazing theatre in which an eternal providence of progressive knowledge, power and love, and all the diversities of virtuous intelligence,—all the forms and hues of *Moral Beauty*, will brighten in an unceasing gradation, and where the harmonious anthems of gratitude and praise, love and enjoyment, will eternally resound.

This ineffably delightful spot, an apostle has enchantingly represented *as the new heavens and the new earth, wherein dwelleth righteousness;*—where God will wipe away all tears from every eye, where there shall be no more death, neither sorrow, nor crying, neither shall there be any more pain; for the former things are passed away; and amongst its various and peculiar privileges will be access to the tree

second veil of this tabernacle called the *sanctum sanctorum*, or holiest of holies, Aaron was forbidden access at all times. Within its sacred enclosure were deposited the golden censer, and the ark of the covenant overlaid with gold, wherein was the golden pot that had manna, and Aaron's rod that budded, and the tables of the covenant, and the cherubim of glory in which God dwelt in the awful cloud that overshadowed the mercy-seat; so in like manner He resides, in the holiest of all in the heavens, as he does not in any other part of the universe. Behold the heaven is his throne and the earth is his footstool. Heaven is the centre of his operations, and perhaps we might say, of his essence.

God, who only gave six days to the work of creation, employed forty days in giving instructions that the tabernacle might be made. For that in which the representation of the world of grace was manifested was by far the most wondrous work. One chapter alone is occupied by Moses in describing the structure of the visible world; more than six in explaining that of the tabernacle; thus we are taught, that the latter is no less to be attended to than the former, since from considering thereof the marvels of Christ are made known to us.—WITSIUS.

of life, denoting a state of immortality. "Blessed indeed are they who do his commandments, that they may have right to the tree of life, and may enter in through the gates into the city."

Notwithstanding our imperfect and inadequate perceptions of the incomprehensible glories of the heavenly state, sufficient has been graciously revealed,* to animate the ravished soul, during her terrestrial sojourn in the tabernacle of this present life of darkness and doubt, dangers and despondency, distress and death, to urge her continually to chant the sonnet of devout aspiration, grateful and adoring praise:

"Who, who would live alway, away from his God;
Away from yon heaven, that blissful abode,
Where the rivers of pleasure flow o'er the bright plains,
And the noon-tide of glory eternally reigns!
Where the saints of all ages in harmony meet,
Their Savior and brethren, transported to greet,
While the anthems of rapture unceasingly roll,
And the smile of the Lord is the feast of the soul!"

* The Christian, however, must propose these questions to himself: "Amidst all this waste of worlds," where is the heaven of his religion? Where is the abode of the body of Christ, which visibly ascended into another place through the firmament above us? The Christian cannot be defrauded of his consolations by the powers of the telescope, nor the loftiest flights of imagination. The God who made the noble universe, gave also Christianity to man, to direct him to an existence in a state of immortality. But if there is a state, or condition, there must also be a place in which we must dwell; and that place we are repeatedly assured, is the same place which the body of Christ now possesses. If St. Stephen was permitted to see the Shechinah, preparatory to his being stoned, his visual faculties shall have been so strengthened that the inconceivable distance between earth and heaven was, as it were, annihilated. St. Stephen, filled with the Holy Ghost, saw, in the flesh, his blessed Redeemer. The heaven of heavens was brought near to man, and the first Christian martyr was enabled to behold it, as a pledge and earnest of his own immortal happiness; and through him a pledge to all those who by the same faith shall offer

But we hasten to offer a few brief and concluding observations regarding the attractive *society* and inviting *associations* of the celestial state ; and which will consist of those glorious spirits who have stood fast in their original integrity, have never swerved from the allegiance of their loyalty to the Majesty enthroned upon the illimitable circle of universal empire. *The children of the resurrection, the children of God,* will hold friendly and intimate intercourse with the purest and most fascinating, the most amiable and lovely intelligences that were ever created, as the representatives of the exuberant beneficience and supreme holiness of Jehovah—whose obedience has never been disturbed by a single emotion of rebellious feeling—whose characters have never been tarnished by one solitary stain of impurity—whose eyes have never been sullied by one momentary tear, and whose hearts have never been seduced by the influence of temptation. As objects of contemplation, angels present to us the delightful spectacle of inherent light, beauty, and greatness. These noble and illustrious beings never indulge in sloth, deceit, wrath, malice, envy, or impiety. "Angels never cheat, corrupt, betray, or oppress. Angels never profane the name of God, perjure themselves, ridicule sacred things, insult the Redeemer, resist the Holy Ghost, nor deny the being, the perfections, the word, or the government of God. Angels never consume their time in idle amusements, or guilty pleasures ; never slander each other, never quarrel, never make wars, and never desire or plunder each other's blessings."

In the survey of those beauteous and resplendent excellencies which, like an ethereal and radiant garment, surrounds and adorns the character and conduct of these love-

themselves living and acceptable sacrifices to God.—Dr. Chalmers, *Astronomical Discoveries.*

ly and affectionate,* immaculate and impeccable inhabitants of the skies, and worshippers in the temple and within the veil of the upper skies, well may Poesy, animated and inspired by such an array of moral virtues, burst forth into the sacred aspiration—

" In *such society* as this,
My willing soul would stay;
And sit and sing herself away
To everlasting bliss."

Another most cheering, elevating, and unspeakably attractive view of the society of heaven, is presented and urged in the joyous expectation and animating desire of meeting and mingling with the most excellent characters that have ever appeared upon the face of this ruined world, —patriarchs, prophets, apostles, martyrs, and the redeemed, " gathered out of every kindred, and people, and nation, and language, and tongue," purified from every earthly imperfection, divested of all infirmity, and clothed with the lustre of the spiritual body—a glorious community, which, in the comprehensive and descriptive declaration of the Scripture, is styled *the general assembly and church of the first born, and the spirits of just men made perfect.*

How enrapturing, too, the thought and belief, that we shall there greet in the *beauty of holiness*, and the worship of the liturgical services of the upper sanctuary, those endeared objects of affection—*the desire of our eyes*—and the children of our love, who have preceded us to the kingdom of glory, delivered from all the infelicities of those dis-

* There is not a single reason to believe that angels ever exercised, even in one instance, personal resentment against the basest and most guilty child of *Adam;* or a revengeful thought against the most depraved inhabitant of hell. No provocation is able to disturb the serenity of their minds. No cloud ever overcasts their smiles, or intercepts the clear sunshine of their benevolence.—DR. DWIGHT.

ciplinary and afflictive dispensations incidental to our present state of existence in this sin-disordered world,—to greet them in those bright and celestial mansions, where the exercise of the refined sensibilities of our spiritualized nature will be liable to suffer no disturbance or interruption from the sufferings of pain, the debility of disease, the vexations of disappointment, the sorrows of unexpected vicissitudes and unforeseen woes, the aberrations of a distempered sensorium,* the avarice which annihilates natural affection, the tormenting reproaches of an awakened conscience, those invasions of mental and moral distress, which in this troublous life besiege and entrench the soul, or the heart-rending separation of the inflexible decree of death! How captivating, then, and supporting the anticipation of thus greeting one another in this goodly and harmonious fellowship† and revealed beatitude of heaven; for Christ has averred, *that in that world, the children of God, being the children of the resurrection, shall be ισαγγελοι, equal or like to the angels*,† invested, adorned, and beatified with the same attributes, knowledge, holiness, dignity, and the ineffable enjoyment of the divine favor!‡

* Amongst the sanitary measures for the recovery of those laboring under mental affliction, as the consequence either of disease or grief, the attendance on the services of sabbatical worship and the observance of religious exercises, are found to be the most soothing, and effectively beneficial; assuredly, then, such a cogent demonstration of the adaptation of Christianity to meet the multiform ailments of our physical nature, as well as the moral necessities of the "*divinity that stirs within us*," it well behooves the *philosopher* to ponder with admonitory astonishment, and the *infidel* with warning consternation.

† I believe there shall never be an anarchy in heaven; but as there be hierarchies amongst the angels, so shall there be degrees of priority amongst the saints.—Sir Thomas Browne, *Christian Morals*.

‡ The bodies of good men, saith St. Augustine, after the resurrection shall be *qualia sunt angelorum corpora*, such as the bodies of angels; and, also, that they shall be *corpora angelica in societate angelorum*, fit for society and converse with angels.

This animating conviction and noble aspiration of a biblical faith, is quaintly, yet strikingly represented in the following expressions of the fervid and devout Isaac Ambrose, in his nervous discourses on the *Communion and Ministry of Angels* : "Adam was kept out of Paradise by cherubims, yet cherubims and seraphims, and all the host of heaven are ready to receive the saints into the glorious city. O! what a joy will be in heaven at the first admittance of these souls! what clasping, closing, kissing, embracing will be at this entrance betwixt saints and angels. Welcome, say the angels, and welcome say the archangels, yea, the principalities triumph, and powers rejoice, and virtues shine, and thrones glitter, and cherubim give light, and seraphim burn, at the soul's arrival, where they shall live together, and love together, and sing together Jehovah's praise!" To which may be added the corresponding sentiments of the eccentric and pious *Skelton* : "What a glow of the infinite sweetness of love and friendship will pervade the 'spirits of good men made perfect;' to see those souls, who perhaps, in this life contended bitterly about the trifles of this world, meeting like 'righteousness and peace, kissing each other,' to see them strike hands, and unite hearts forever. Among this glorious company there is none that doth not contribute largely to the satisfaction and entertainment of the rest. There is no weak reasoning, no biassed judging, no tedious searches after knowledge; no ill-natured ridicule, no trifling, no impertinence; no pride, nor jealousy, nor envy."

Amidst the trials, and temptations, and bereavements of this probationary scene of mortality, how consolatory and sustaining the hope, and stimulating the promise of the living oracles of inspired truth, of an admission into *that building of God, the house not made with hands, eternal in the heavens :*

"Where numerous households meet at last,
In one eternal home."

But the unspeakable majesty, the crowning glory, the splendid magnificence of the residence and society of heaven will consist of the presence of JESUS CHRIST, as seated on the throne of everlasting love and universal empire. In this transcendentally overpowering contemplation of heaven, *hope*, brightens; *faith*, adores; and *charity*,—the favorite and radiant guest of a blissful eternity—burns with fresh accessions of divine ardor. As the reward of Redemption,—as the trophies of his victory over death and the grave,—as the purchase of his precious and atoning blood, the adopted children of God, sanctified by the gracious influences of the promised Paraclete, will forever stand around the flaming throne of his sovereignty, irradiate in the dazzling effulgence of the ineffable complacency of the Godhead,—in that resplendent pavilion and sacred temple of celestial regality, which an elegant writer has thus represented:—"Whatsoever heaven is higher than all the rest of the heavens; whatsoever sanctuary is holier than all which are called holies; whatsoever place is of greater dignity in all those courts above, into that place did Christ ascend, where in the splendor of his Deity, he was before he took upon himself our humanity."

But before dismissing our reflections on this august and mysterious subject, we desire with respectful remonstrance, earnest expostulation and Christian sincerity, prompted by the unswerving loyalty of our *faith*, to address those who *seek to cast Christ down from his excellency*. Give a negative to the Deity Christ, and discord is instantly introduced amongst the attributes of Jehovah! Reject the Deity of Christ, and the melting tragedy of the sacrificial and ensanguined summit of Calvary becomes a solemn mockery, and dreadful delusion ; extorting with a bitterness which no language can portray, the dolorous lamentation and afflictive announcement of apostolic averment, "We are of all men indeed the most miserable." Deprive Christ of his Deity, and instantly the key stone is displaced out of the arch of salvation which tumbles into inevitable ruin and irrecoverable destruction! If Christ be not divine, then *Heaven* is annihilated, and creation also deprived of her Maker and Lord, Benefactor and Upholder! The denial of the Deity of Christ involves the awful and petrifying alternative of making God a liar, and violating, by a forbidden idolatry, the second commandment of the decalogue, which *was received by the disposition of angels*, amidst the blackness and darkness, the thunder and lightnings of the august and terrific scenery enacted upon the smoking summit of the trembling mount of Sinai.*

For there are three that bear record in heaven, the Father, the Word, and the Holy Ghost; and these three are one. If we receive the witness of men, the witness of God is greater; for this is the witness of God which he hath testified of his Son. He that believeth on the Son of God hath the witness in himself; he that believeth not God hath made him a liar, because he believeth not the record that God gave of his Son. 1 John v. 7, 9, 10.

For I testify unto every man that heareth the words of the prophecy of this book, If any man shall add unto these things, God shall add unto him the plagues which are written in this book: and if any man shall take away from the words of the book of this prophecy, God shall

* The late Dr. Channing, (the intellectual champion and most eloquent writer amongst the Unitarians of this country,) in his essay upon heaven, represents it as scarcely better than a nursery for the improvement of our mental faculties. What a difference—what an impassable gulf—between the heaven ot the Socinian and the Christian.—G. C.

take away his part out of the book of life, and out of the holy city, and from the things which are written in this book. Rev. xxii. 18, 19.

Ashamed of Jesus ! sooner far,
Let evening blush to own a star;
Ashamed of thee, whom angels praise,
Whose glories shines through endless days.

Ashamed of Jesus ! that dear friend,
On whom my hopes of heaven depend;
No ! when I blush, be this my shame,
That I no more revere his name.

Ashamed of Jesus ! yes I may,
When I've no sins to wash away,
No tear to wipe, no good to crave,
No fears to quell, *no soul to save.*

Till then—nor is my boasting vain,
Till then, I boast a Saviour slain,
And oh ! may this my glory be,
That Christ is not *ashamed of me.*—GRIGG.

Whosoever therefore shall confess me before men, him will I confess also before my Father which is in heaven. But whosoever shall deny me before men, him will I also deny before my Father which is in heaven.

TRADITIONARY AND DELINEATIVE.

The Talmudists appear to have regarded, in the theory of their legends, the garden of Eden as an intermediate state, in the light of a residence for the souls of the righteous immediately after death; and also adopted the belief that the bodies of Enoch, Elias, and St. John the Evangelist were translated thither, in order that they might not undergo the process of death and decomposition; and that they will remain there until the end of the world;—making the dimensions of Paradise one hundred and sixty times larger than the terrestrial globe, stating that Paradise and hell were among the seven things which God created before the formation of the material universe.

The Jews retain a tradition that Moses their leader having ascended to Heaven to intercede before God on their behalf, he received from the hands of Jehovah the two tables of stones, carved from the sapphire of the throne of his preciousness, and during his stay there, when Jah gavė to him the law and commandments, the wicked of that generation arose and made a golden calf. When Moses returned, bearing the two tables, learning the offences of the people, his hands became heavy, and they fell from him, and were broken. After this serious catastrophe Moses re-ascended to propitiate Jah, on account of the rebellious wickedness of the children of Israel; Rabbinical writers affirming that in his second entrance into heaven, Moses having prayed for the people, and propitiated the displeasure of Jah, received the revelation of the institutions of divine worship, and also heard the dreadful voice of the holy and blessed God.

St. Athanasius poetically described the spicy gales which breathe over the Indian seas, to have come from the neighborhood of Paradise, which God planted in the East; whilst Origen resolved the second chapter of Genesis altogether into an allegory, referring Paradise to the third heaven; transforming the trees into angelic virtues, and its rivers into waters above the firmament. St Augustine also composed a hymn entitled *de Gloria Paradisi*, glowingly descriptive of the loveliness and luxuriant fruitfulness of the gardens designed and prepared for the blest.

Some suppose Eden to have been the earth in miniature, and to have contained specimens of all natural productions, as they appeared, without blemish, in an unfallen world, in the utmost profusion.

The North American Indians believe that beyond the most distant mountains of their country, there is a great river, and beyond that river a vast territory, and on the other side of that region a world of water, and in that water a thousand islands, abounding with fruitful trees, and transparent streams, and that a thousand buffaloes and ten thousand deer graze on the grassy hills and ruminate in the verdant valleys, and that when they die the Great Spirit will conduct them to this happy and distant land of souls.

No man, it is presumed, ever read the history of our first parents contained in the second chapter of Genesis, without being deeply interested in their state as well as their character. The Paradise allotted to them as their proper residence, has, in a high degree, engaged the attention, and awakened the delight of every reader. Its majestic trees laden with luscious fruits, its fields arrayed in verdure and adorned with variegated flowers, the life which breathed in its fragrant winds and flowed in its crystal rivers, the serenity of its sky, and the splendor of its sunshine, together with the immortality which gilded and burnished all its beauteous landscapes and enchanting scenery, have filled the heart with rapture, and awakened the most romantic visions of the imagination. The poets of the West, and still more those of the East, have, down to the present hour, kindled at the thought of this exhibition of perfection and profusion, production and perfume; and the very name of Eden has met the eye as a gem, in the verse which it adorned. Nay, it has been transferred by God himself to the world of glory, and become one of the appropriate and favorite designations of Heaven, in reference to the attainment of salvation, as the noblest and all-satisfying recompense of reward to the faithful adherents of Christianity. *To him that overcometh,* saith our Saviour, *I will give to eat of the tree of life, which is in the midst of the Paradise of God.*

The pagans, as well as the ancient philosophers, entertained a strange variety of opinions respecting the locality and constitution of the heavens or firmament, and the occupations of its multitudinous inhabitants. In ancient astronomy, the ethereal heavens were represented as an orb, or a circular region, in which the number of the heavens varied according to the different or apparently independent motions of the celestial bodies. Other philosophers make their enumeration to correspond with that of the seven planets. The region of the fixed stars was denominated the stellar firmament. Ptolemy included in his system nine heavens, to which Alphonso, king of Castile, added a tenth or crystalline heaven, to remedy some irregularity in his astronomical theory, and over which was drawn the empyreal heaven, which was appropriated as the particular residence of Deity. Others, again, admitted into their hypotheses a large plurality of heavens. Eudoxus specifies twenty, Callipus thirty, Regiomontanus thirty-three, Aristotle forty-seven, and Francastor seventy. Amongst the heathens, heaven was considered as the special residence of their gods, into which no mortals were admitted, after death, unless they were accounted worthy of deification, whilst the souls of good men were assigned to the Elysian fields.

In modern astronomy the term heaven is employed to denote the ethereal expanse in which the stars, planets, comets, &c., are disposed, and called by Moses the firmament, recorded as the work of the second day's creation; whilst recent scientific discoveries have ascertained more correctly the laws which regulate the planetary motions of the solar system, and accordingly exploded the errors of ancient and numerous theories.

Plato gives a description of heaven, bearing so close a resemblance to the magnificent representations of Isaiah and St. John, that Eusebius charges the philosopher with plagiary.

Description of Plate.—The plate is designed to represent the scriptural residence of angels. In the centre is an hieroglyphic of the Trinity, on each side of which is presented an emblematic figure of the second and third Persons of the Godhead, encircled by adoring angels and worshipping saints, as described by Saint John the apostle:—" And round about the throne were four and twenty seats; and upon the seats I saw four and twenty elders sitting, clothed in white raiment, and they had on their heads crowns of gold. The four and twenty elders fall down before Him that sat upon the throne, and worship him that liveth for ever and ever, and cast their crowns before the throne, saying, Thou art worthy to receive glory and honor and power; for thou hast created all things, and for thy pleasure they are and were created." Rev. xiv. 4, 10, 11.

" Princes to his imperial Name,
Bend their bright sceptres down;
Dominions, Thrones, and Powers rejoice,
To see Him wear the crown.

" Archangels sound his lofty praise
Through every heavenly street;
And lay their highest honors down,
Submissive at his feet."—WATTS.

" Legions of Angels, strong and fair,
In countless armies shine;
And swell his praise with golden harps,
Attuned to songs divine."—GREGG.

THE *UBI*;
or
Residence of Angels.

EMPLOYMENTS AND PURSUITS.

We have now reached and cheerfully ascend the Pisgah of our interesting and important subject, from whose elevated and sequestered summit, with the eye of our faith undimmed, and the force of our hopes unabated, we are vouchsafed a goodly and animating prospect of that heavenly Canaan which we anticipate, when it shall please the Lord God to speak to us in the summons of death, and withdraw us from the turmoil, vocations, and entanglements of the devious windings of our passage through this wilderness world, being called to worship Him in the eternal rest and unfading beatitude of the promised city and glorious temple of the celestial Jerusalem.

Before we proceed further, however, it may be expedient to advert to the objection which has been mooted, *of the improbability of the continued agency and ministrations of angels*, because of their non-appearance, in visible forms, since the days of the apostles, and to which objection it is deemed only requisite to reply, that the canon of Scripture being closed, and the last dispensation of Divine purpose having been ushered in by those signs and wonders, instrumentalities and manifestations, whose miraculous interventions were needed to establish the divine origin and permanent continuance of the economy and institution of Christianity—until the "consummation of all things," according to fulfilled, as well as unfulfilled prophecies,—are now withdrawn, as not requiring any additional confirmation of their truth and binding obligations. "*To the law and to the testimony, if they speak not according to this word, it is because there is no light in them.*" Isaiah viii. 10. *If they hear not Moses and the prophets, neither will they be persuaded, though one rose from the dead.* Luke xvi. 31.

During the patriarchal, Mosaic, and prophetical dispensations, Jehovah was pleased to manifest his will, and foreshow his gracious purposes, and foretell his threatened judgments by instructive dreams, informing visions, audible voices, and the apparition of angelic messengers, to awaken the attention, excite the obedience, and confirm the faith of those who put their trust in Him, in relation to the procedures of his providence, and the promises of Almighty grace, during the dawning periods of Christianity, prefigured in the types and shadows of the Aaronic priesthood, until their complete accomplishment in the meridian glory of the present and final economy of divine purpose in the Revelation of Christ Jesus, the Great Antitype, *who hath brought life and immortality to light by the gospel;* and, therefore, we conclude, that with the age of miracles, the supernatural interposition of the visible appearance of angels is withdrawn, as unnecessary, and contrary to the wisdom of God, in the superfluous exhibition of miraculous operation and confirmatory evidence, beyond the necessities of human reason and the requisite apprehensions of an acquiescent faith.*

No less futile is the suggestion, that the doctrine of angelic ministration is of too speculative a character to pro-

* God sends not angels now to propose new articles of faith, or to give new laws to men, he having fully furnished the rule of our religion by Jesus Christ. And as for interpretations of Scripture, none must be received that agree not with the context and the analogy of faith.—*Pneumatologia.*

GUARDIAN ANGEL.

duce sufficiently edifying results. The eternal love of God and the blessings of free grace,—the inscrutable decree of the sovereignty of a special and divine election,—justification by faith, together with our adoption as the children of God—the mediation and intercession of Christ,—the joys of heaven, and the sanctifying influences of the Holy Ghost—as the essential doctrines of an orthodox Christianity, are not a whit less speculative, as regards the tendency of their practical effects, and especially designed to promote a life of holiness, and a preparation for the worship and employments of the heavenly state.

By such a process of intangible objections, it is evident that we should be deprived of the very vitalities and principles of an evangelical faith, rendering our hopes nothing better than a fleeting shadow, instead of an invaluable substance,—a lifeless skeleton, instead of an animated body.

Various have been the opinions of expositors as to the time when the angels commenced their ministrations on this earth; some supposing, that they are exercised as soon as we are quickened into existence, in the womb, founded on the following passages.—Psalm cxxxix. 14–16; Luke i. 41. Others, at the time of birth, of baptism or regeneration. Every supposable case of danger to which infancy and childhood are liable, angels are supposed to watch and provide a suitable protection. The imprudences of mothers, the carelessness of nurses, the generally unguarded and hazardous circumstances to which the young from the earliest dawn of existence are exposed, receive the especial notice and provision of these celestial and benevolent intelligences, as their guardian angels.*

* Plato was of opinion that children are no sooner born, but they have angels to attend them, which first produce and then conjoin the soul to the body, and after they are grown to maturity, teach and govern them.

The ancient philosophers, as well as some modern commentators, believe that every individual has appointed unto him a guardian angel that attends upon his welfare through all the different stages of this mortal life; whilst in the Scriptures we find mention of several instances in which angels were sent by divine commission to instruct and protect the favorites of God's special regard, or to act as the executioners of the divine displeasure against all ungodliness of men, or to make known his purposes respecting the dispensations of his mercy to mankind. It was through the instrumentality of an angel that the prediction was given to Hagar respecting the future character and prosperity of Ishmael. The angel Gabriel informed Daniel of a variety of events which would befall the Jewish nation; and also visited with divine messages and announcements, Zacharias, and the Virgin Mary. They were angels that were entertained by the hospitable and venerable patriarch, and who communicated to Abraham the will and gracious purposes of Jehovah respecting the birth of Isaac, and the wonderful events which were to happen to the nations who were to spring from him. Throughout the extraordinary and eventful periods of his pilgrimage, angels constantly appeared to the patriarch Jacob, and conveyed to him counsel, and ministered to his behalf, and that of his family. Angels rescued Lot and his daughters from the destruction of Sodom. An angel of the Lord attended the Israelites during their journeyings in the wilderness; and the moral law was received by the disposition of angels on Mount Sinai.

Joshua, the successor of Moses, was encouraged by the appearance of an angel in the martial character of the *captain of the host of the Lord*, whilst he was meditating an attack on the city of Jericho (Joshua v. 13, 14); but who, however, by most commentators, has been considered as the Angel-Jehovah. An angel appeared to the valorous Gideon, bidding him deliver the Israelites out of the hands of the Midianites—whilst a mighty angel destroyed in one night an hundred fourscore and five thousand of the veterans of the army of Sennacherib.*

In the New Testament the employments of angels on behalf of those who are chosen of God, by the redemption which is in Christ Jesus, are rendered prominently conspicuous. "*Are they not all ministering spirits*," says St. Paul, "*sent forth to minister for them who shall be the heirs of salvation?*" In this passage we are obviously taught, that ministering to the saints, without any distinction or exception of rank or station, is a permanent employment of angels. They conducted Joseph and Mary to Egypt, Philip to the eunuch, and Cornelius to St. Peter, who obtained from the apostle a knowledge of the Gospel, to the salvation of himself, his family, and his friends. They also comforted the apostle and his companions after the resurrection, Paul, immediately before his shipwreck, and the church of Christ universally. Often when the children of affliction are murmuring under the disciplinary dispensations of God's Providence and Grace, some ministering angel is on the wing, bearing the succor they require, the comfort they need, and putting to the blush the language of their unbelieving hearts.†

* Otway tells us, in describing the horrors of the plague, which almost depopulated London, that the "Destroying Angel" stretched his arms over the city.

"Till in th' untrodden streets unwholesome grass
Grew of great stalk and color gross,
A melancholic poisonous green."

† The afflicted soul makes sad complaints sometimes. 'I am quite forsaken; I am left alone; I have none to take my part; no friends left me in

One particular employment of angels is to attend the beds of dying saints, and sustain them by the consolations and hopes of faith, preparatory to their entrance on the joys and fruition of heaven. In a peculiar sense, during their trials, temptations, sufferings, and on the eve of their departure from this world of tribulation and woe,

"Bright seraphs dispatched from the throne,
Repair to their stations assigned;
And angels elect are sent down
To guard the elect of mankind."

Conjecturally, some special office is assigned to each one of the heavenly host. One indeed may superintend the affairs and prosperity of a kingdom, while another watches the slumbering babe in a cottage cradle,—others are appointed to meet the several necessities of the adopted children of God who are constantly assailed by the opposition of Satan and his angels; thereby hindering their growth in Christian graces, and their advancement in the way of holiness and heaven. Accordingly, in the apocalyptic representations of St. John, we behold them controlling evil spirits; wielding the elements of this world; producing, directing, and bringing to a termination the great convulsions of time; convey-

all the world!" Oh, do not say so;—all the holy angels are thy hearty friends, and have charge of thee, and with the greatest alacrity and cheerfulness attend that charge.—*Pneumatologia*, 1701.

Therefore, most likely, 'tis as God made the stars to have their influence on the plants and animals, so he made the angels that are higher than the stars, for some service in the world, to be the instruments of his providence. —*Idem.*

How merciful art thou, O Lord, that thou thinkest us not safe enough in our weak and slender walls, but thou sendest thine angels to be our keepers and guardians.—AMBROSE, *Ministration and Communion of Angels.*

It is better to think that there are guardian spirits than that there are no spirits to guard us.—SIR T. BROWNE, *Christian Moral.*

Serrell & Perkins — No. 75 Nassau St.

THE JUDGMENT DAY,
Heralded by Archangels.

ing the souls of the just to the paradise of God, and severing the wicked from the good at the day of judgment.

One of the most solemn and affecting exhibitions of angelic ministration is presented in the dolorous narratives of the Evangelists, which relate the descent of angels to relieve our Savior in the wilderness of Satanic temptation, and during his agony in the garden of Gethsemane. What a mysterious, solemn, and wonderful mission for holy angels to perform, in rendering such services and homage to Him who was the *Lord of Angels*.

The "innumerable company of angels,"—of the glorious host dispersed throughout the illimitable universe, is clearly intimated by the apostle as beyond all the computation of mortal arithmetic, nevertheless, several references in Scripture will somewhat aid our conceptions in this particular. To Jacob, at Bethel they appeared on the mystic ladder, ascending and descending, in multitudes; and when he returned from Padan-aram, "the angels of the Lord met him," and he called the place "*Mahanaim*," or the two hosts. They are represented by the Psalmist as constituting many hosts,—Psalm ciii. 21; cxlvii. 2. Micaiah, the prophet, "saw the Lord sitting upon his throne, and all the hosts of heaven standing by him, on his right hand and on his left."—1 Kings xxii. 19. "The chariots of God are twenty thousand, even thousands of angels."—Psalm lxviii. 17. Elisha's servant, when "the Lord opened his eyes and he saw; and behold the mountain was full of horses and chariots of fire round about Elisha."—2 Kings vi. 17. Daniel beheld in the vision of God, "thousand thousands minister unto him, and ten thousand times ten thousand stand before him."—Dan. vii. 10. St. John, "I beheld, and I heard the voice of many angels round about the throne, and the number of them was ten thousand times ten thousand and thousands of thousands."—Rev. v. 11.*

Respecting the pursuits of angels in the heavenly state, we can form but a very inadequate conception, in the present life, and must await our arrival in those bright and blessed mansions which Christ has prepared for them that love Him. But from the declarations of Scripture we know that they are deeply occupied in investigating, with intense earnestness, the astonishing developments of the Divine Majesty in the works of creation and providence, and the wondrous economy of grace and salvation. In the celestial temple angels are engaged in the most exalted services, contemplating the perfection, and celebrating the praises of the Great Eternal.

To such ennobling and glorious pursuits who would not aspire, and devoutly prepare with a moral and spiritual meetness, to join the resounding *trisagion* of the celestial hierarchy.

Holy, holy, holy, Lord God Almighty, which was, which is, and is to come. Thou art worthy, O Lord, to receive glory, honor, and power, for thou hast created all things, and for thy pleasure they are and were created.

TRADITIONARY AND ANECDOTICAL.

The Talmudical traditions and Rabbinical writings, with their characteristic fecundity, abound with singular fictions respecting the guardianship and employment of angels;—the Jews indulging the vain conceit that the appearance of angels, and their ministrations by the commission of God, were only manifested

* Some of the fathers, with the view of representing the number of the angels compared with mankind, refer to the parable of the ninety-nine sheep left by the shepherd on the mountains, while he went in search of the strayed one, meaning apostate humanity.

in Judea. Regarding the presidency of angels, the Rabbinical writers give the following statement, over the seventy nations into which they say the human family was divided at the confusion and subsequent dispersion of Babel.

"The Lord said to the seventy angels which stood before him, come now, and let us go down, and there let us confound their language, so that a man may not understand the language of his companion. And the word of the Lord was discovered against that city, and with it the seventy nations,—and their respective languages, which each angel respectively wrote with his hand." Another says, "The earth consisted of seven climates, and every climate divided into ten parts. Then was each country and people assigned to its respective prince, and these princes are called gods of the world. Thus were the seventy nations divided amongst the seventy princes; the blessed God taking no part in them, because He is pure. One rabbi assigns to these angels the function of "moving the heavenly bodies; another affirms them to be "the souls of the heavenly bodies;" and another asserts them to be no other than the "stars and planets." Among some of the employments of angels, the rabbies say, that the ark had no rudder, and was steered and guided by them; and that God used their services in calling together "every living thing of all flesh, cattle, and creeping things of all sorts," when God commanded Noah to assemble them for embarkation.

Guardian angels, according to the notions of the Jewish rabbins, perform very important services in favor of men. They say, "Every man has his angel who speaks for him, and prays for him; as it is said (Psalm lxv. 2), "O Thou that hearest prayer;" that is, the prayer of the angel, who is the *Mashal* or guardian of men. It follows, "Unto thee shall all flesh come." *Wherefore,* the angels are not allowed to say their hymns above, till the Israelites have said them here below; for all that a man does is imitated by his *Mashal,* who performs it above, in the same manner in which it is performed here below. A man should never ask his necessaries of God in the Syriac or Chaldaic language. The ministering angels do not attend, to carry any one's prayers before God, who petitions for his necessaries in the Syriac language. This is meant of one single man who prays for himself; by a whole congregation it may be done in all languages, because the presence of God is amongst them. There are three who weave or make garlands out of the prayers of the Israelites; the first is Achtariel, the second Metraton, and the third Sandalphon. Behold! these three, who make garlands, do not attempt to make garlands of any other prayers; but only of such as are made in the Hebrew tongue.

The rabbies represent the removal of men from the present life as effected by the instrumentality of angels, whom they denominate *angels of death.* The execution of the mortal sentence, on those who die in the land of Israel is assigned to Gabriel, whom they style *an angel of mercy;* and those who die in other countries are dispatched by the hand of Samnael, the prince of demons." These two are deputies of Metraton, to whom God daily makes known those who are appointed to die. These deputies do not themselves bring away any souls out of the world; but each of them employs some of his host for that purpose.

The Jewish cabalists single out some particular angels as preceptors to the patriarchs;—to Adam was given Raziel,—to Abraham, Zidekiel,—to Moses, Metraton,—to Elias, Malashiel,—and to David, Gerviel, &c.

Amongst the chief spirits of the Mahometan heaven, such as Gabriel, the angel of revelation,—Israfil, by whom the last trumpet is to be sounded,—and Azrael, the angel of death, there were also a number of subaltern intelligences, appointed to preside over the different stages or ascents into which the celestial world was divided. Thus Kelail governs the fifth heaven, while Sadiel, the presiding spirit of the third, is employed in steadying the motions of the earth, which would be in a constant state of agitation if this angel did not keep his foot planted upon its orb.

Amongst other miraculous interpositions in favor of Mahomet, recorded in the Alcoran, was the appearance of five thousand angels on his side, at the battle of Bedr.

The Grecian academies entertained the belief that spirits behold all the actions of men, and rendered them assistance accordingly. That they, moreover, are acquainted with all our apprehensions, cogitations, and circumstances; and when the soul is delivered from the body, they bring it before the high Judge. That then they are questioned about our good or bad actions, their testimony being much prevalent either to exonerate or aggravate our doom. Porphirius asserts that many spirits or genii have the charge and custody of every man; one having a care of his health—another indulgent over his beauty and features—and another to infuse into him courage and constancy.

The ancient Persians supposed that Ormund appointed thirty angels to preside successively over the days of the month; and twelve greater ones to assume the government of the months, themselves; among whom Bahman (to whom Ormund committed the custody of all animals, except man) was the greatest Mihr. The angel of the seventh month was the spirit which watched over the affairs of friendship and love. Chūr had the care of the disk of the sun. Mah was agent for the concerns of the moon. Isphandārmaz was the tutelar genius of good and virtuous women. The Persians, also, had a certain office or prayer for every day of the month, addressed to the particular angel who presided over it, and whom they called Sizouzé.

The subjoined anecdotes are chiefly extracted from Isaac Ambrose's *Discourses on the Communion and Ministry of Angels*; respecting whom, in a biographical sketch, the following particulars are given:—He was a native of Lancashire, England, and descended from a highly respectable family. In 1621 he matriculated in Brazen-nose College, of the University of Oxford, and took the degree of bachelor of arts. In consequence of some difference of opinion and the laxity of morals, which then prevailed, he seceded from the Church of England, though he invariably retained her form of episcopal worship against the remonstrances of the Independents, with whom he had ecclesiastically connected himself. Having notified to his friends, a few days preceding the time of his death, he was found dead in his chair, in his study, having that morning sent to the printer the last page of his work on *Angels*. "His character may be comprised in a few expressions. He was holy in life, happy in his death, favored of God, and held in high estimation by all good men. His writings, like those of *Baxter*, have a vigorous pulse beating in every page, and it would be difficult to select a paragraph in which the author does not appear in earnest for the salvation of his readers. He was one of those excellent divines who distinguished and adorned the turbulent age in which he lived, amidst those ecclesiastical troubles for which it was remarkable; and who, in their combined influences, irradiated the moral gloom which then overspread the land; and it is to their indefatigable exertions that we are indebted for many of the religious blessings which we now enjoy. He was a star of no common magnitude and effulgence in that bright constellation of worthies, who have enriched the world by their writings, bequeathing a noble example to posterity, of whom, indeed, the world was not worthy."

God does, by his angels, preserve and keep good ministers from the hands of their persecutors, as is reported by great divines of unquestionable credit, in the following instance:—"One Grynæus, a German divine, a learned and holy man, coming from Heidelbérg to Spire, and going to hear a certain preacher in that city, that did then let fall some erroneous propositions of Popish doctrine, was thereat greatly offended, and presently went to the preacher, exhorting him to abandon his error; the preacher seemed to take it well, and pretended to be desirous of some further discourse with him, and so they parted. Grynæus going to his lodging, reports the passages of the late conference to those that sat at table with him, amongst whom Melancthon was one; he was called out of the room to speak with a stranger newly come into the house, and going forth he finds a grave old man of a goodly countenance, seemly and richly attired, who, in a friendly and grave manner tells him that within one hour there would come to their inn certain officers to apprehend Grynæus, and to carry him to prison, willing him to charge Grynæus with all possible speed to fly, and requiring Melancthon to see that this advantage was not neglected. Instantly Melancthon returned to the company, related the words of this strange monitor, and hasted Grynæus away, who had no sooner taken boat but he was eagerly sought for at his said lodging. No doubt this was an angel which God had sent to deliver this goodly minister from persecution.

Another worthy minister who was sought after by his persecutors, crept into a dark hole in the house, to hide himself, and as soon as he was got in, a spider drew a web over the mouth of the hole. When the searchers came, one of them would have looked in there for the man, where, indeed he was, but the other observing that there was a spider's web over the hole, concluded he could not be there, and therefore they ceased their search. What an artifice of the good man's angel-guardian was this to preserve him? Though persecutors are crafty and cruel, yet our keepers are more cunning than they, and can out-wit them.

Mr. Hawks being burnt to death, was desired by his friends to give them (if he could) some sign, by lifting up his hand, if he found his pains such as were tolerable, and might be borne with patience, and he did so; when his speech was gone, his body burning, and he thought to be dead, he lifted up his hands over his head, all on fire, and clapt them thrice together, which caused a great shout amongst his friends.

Mr. James Bingham, when the flames had half consumed him, cried out in the fire: "O ye papists! ye look for miracles; here now ye may see a miracle; for in this fire I feel no more pain than if I were on a bed of roses!" If angels could keep Shadrach, Meshach and Abednego in the fiery furnace without any hurt, why might they not keep this holy martyr in the flames without pain, though he died in them? He is a very uncharitable wretch that will not believe he found as he spake. 'Tis, I confess, a wonderful instance, that 'tis usual for God to indulge his martyrs more than ordinary support in fiery trials."

Mr. Holland, the day before his death, on a sudden, while one was reading, said, "O stay your reading. What brightness is this I see? It is my Savior's shine. Now farewell world, welcome Heaven. The day-star from on high has visited my heart." And then turning to the minister who preached his funeral sermon, he said, "I desire you speak this for me, that God deals familiarly with man; I feel his mercy, I see his majesty, whether in the body or out of the body, I cannot tell, God he knoweth; but I see things that are unutterable."

Many have told the very day and hour of their departure; and, says Bishop Hall, these revelations and ecstacies whence are they? If a man without all observation of *physical criticism*, shall receive, and give intelligence many days before, what day and hour shall be his last, what cause can we attribute this to but our attending angels? And when joy arises not to such an overflowing height, yet does it frequently begin our heaven on earth, and the fears of death are fully vanquished, and the good man can see it, and feel it coming without any regret.

Angels are with the saints in the very minute of dying, taking away the terribleness of it. There is an aversion in nature to death; but, says Mr. Ambrose, the body's passage through the grave, though it be dark and dismal, yet it is safe and secure. The grave is but a sleeping-place (*they shall rest in their beds*), and their soul's angels guard safe to heaven, and thus minister to the saints in death.

"Oh would God, ye saw what I see (said Mrs. Stubbs, on her death bed). Behold, I see infinite millions of angels stand about me, with fiery chariots to defend me, these are appointed of God to carry my soul unto the kingdom of heaven."

Immediately after the separation of the soul from the body, the angels receive it, and carry it to heaven. They are a convoy for the departing souls of the godly, to bring them to their felicity, though how they do it we cannot understand. They keep them company at least, and they are a guard to them as they pass through the Devil's territories; for the Devil is called the Prince of the power of the air. He, with all his hellish crew, are the inhabitants of that region, and souls in their journey to heaven must pass through the air, and the angels wait upon them as a convoy.

The Devil drags the souls of wicked men to hell, when they die; and angels conduct the souls of good men to heaven. Such honor have all the saints. The poorest and meanest of them will be thus royally attended. Lazarus was a beggar, and he went in state to heaven.

Description of Plates.—Plate 1.—The guardian angel, attracted by the simplicity and innocency of childhood, presses his charge close to his side, with his arm around her neck; whilst the child, with a natural and confiding fondness, leans against him. With a dignified and benignant countenance, the angel extends his arm in the attitude of protection, as if warding off approaching danger. Plate 2.—Represents the angelic hosts celebrating the completion of the finished work of creation,—"When the morning stars sang together, and all the sons of God shouted for joy?"—Job xxxviii. 7. Plate 3.—Represents the final employment of angels in this world, on the arrival of the resurrection morn and the judgment day. Christ "on the throne of his glory," attended by holy angels. On one side is the recording angel, opening the book of life, in which are enrolled the names of the "heirs of salvation." In the space between the judgment seat, and those arising out of their graves, the archangel is sounding the trumpet which summons the assembling universe.

MORAL AND CONCLUSION.

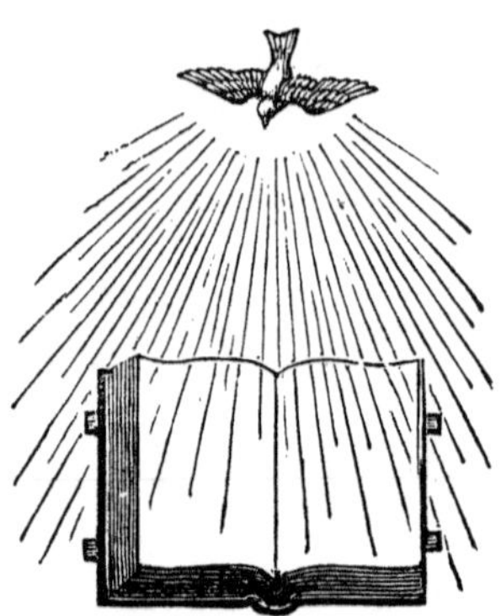

Verbum Domini manet in eternum.

All Scripture is given by inspiration of God, and is profitable for doctrine, for reproof, for correction, for instruction in righteousness.—2 Tim. iii. 16.

Upon the opening of our divine and delightful subject, we intimated the intention of furnishing a synopsis of some of the confirmatory proofs, and illustrative facts demonstrative and recommendatory of the authenticity, antiquity, literature and inspiration of the Scriptures, to be received as the unimpeachable standard of *faith* and *practice*, requiring the entire dissociation of all negative assertions and mental reserves or suppositions, originating either in the unhallowed pride of the human intellect or the Pharaoh-like reluctance of the heart to yield an implicit obedience or acquiescent submission to the authority and precepts, the truths and doctrines contained in Holy Writ.*

* The mass of evidence in favor of the divine inspiration of the Bible is

From the days of the apostles, (when the philosophizing Greeks arrogated to themselves the pompous title of Σοφοι and φιλοσοφοι, *wise men and philosophers*,) to the present period, this state of mind and disposition have been the principal source from which have arisen all those heresies which have disfigured the benevolent character and perverted the gracious designs of Christianity, producing the most horrible persecutions, to all that superadded variety of evil in religion, morals and society, engendered by the violence of a sanguinary discord, the pretensions of a pseudo-philosophy, and the blasphemous negations of a presumptuous infidelity, whose name, indeed, is Legion.

Even those who have professed to have received the revelation of the Bible, too frequently employ themselves in endeavoring to help out other systems and formula of beliefs, for which no sanction can be shown, in the obvious bearing and spirit of the Sacred Scriptures, under the disguise of new constructions, rejection of alleged interpolated passages, allegorical explanation of inferences of a directly antagonistical tendency; and for which conduct nothing can be more irrational, inconsistent and injurious to the reception and

too great to be set aside by anything short of scientific demonstration. Were the Scriptures to teach that the whole is not equal to its parts, the mind could not, indeed, believe it. But if it taught a truth which was only contrary to the probable deductions of science, science, I say, must yield to the Scriptures; for it would be more reasonable to doubt the probabilities of a single science, than the various and most satisfactory evidence on which revelation rests. I do not believe that the probabilities of any science are in collision with Scripture. But the supposition is made to show how strong are my convictions of the evidence and paramount importance of the Bible.

DR. EDWARD HITCHCOCK, *Religion of Geology*.

Adam no sooner fell, but philosophy fell with him, and became a common strumpet for carnal reason to commit frolic with, and oh! how have the lascivious wits of lapsed human nature, ever since, gone a whoring after vain philosophy.—GALE, *Preface*, *Court of the Gentiles*.

utility of the Scriptures than to profess to accept them as a divine Revelation, and at the same time to constitute human opinion as the standard by which their declarations are to be tested; virtually invoking the awful consequences of sitting in judgment upon Deity, (who is the acknowledged author of them,) and to determine whether He has declared truth or spoken falsehood! Verily! must not angels wonder to see frail and fallen humanity thus engaged?

As corroborative of the importance and doctrine of the subject which we have discussed, and now deferentially submit to the candid and serious consideration of the Christian, as well as the philosophic and general reader, we offer the following appropriate and conciliatory remarks of President Dwight:—"In the Scriptures we find an order, or rather a kind of beings described, which were never known, nor imagined by any person who did not derive his acquaintance with them from that book. They are beings who have a character as appropriate as that of man, as far, as finite intelligences can be supposed to differ from each other. Yet the character is complete, entire, and of a piece with itself. Every attribute is suited to every other; all are angelic; all are heavenly. A station is also assigned to them, of a dignity and importance, perfectly fitted to their character, and worthy of being filled by such beings. Employments are also marked out for them, altogether becoming both the station and the character; angelic employments—suited to the Sons of God, the Morning Stars of Heaven. Can it be reasonably supposed that these things were devised by human imagination? Have similar things been ever thus devised? The fancy of man has, in all nations and ages, delighted itself with the employment of fashioning imaginary beings, of a nature superior to ours. What have been its productions? The gods, demons, and genii of ancient, and the elves, sylphs, and fairies of modern times. But how do all these shrink from a comparison with angels? They are little, base, trifling, sordid, and sinful enough to have been copied with a few easy additions from the characteristics of men. But where does this world furnish materials for the composition of an angelical character? What originals has it presented, from which the portrait could be drawn?*

A multitude of writers in the Scriptures, *fifteen at least*, have described these glorious beings with the most perfect harmony, and without a single discordant idea. In the mean time their descriptions are extensively various, comprising many particulars, and wholly independent of each other. All the writers are in this respect, as well as others, originals. Not one is a copier; not one a plagiary; yet their representations are universally noble, sublime, dignified, beautiful and lovely, beyond anything found in the most perfect writings of uninspired men. To which may be added a similar testimony to the authority of the Bible, from the eccentric, erudite and ironical Gale, in his preface to the "*Court of the Gentiles.*" "But such was the infinite benignity and condescension of sovereign light and love, as that he vouchsafed to irradiate a spot of the lapsed world, even of his holy land and elect seed, with fresh and glorious rays of the light and life conveyed in and by the sacred Re-

* If then, we find a book which professes to be a revelation from heaven, a system of moral laws which can clearly be shown to be the basis of the moral order of the universe, and which are calculated to secure the eternal happiness of all intellectual beings, it forms a strong presumptive proof, if not an unanswerable argument, that the contents of that book are of celestial origin, and were dictated by Him who gave birth to the whole system of created beings;—a moral demonstration that a power and intelligence superior to the human mind, must have suggested such sublime conceptions and such astonishing ideas, since there are no such prototypes to be found within the range of the human understanding.—Dr. Dick, *Philosophy of Religion.*

velation. And oh! how bright, how ravishing were those heavens of divine light which shone on Judea? Were not all the adjacent parts illuminated thereby? Yea, did not Greece itself (esteemed the eye of the world) light her candle at this sacred fire? Were not all the Grecian schools hung with philosophic ornaments, or contemplations stolen out of the Judaic wardrobe? Were not Pythagoras's college, Plato's academy, Aristotle's peripatum, Zeno's stoa, and Epicurus's garden all watered by rivulets, though in themselves corrupt, originally derived from the sacred streams of Siloam? Whence had Phenicia, Egypt, Chaldea, Persia, with our occidental parts, their barbaric philosophy, but from the sacred emanations of Zion?"

Our design in favor of the positive, prophetic, and miraculous evidence of the Inspiration of the Holy Bible, is so ably set forth by Dr. Townsend (whose classical learning and sincere Christianity no man will attempt to question), in the annexed statement, that we make no apology for its insertion or length, assured of the pleasure which its perusal will afford the reader, and his approbation accordingly.

From the period of the dispersion of the Jews among the Egyptians and Babylonians, we find that the Greeks began to have more exalted and refined ideas of a Deity; and that they applied themselves more particularly to that philosophy and literature, which contributed so eminently to raise them to the highest intellectual rank among ancient or modern nations. All the sects and schools of philosophy, in ancient Greece, originated from the Ionic and Italic sects. The Ionic sect was founded by Thales, the Italic by Pythagoras. Thales was born about the year 640 before Christ, and is remarkable for being the first Grecian who taught a regular system of philosophy, and left a succession of disciples to establish and maintain it. He traveled into Egypt when he was a young man, and resided there several years. If he went into that country when at the age of twenty or twenty-five, and resided there ten or more years (and this period was not beyond that which was usually passed by the students in Egyptian learning), he would have been in Egypt when Jehoahaz, king of Judah, was brought there as a prisoner by Pharaoh Necho. The attention of the curious Greek must have been attracted by the various captives, strangers thus introduced into Egypt; and while he improved himself in those sciences in which the Egyptians excelled, it is highly probable that from conversing with these Jewish captives, he acquired some of those great and truly philosophical notions which he afterwards taught at his native Miletus, and in Greece.

The chief of these opinions were, that the world was not eternal, but was made by God the Spirit, out of water,—an opinion which seems to have been derived from the Mosaic and Christian doctrine, "the Spirit of God moved on the face of the waters;" that the world being God's workmanship, was exceedingly good and perfect; that the universe was filled with invisible spirits, who inspect the actions of men.

Thales was the first of the Greeks who made any philosophical inquiries into the nature and perfections of God; for though, as Gale remarks, Orpheus, Linus, Homer, and Hesiod, had some traditions of God, their value was obscured by a mixture with pagan fables. Thales however delivered his knowledge concerning God in a more plain and simple manner. He first maintained amongst the Greeks that God was the most ancient of beings; and are evidently derived from purer sources than from invented traditions or speculative heathen philosophy. From the Jews alone, therefore, with whom Thales became acquainted in Egypt, could he have received those ideas of God and his Providence, which shine like a meteor through the dark mist of the ignorance and blindness of that superstitious age.

Thales was succeeded by Anaximander, Anaximines, and Anaxagoras, the friend and tutor of Pericles; by Diogenes Apolloniates, and by Archelaus the instructor of Socrates. The various sects which are referred to the Ionic school, are the Socratic, founded by Socrates, among whose disciples and followers are Xenophon, Plato, Euclid, and Alcibiades; the Cyrenaic sect, founded by Aristippus; the Megaric, established by Euclid at Megara; the Eretriac or Elïac school, instituted by Phædo at Elis; the Academic, founded by Plato, whose school, after his death, was divided into the old, middle, and new academies; the Peripatetic, founded by Aristotle; the Cynic, by Antisthenes; the Stoic, by Zeno. These sects continued till the time of Christ; and when St. Paul visited Athens, he found the Greeks still engaged in disputes, and inquiries into the mysteries and difficulties of philosophy. Although the purest and most refined speculations of the best and most celebrated of these philosophers fall far short of the principles and morality inculcated by the Christian dispensation, they still served to advance the progress of Christianity, or rather they tended to diminish the superstitious reverence paid to the pagan deities. The commonest people became at least sensible that their philosophers only adhered to the religious ceremonies of the established superstition, from mere compliance with popular custom; and the reflecting part of the community were divided, in a state of doubt and uncertainty: Socrates, in particular, declared that a teacher from heaven was necessary to impart instruction to mankind.

Moral philosophy may be considered as a light to the dark and ignorant age in which it flourished; but when compared with Christianity, it is little less than the very darkness it so partially illuminated. Philosophy, at the height of its splendor, displayed only the corruption, the folly, and the degradation of the human mind when deprived of revelation. It was like the taper in a charnel house at midnight, which disperses the darkness of the tomb, and shows to the sickening spectator how melancholy is the sight of humanity, when bereaved of life and spirit.

Though the accounts of Pythagoras are mingled with fable

there is abundant authority to induce us to believe that this philosopher conversed likewise with the Jews of the dispersion, at Tyre, in Phœnicia, and probably at Mount Carmel, where it is said his walk was long shown. It is certain that he was in Egypt, and many suppose he was taken prisoner into that country either by Nebuchadnezzar, or by Cambyses. From Egypt he either went or was taken to Babylon, where again he must have acquired an intimate knowledge of the Jews; and in this latter place he is said to have had for an instructor Zabratus, or Nazaratus—whom the learned Selden supposes to have been Ezekiel—and Prideaux, Zoroaster. The exact period of the birth of Pythagoras is not certainly known. The accounts of his life, now extant, are uncertain and contradictory ; that which appears most probable and satisfactory informs us, that at the age of eighteen he consulted Thales at Miletus, who recommended him to visit Egypt.

From Miletus he proceeded to Tyre (the place of his nativity, though educated at Samos) ; from thence he travelled to Egypt, with letters to Amasis from Polycrates, tyrant of Samos. He quitted Egypt for Babylon, where he continued twelve years, and conversed with Zabratus or Nazaratus. He is then supposed to have returned to his own country, and to have been at that time about fifty-six years of age.

In the year 563 before Christ, the whole country of Judea was still desolate—not having recovered from its last ravage by Nebuzzaradan. In this year Nebuchadnezzar was restored from his lycanthropy, and the Jews were rising into distinction in the Persian empire. Leaving Judea and its refugees, whom he might have found both at Tyre and Carmel, Pythagoras proceeded to Egypt. He would there meet with many of the Jews who had fled with Jeremiah from Judea, nineteen years preceding. From them, as well as from the natives, he would learn the fulfilment of that prophet's predictions respecting Apries. This and other circumstances exciting his curiosity, he at last visited Babylon, where he is supposed to have arrived in the year 541, and two years before the death of Beltshazzar.

During his residence of twelve years in Babylon, Pythagoras must have been a spectator of the wonderful events recorded in the Book of Daniel. The greatest statesman of the day in Babylon was a Jew. As the time and manner of Ezekiel's death are unknown; and as in this year, Ezekiel, if alive, would not be more than fifty-three years of age; it is by no means improbable that he might have conversed, as tradition asserts, with that prophet. Pythagoras must have been informed of the decree of Cyrus, before Christ 536, for the return of the Jews, and he must have been acquainted with prophecies thereby fulfilled;—it is not improbable that he was a wondering spectator of their departure for their own lands. At Babylon he undoubtedly saw the school or universities established by the Jews; for he introduced into his own country institutions which were characterized by regulations similar to those adopted by the Jews.

Struck and astonished at all he read or heard or saw of this persecuted and favored people, we cannot be surprised that he should have engrafted many of the purer truths of morality on his system of philosophy.

Pythagoras quitted Babylon in 529, the same year that Cyrus died. It is probable his departure was accelerated by the cruel and tyrannical government of Cambyses, his successor. In this year the Greek philosopher returned home; and dissatisfied with the political state of affairs at Samos, he taught his new system called the Italic philosophy, in the towns of Magara Grecia. The philosophy of Pythagoras, so far as it is known, may be described as a mixture of Persian, Grecian, and Egyptian superstitions, interwoven with Jewish doctrines, institutions, and customs. The numerous coincidences between his enactments and those of the Jews, are found in the similarity of discipline established in his schools and colleges; in his distinction between the perfect or the initiated, and the service the τελειος and the *νεοφυτος*, or the תמים and נקיע of the Jews; in the covenant among the members of his colleges, in the use of salt as a sign of union or agreement, as well as some others.

The doctrines of Pythagoras must have tended to remove many of the evils of polytheism and idolatry. He acknowledged but one God, the Creator of the world. He had some idea of the sacred name of the Petragammaton of the Jews, which he revealed as a mystery to his disciples. He described the Deity in the very words of the Hebrew Scriptures, as the א, the *το ὀν*, *the self-existent.* He taught by this definition that God was infinite and eternal; a truth which human reason, unassisted by divine revelation, has never yet discovered. He likewise instructed his disciples in the doctrine of a peculiar providence, particularly over good men—the necessity of pure worship—the immortality of the soul—the incorporeality of the Deity. His morality evidently sprung from a purer source than from the profane worship of pagan deities; his golden verses (if they are certainly his) are evidently transcripts of the Mosaic precepts; and virtuous will be the life, and tranquil the death of that man who habitually observes the precepts they contain, and thrice reviews the actions of the day, before he resigns himself to rest at night.

The Italic sect flourished till the end of the reign of Alexander. It gave rise to the Eleatic, the Heraclitean, the Epicurean, and the Phyrrhonic sects, whose doctrines, however, differ materially from those enforced by Pythagoras himself. When the best pagan philosophy, considered as a system, is compared with Christianity, the observations already made on the speculations of Thales are equally applicable. But when we consider this philosophy as a virtuous effort of the human mind to penetrate through the darkness and superstition by which it was surrounded; and gaining by these efforts, and the light borrowed from revelation, more pure ideas of morality, and more just notions of a Deity, we are called upon to acknowledge that philosophy was beneficial to man, and that those who acquiesced in the doctrines of Pythagoras, and received the better part of his system, must have been wiser and purer than their more ignorant or prejudiced countrymen. That the Greeks, therefore, were indebted to their intercourse with the Jews for the origin of their philosophy, is highly probable; it is, therefore, no less probable, that their literature may be partly traced to the same source. From the temperance Pythagoras uniformly practised, it is probable that his life was extended to a late period. He is supposed to have perished in consequence of a political disturbance in the seventieth olympiad, about the year 563 before Christ. If this tradition be correct, he must at this time have entered his eighty-third or eighty-fourth year.

Æschylus, the founder of the Greek drama, in its present form, would have been at that time about twenty-five years of age; and though we are not acquainted with the particulars of his early life, we may naturally conclude that one so eminent would have carefully instructed himself in all the philosophy and learning of his age. A Pythagorean in principle, many of his sentiments are the same as those taught in the golden verses of Pythagoras. We very justly conclude, therefore, that the great tragedian was either personally acquainted with, and a disciple of the Samean; or that he was well versed in the system promulgated by that philosopher. Like many of his countrymen he gave offence to the people, by deviating from received opinions. In the mythology of Æschylus, Dr. Gray observes, there is frequent reference to principles originating in revelation. In the passage cited by Eusebius, he describes the Supreme God as a being who is carefully to be distinguished from mortals, having nothing resembling the body of man. At one time he declares, that God shines forth in unapproachable fire; at another, he invests Him in the elements, appearing in the wind, the thunder, and the lightning! He represents the ocean, the rocks, and the fountains as ministering to the Supreme Being; the hills, and the earth, the depths of the sea, and the summit of the mountains, as trembling at His presence. The piercing eye of God he describes as overlooking all things, for the glory of the highest God is powerful. His celebrated scene in Persia, in which the shade of Darius is summoned by Atossa, is very similar to the account of the appearance of Samuel to Saul, as related in the narrative of the Witch of Endor. Many of the Christian fathers have asserted that the character of "Prometheus" could not have been drawn, unless the author of the drama had been acquainted with the Sacred Writings, or with at least many of the prophetic books, of which it exhibits the most decisive evidence in several of its passages. It is probable that the Sacred Writings were partly made known to him by his tutor, and contemporary, Pythagoras. Similarity of description only, with identity of expression, would demonstrate this point; these, it is true, might be mere coincidences; but where the same personifications are used, we may justly conclude, that the resemblance is not accidental. In Jeremiah xlvii. 6, we meet with this bold personification—"O thou sword of the Lord, how long will it be ere thou be quiet? put up thyself into thy scabbard, rest, and be still. How can it be quiet, seeing the Lord hath given it a charge against Ashkelon?" The same metaphor is adopted by Æschylus. Also, "Thus saith the Lord God, I will spread my net over him, and he shall be taken in my snare," and the same expression is employed in other portions of Scripture to describe a state of inextricable difficulty, of distress, or ruin. The same metaphor is applied by Æschylus to describe the destruction of Troy. The tragedian who followed Æschylus, although perhaps inferior to him in sublimity, maintained an exalted nobleness of moral sentiment. A higher tone seems to have been given to the public mind in Greece, which cannot entirely be attributed to their political institutions, or the incessant agitation and restlessness of mind induced by their party dissensions. We must refer this intellectual elevation to a more intellectual source; to the spirit of their philosophy, morality, and poetry, which was partially derived from the purer fountains of the Hebrew Scriptures, and the peculiar object of Providence, in thus communicating to the Greeks, through the dispersion and captivity of the Jews, some knowledge of a purer creed was shown in subsequent ages, when that language was selected to impart the knowledge of the Scriptures to the world. The universality of the Greek language may be attributed to the general interest excited by the Greek Drama, the splendid composition of the poets, and the more exalted speculations of their philosophers. The pagan nations did not, it is true, eat of the fruit of the tree of life, yet they were blessed with some few of its leaves, and the very "leaves of that tree which are for the healing of the nations."

Bishop Watson finely and strikingly remarks: "To read the prophecies of Daniel with attention, intelligence and an unbiassed mind, is sufficient to convert an unbeliever from Deism to Christianity." They were declared several hundred years before the birth of Christ; they extend through many ages; and have ever been considered as the foundation of all modern history; revealing the successive rise and fall of the four great monarchies of the world; the establishment of the Messiah's kingdom upon earth; his death and sufferings; and passing from earth to heaven, they terminate only in eternity.

The psalms present every possible variety of Hebrew poetry. They may all, indeed, be termed poems of the lyric kind, that is, adapted to music, but with great variety in the style of composition. Thus some are simply odes, giving a narrative of facts, either of public history or private life, in beautiful and figurative language. Others, again, are *ethic* or *didactic*, "delivering great maxims of life, or the precepts of religion, in solemn, but for the most part, simple strains. To this class we may refer the hundred and nineteenth, and other *alphabetical psalms*, which are so called, because the initial letters of each line or stanza follow the order of the alphabet. Nearly one-seventh part of the psalms are elegiac or pathetic compositions on mournful subjects. Some are enigmatic, delivering the doctrines of religion in enigmatic sentences contrived to strike the imagination forcibly, and yet easy to be understood; while a few may be referred to the class of idyls or short pastoral poems. But the greatest part, according to Bishop Horsley, is a sort of dramatic ode, consisting of dialogues between certain persons sustaining certain characters. In these dialogue psalms, the persons are frequently the Psalmist himself, or the chorus of priests and Levites, or the leaders of the Levitical band, opening the ode with a poem declarative of the subject, and very often closing the whole with a solemn admonition drawn from what the other persons say. The other persons are, Jehovah, sometimes as one, sometimes as another of the three persons; Christ in his incarnate state, sometimes before, sometimes after his resurrection; the human soul of Christ, as distinguished from the divine essence. Christ, in his incarnate state, is personated sometimes as a priest, sometimes as a king, sometimes as a conqueror; and, in those psalms in which he is introduced as a conqueror, the resemblance is very remarkable between this conqueror in the Book of Psalms, and the warrior on the white horse in the Book of Revelations, who goes forth with a crown on his head, and a bow in his hand, conquering and to conquer; and the conquest in the Psalms is followed, like the conquest in the Revelations, by the marriage of the conqueror. These are circumstances of similitude, which, to any one versed in the prophetic style, prove beyond a doubt that the mystical conqueror is the same personage in both.

In praise of the Psalms, all the fathers of the church are unanimously eloquent. Athanasius styles them an epitome of the whole Scriptures; Basil, a compendium of all theology; Luther, a little Bible, and the summary of the Old Testament; and Melancthon, the most elegant writing in the whole world. How highly the Psalter was valued subsequent to the Reformation, we may easily conceive by the very numerous editions of it which were executed in the infancy of printing, and by the number of commentators who have undertaken to illustrate its sacred pages. Carpzor, who wrote a century ago, enumerates upwards of one hundred and sixty; and, of the subsequent modern expositors of this book, it would perhaps be difficult to procure a correct account. "The Psalms," as Bishop Horne, their best interpreter in our language, has remarked with equal piety and beauty, "are an epitome of the Bible, adapted to the purposes of devotion. They treat occasionally of the creation and formation of the world; the dispensations of providence, and the economy of grace; the transactions of the patriarchs; the exodus of the children of Israel; their journey through the wilderness and settlement in Canaan; their law, priesthood, and ritual; the exploits of these great men, wrought through faith; their sins and captivities; their repentances and restorations; the sufferings and victories of David; the peaceful and happy reign of Solomon; the advent of the Messiah, with its effects and consequences, his incarnation, birth, life, passion, death, resurrection, ascension, kingdom, and priesthood; the effusion of the Spirit; the conversion of the nations; the rejection of the Jews; the establishment, increase, and perpetuity of the Christian church; the end of the world; the general judgment; the condemnation of the wicked, and the final triumph of the righteous with their Lord and King. These are the subjects here presented to our meditation. We are instructed how to conceive of them aright, and to express the different affections, which, when so conceived of, they must excite in our minds. They are for this purpose adorned with figures, and set off with all the graces of poetry; and poetry itself is designed yet further to be recommended by the charms of music, thus consecrated to the service of God; that so delight may prepare the way for improvement, and pleasure become the handmaid of wisdom, while every turbulent passion is calmed by sacred melody, and the evil spirit is still dispossessed by the harp of the son of Jesse. This little volume, like the paradise of Eden, affords us in perfection, though in miniature, everything that groweth elsewhere, "every tree that is pleasant to the sight, and good for food," and, above all, what was there lost, but is here restored—*the tree of life in the midst of the garden.* That which we read as matter of speculation, in the other Scriptures, is reduced to practice when we recite it in the Psalms; in these, repentance and faith are described; but in those they are acted; by a perusal of the former, we learn how others served God, but, by using the latter, we serve him ourselves. "What is there necessary for a man to know," says the pious and judicious Hooker, "which the Psalms are not able to teach? They are to beginners an easy and familiar introduction, a mighty augmentation of all virtue and knowledge in such as are entered before, a strong confirmation to the most perfect among others. Heroical magnanimity, exquisite justice, grave moderation, exact wisdom, repentance unfeigned, unwearied patience, the mysteries of God, the sufferings of Christ, the terrors of wrath, the comforts of grace, the works of Providence over this world, and the promised joys of that world which is to come, all good necessarily to be either known, or done, or had, this one celestial fountain yieldeth. Let there be any grief or disease incident unto the soul of man, any wound or sickness named, for which there is not, in this treasure-house, a present comfortable remedy at all times ready to be found."

Many of the Psalms, which bear the royal prophet's name, were composed on occasions of remarkable circumstances in his life, his dangers, his afflictions, his deliverances. But of those which relate to the public history of the natural Israel, there are few in which the fortunes of the mystical Israel are not adumbrated; and of those which allude to the life of David, there are none in which the son of David is not the principal and immediate subject. David's complaints against his enemies are Messiah's complaints, first of the unbelieving Jews, then of the heathen persecutors, and of the apostate faction in later ages. David's afflictions are Messiah's sufferings. David's penitential supplications are Messiah's, under the burden of the imputed guilt of man. David's songs of triumph and thanksgiving are Messiah's songs of triumph and thanksgiving, for his victory over sin, and death, and hell. In a word, there is not a page of this Book of Psalms, in which the pious reader will not find his Savior, if he reads with a view of finding him.

In the language of this divine book, therefore, the prayers and praises of the church have been offered up to the throne of grace, from age to age, and it appears to have been the manual of the Son of God in the days of his flesh; who, at the conclusion of his last supper, is generally supposed, and that upon good grounds, to have sung a hymn taken from it; who pronounced on the cross, the beginning of the twenty-second Psalm, "My God, my God, why hast thou forsaken me? and expired with a part of the thirty-first Psalm in his mouth: "Into thy hands I commit my spirit." Thus He, who had not the spirit by measure, in whom were hidden all the treasures of wisdom and knowledge, and who spake as never man spake, yet chose to conclude his life, to solace himself in the greatest agony, and at last to breathe out his soul, in the Psalmist's form of words, rather than his own. "No tongue of man or angel," as Dr. Hammond justly observes, "can convey a higher idea of any book, and of their felicity who use it aright."

The Psalms have been thus classified according to their several subjects, as adapted to the purpose of private devotion under the following divisions: 1st. Prayers, for pardon of sin,—when deprived of the opportunity of the public exercise of religion—when deprived of consolation under the pressure and despondency of external afflictions and internal grief—supplications for divine assistance under conscious integrity of heart, and the justice of the suppliant's cause—expression of confidence and trust in God under trials—prayers of intercession on behalf of the people of God—with others suited to their experience under every variety of trouble and distress. 2d. Psalms of thanksgiving for mercies vouchsafed to particular persons and the Israelites in general. 3d. Psalms of praise and adoration displaying the attributes of God, including the acknowledgment of his goodness, mercy, care, and protection of good men, with reference to the power, majesty, and glory of God. 4th. Instructive Psalms, describing the happiness of good, and the misery of bad men. 5th. Psalms especially prophetical. 6th. Historical Psalms.

The Bible, then, as the bulwark of civil and religious freedom—as the Magna Charta of divine principles and privileges, guaranteeing the reversion of our immortal hopes and title to the inheritance "incorruptible, undefiled, and that fadeth not away;"—as the water of life distilled through the crystal conduits of revelation, each and all claim from our reason a reverential and grateful reception of Holy Writ, as the only admitted standard of faith and practice.*

What infatuation! what impiety! to renounce this sacred Book; which, after the similitude of a celestial *lighthouse*, a gracious Jehovah has established on the Rock of Ages, and in the manifold wisdom and grace of God, placed along the shining banks of immortality, whose reflected beams, espied by the telescope of faith, will safely pilot the frail bark of mortality, tempest-tossed upon the crested billows of adversity, and amidst the dangerous and deceitful shoals of temptation as it nears the haven of eternal rest, and enters the harbor of the delectable city of the heavenly Jerusalem!

Another corollary which we would deduce from the con-

* With such purposes and such feelings have I perused the books of the Old and New Testaments—each book as a whole, and also as an integral part. And need I say that I have met everywhere more or less copious sources of truth and power and purifying influences; that I have found words for my inmost thoughts, songs for my joy, utterances for my hidden griefs, and pleadings for my shame and feebleness? In short, whatever finds me, bears witness for itself, that it has proceeded from a Holy Spirit, even from the same Spirit, *which remaining in itself, yet regenerateth all other powers, and in all ages entering into holy souls, maketh them friends of God and prophets* *Wisd.* vii.—COLERIDGE, *Con. Inq. Spirit.*

sideration of our delightful and important subject *is the wonderful dignity and destiny of man.*

If our good-hearted philosopher, in his *Hydriotaphia*, could speak of man amidst corruption and decay, as "splendid in ruins, and pompous in the grave," how much more ennobling a view is the Christian permitted to take of him, in connection with the declarations revealed and contained in the volume of Inspiration,—as the candidate for immortality—the heir of salvation—the child of the resurrection, and the adopted son of God, destined to be made equal to the angels,—those glorious beings who have never fallen from the high and original righteousness of that radiant condition in which they were created.

In the aphoristic expostulation of the royal Preacher—*Let us hear the conclusion of the whole matter :* With what adoring gratitude and reverential humility does it behoove us to receive the redemption which is in Christ Jesus. But for the mediation, the atonement, and the intercession of Christ, seated on the right hand of the Majesty on High, we should have been hopelessly deprived of all those present benefits and prospective privileges for our bodies and souls,* in time and eternity, which flow directly from the passion of His agony, the merits and ransom of His death, when He offered himself up as a sacrifice to satisfy Divine justice! But for the *atonement of Christ*, angels would have never ministered to us amidst our necessities and distresses—would never have attended us through the dark *valley of the shadow of death*,—and then on the downy cha-

* The visible world, so magnificent and so beautiful, is a temple worthy of God, the Creator; the spiritual world described in the pages of the Scriptures is a temple equally worthy of God, the Redeemer. Both equally demonstrate the mercy and love of the same all-wise Providence to the bodies and the souls of men.—DR. TOWNSEND, *Introduction to the Old and New Testament.*

riots of their soft and silvery pinions escort us into the presence of their God and our God, their Savior and our Savior!

In this my present unpretending attempt, I now bid ye, blessed angels, a courteous but reluctant and too abrupt a farewell; receiving, as the mantle of your departure, this gracious exhortation—this animating benediction, for my candid readers; happy, thrice happy they, who, in setting out on the uncertain voyage and agitated sea of this mortal life, having weighed the *anchor* of a Christian hope, have decided to take for their polar light, the guiding star of Bethlehem;* for their *compass*, the magnetic attractions of the cross; for their *chart* the discoveries of a divine revelation; with their *canvass* spread, for the propitious gales of spiritual influences to waft and speed them heavenward, in their perilous course; wisely turning a deaf ear to the syren songs of temptation, and avoiding the more fatal under-

* Once on the raging seas I rode;
The storm was loud, the night was dark;
The ocean yawn'd, and rudely blow'd
The wind, that toss'd my found'ring bark.

Deep horror, then, my vitals froze;
Death-struck, I ceas'd the tide to stem;
When suddenly a star arose—
It was the star of Bethlehem.

It was my guide, my life, my all,
It bade my dark forebodings cease;
And through the storm and danger's thrall,
It led me to the port of peace.

Now safely moor'd, my perils o'er,
I'll sing first in night's diadem,
For ever, and for evermore—
The star!—the star of Bethlehem.

HENRY KIRKE WHITE

currents and vortices of carnal lusts, shall escape making "shipwreck of faith and a good conscience" upon the dangerous rocks and deceitful shoals of fatal pleasures ;—and after having, by prayerful vigilance, resolutely encountered every hurricane of woe, and bravely outrode every tempest of tribulation, shall be safely launched on the unruffled ocean of a glorious eternity, over whose boundless surface no storms will ever arise, and the duration of whose unalloyed felicity shall be commensurate with the illimitable expanse of its shoreless extent, and the seraphic fervor of whose adoration will correspond with the crystal holiness of the transparent waters of its unfathomable depth !

BIBLICAL AND CURIOUS.

In the last century, all the manuscripts that could be obtained of the Bible were collated with the greatest care, and collections of the various readings have been published to the world. But amongst all the various readings, both of the Old and New Testaments, none have been found to affect any point of doctrine or moral practice; so that the sacred volume has been handed down to our time, in such a state, as to demand from all its friends a grateful acknowledgment of the divine providence in its preservation.

There are not wanting proofs of the most scrupulous care of the Hebrew text on the part of the Jews: they have counted large and small sections, the verses, the words, and even the letters, in some of the books. Father Simon says he had seen a manuscript of Perpignan, which contained the following computation:

	Great sections.	Small sections.	Verses.	Words.	Letters.
Genesis,	12	43	1,534	20,713	78,100
Exodus,	11	33	1,209	—	63,467
Leviticus,	10	25	859	11,902	44,989
Numbers,	10	33	1,288	16,707	62,529
Deuteronomy,	11	31	955	16,304	54,892

They have likewise reckoned which is the middle letter of the Pentateuch, which is the middle clause of each book, and how many times each letter of the alphabet occurs in all the Hebrew Scriptures.

Aleph, . .	42,377	Lamed, . .	41,517
Beth, . .	38,218	Mem, . .	77,778
Gimel, . .	29,537	Nun, . .	41,696
Daleth, . .	32,530	Samech, . .	13,680
He, . .	47,554	Ain, . .	20,175
Vau, . .	76,922	Pe, . .	22,725
Zain, . ,	22,867	Tzaddi, . .	21,882
Cheth, . .	23,447	Koph, . .	22,972
Teth, . .	11,052	Resh, . .	22,147
Jod, . .	66,420	Shin, . .	32,148
Caph, . .	48,253	Tau, . .	59,343

The most notable editions of the Bible are those which have been issued under the titles of the *Wickliffe*, about the year 1370, *Tindal and Coverdale's*, about 1527 and 1535; *Matthew's*, about 1537; *Cranmer's*, 1539; *The Bishop's*, 1569, and *King James's*, prepared by a conclave of the most able scholars and eminent divines in Hampton Court, in the year 1603, which is the present authorized version, and though upwards of two centuries have elapsed since it first appeared, and during this interval, notwithstanding many passages in particular books have been variously elucidated by learned men, with equal felicity and ability, perspicuity and excellence, their united labors have contributed to give the present translation a high and distinguished place in the judgment of the Christian world, wherever the English language is spoken and studied.

The middle chapter, and the shortest in the Bible, is the 117th Psalm; the middle verse is the 8th of the 118th Psalm; the 21st verse of the 7th chapter of Ezra, in the English version, contains all the letters of the alphabet; the 19th chapter of the 2d Kings, and the 37th chapter of Isaiah are alike.

The Old Testament comprises 39 books, 929 chapters, 23,214 verses, 592,493 words, 2,728,100 letters. The New Testament 27 books, 260 chapters, 181,253 verses, 838,380 letters, making a total of

Books, . .	66	Verses, . .	31,173
Chapters, . .	1,189	Words, . .	773,746
	Letters, . .	3,566,480.	

Independently of all considerations of its religious advantages, no book has conduced more than the Bible to the high cultivation and moral advancement of the human mind. The labor bestowed by so many of the learned, upon the just interpretation of this inestimable book, is of itself an attestation of its worth, and countenances the supposition, that Divine Providence has appointed it for the attainment of great designs.

The Bible, *το Βιβλιον*, is the name applied by way of eminence to the collection of sacred writings, otherwise called in Holy Scripture the Old and New Testament. "This volume to which both Jews and Christians respectively appeal; the former, to the Old Testament Scripture exclusively; the latter, to the Old and New Testament combined, which is emphatically termed the Bible. It comprises a great number of narratives and compositions written by inspired persons, at distant periods, in different languages, and on various subjects. Collectively, they claim to be a *Divine Revelation*, that is, a discovery afforded by God to man of Himself, or of his will beyond what He has vouchsafed to make known by the light of nature or reason."

Bishop Horne forcibly and beautifully remarks: "The Scriptures are the appointed means of enlightening the mind with true and saving knowledge. They show us what we were, what we are, and what we shall be. They show us what God has done for us, and what He expects us to do for him. They show us the adversaries we have to encounter, and how to encounter them with success. They show us the mercy and justice of God, the joys of Heaven, and the pains of Hell. Thus will they give to the simple an understanding of such matters as philosophy, for whole centuries, taught in vain."

COLLECTANEA:

OR,

A PARTERRE

OF

SENTIMENTS,
SIMILITUDES,
SPIRITUALITIES,
SPECULATIONS,
SINGULARITIES, &c.

SPARSOS COLLIGERE FLORES ET FRONDES.

COLLECTANEA.

Abraham's Wife; *tradition respecting her beauty.*

The rabbies have invented the following singular account of Abraham's conveyance of Sarah into Egypt. "He put her into a chest, and locked the cover of the same upon her face, jealous of her beauty being noticed. When he was come to the toll or custom-house, they said, 'Pay us custom,' and he said, 'I will pay the custom.' They said to him, 'Thou carriest clothes;' and he said, 'I will pay for the clothes.' They said to him, 'Thou carriest gold;' and he answered them, 'I will pay for my gold.' They said to him further, 'Thou carriest the finest silk;' then he said to them, 'I will pay for the finest silk.' Farther, they said to him, 'Thou carriest pearls;' and he said to them, 'I will pay for the pearls,' and he was willing to pay custom as if he had carried such valuable things. But they said unto him, 'It cannot be, but thou must open, and show us what is within.' And when he had opened the chest, the whole land of Egypt was brightly illumined by the lustre of Sarah."—Allen.

Adam's *designation of the Animals in Paradise allegorized.*

The beasts of the field which God brought to Adam, in order that he might give them names, are the unreasonable motions of the flesh. Fowls of the air, are idle thoughts, and empty speculations. The garden of Eden the spiritual purity of the mind and the region of heavenly truth into which Paul was wrapt.—Heywood.

There is a tradition that our first parents were forty days in Paradise.

Christ, *his nativity, intercession, gracious and miraculous operations spiritualized;—Nature's recognition of her Deity;—and parallelisms illustrating the Mosaic and Christian dispensations.*

Unexpressible is the Sacrament of the nativity of our Lord the God of life, which we ought rather to believe than examine. A virgin conceived and brought forth, which nature affordeth not; use knew not; reason was ignorant of; understanding conceived not. This, at which heaven wondered; earth admired; the creature, was stupefied, what human language is able to deliver! Therefore, the Evangelist, as he opened the conception and birth in a human phrase, so he shut it up in a divine secret. And, this he did to show, that it is not lawful for a man to dispute that which he is commanded to believe. And, again, how can there be the least damage unto modesty when there is interested a Deity? when an angel is the messenger; faith, the bridesmaid; chastity, the contract; virtue, the espouser; conscience, the priest; God, the cause; integrity, the conception; virginity, the birth; a maid, the mother? Let no man, therefore, judge that thing after the manner of man which is done by a divine sacrament; let no man examine a celestial mystery by earthly reason, or a secret novelty, by that which is frequent and common. Let no man measure that which is singular, by example; nor derive contumely from piety; nor run into danger by his rashness, when God has promised salvation by his goodness. What was the necessity that Mary the blessed virgin should be espoused unto Joseph? but, either because that mystery should be concealed from the devil; and so the false accuser should find no cavil against her chastity, being affianced unto an husband; or else that after the infant was born, he should be the mother's conductor into Egypt and back again. For Mary was the untouched, the unblemished, the immaculate mother of the only begotten Son of God;—the almighty Father and Creator of all things,—of that Son who, in heaven, was without a mother;—on earth, without a father;—in heaven, (according to his Deity,) in the bosom of his Father; on earth, (according to his humanity,) in the lap of his mother.—HEYWOOD.

Father, forgive them, for they know not what they do!

Philosophy, therefore, if it required a lesson in humanity, may come to school here. The feeling which prompted these words touched the highest culminating point of human nature, where divinity itself begins.—SIR THOMAS BROWNE.

The fountain with which Paradise was watered is Christ: of the four rivers into which it is often parted, Pison is prudence; Gihon, temperance; Tigris (Hiddekel), fortitude; Euphrates, justice.

That of three things the world has great cause to wonder—of Christ's resurrection after death,—of his ascension to heaven in the flesh,—and that by his Apostles, being no better than fishermen, the whole world should be converted. There be four miraculous imitators made by Christ—a fisherman, to be first shepherd of his flock—a persecutor, to be first master and teacher of the Gentiles—a publican, to be the first evangelist—a thief, that first entered heaven.

Would we be acquainted with the mysteries of the kingdom of heaven, we must make application not to angels, for they are themselves learners, but to Christ himself.—AMBROSE.

As in the earthly Paradise there were four rivers which watered the whole earth; so in Christ, who is our Paradise, we may find four fountains; the first is the fountain of mercy, to wash away our sins by the waters of remission; the second is the fountain of wisdom, to quench our thirst with the waters of discretion; the third is the fountain of grace, to water the plants of good works with the springs of devotion; and the fourth is the crystal fountain of everlasting life whose refreshing waters issue from the mount of the heavenly Zion.

The heavens knew him, which lent him a bright star to light him into the world. The sea knew him, which against its own nature, made itself passable for his feet. The earth knew him, which shook and trembled at his passion. The sun knew him, which hid its face, and withdrew his beams from beholding so execrable an object as the crucifixion. The stones and buildings knew him, which split and rent themselves asunder. The grave and hell knew him, the one, by yielding up the dead; the other, by witnessing his descension.

The Jews reckoned up five several marks of divine favor which distinguished the first temple, and were wanting in the second. The ark of the covenant and the mercy seat which was upon it; the Shechinah or the divine presence; the Urim and Thummim; the holy fire upon the altar; and the spirit of prophecy. Now the absence of those several things was abundantly supplied by the presence of that Divine Person of whom each of them was in some measure typical. Christ may be called the ark, as he was the material representative of the Deity, in whom was deposited the perfect law of God. Like the cedar of which the ark was composed, Christ was incorruptible; and the golden crown of divinity and glory was upon him, as it was upon the ark. Angels attended him in his humiliation. and desired to penetrate the mystery of his incarnation, as the cherubim bent over the mercy seat; so is Christ the meeting place between God and man. Christ was the Shechinah, for he dwelt in the tabernacle among men, the true glory of the Shechinah. The Urim and Thummim were not required when the Messiah was on the earth. He only has given those clear oracular answers, which shall ever instruct the world; the others were but typical of that union of light and perfection which met in Him alone. Never but in him were united perfect knowledge and perfect holiness. He is the Great High Priest, who has spoken with the mouth of God. The holy fire was not necessary, it was but typical of that eternal flame of devotion, and purity, and love, which God requires, and Christ exemplified. The spirit of prophecy was not wanted, for on him rested the spirit without measure. He was the prophet like unto Moses, in bringing in a new dispensation; though greater than Moses, for he was perfect in himself, and grace and truth are better than the law. Christ united in himself all these ornaments of the first temple, and He excelled them all, inasmuch as the substance is superior to the shadow. These things, it is true, made the first temple glorious; but the glory of the second temple was indeed greater than that of the first; when Christ uniting all the realities of which the first temple were but typical, presented himself in the second temple, to the admiring and wondering crowd as the true Messiah, the expected Hope and Savior of Israel.

Socinius and his followers believed in the actual translation of Jesus to some celestial region in the interval between his baptism and his entrance upon his public ministry.

CREATION; *allegorized.*

"That God has taught us by the course he took in framing and fashioning the world, how we must proceed to become a new creation or a new heaven and a new earth, renewed both in soul and body. In the first day, he made the light; therefore the first thing of the new man ought to be the light of knowledge, for saith St. Paul, 'he that cometh to God must know that he is.' On the second day, he made the firmament, so called because of its steadfastness; so the second step in man's new creation must be *firmamentum fidei*—the sure foundation of faith. On the third day, the seas and trees bearing fruits; so the third step in the new man is, that he become waters of relenting tears, and that he bring forth fruit worthy of repentance. On the fourth day, God created the sun, that whereas on the first day there was light without heat, now on the fourth day there is light and heat joined together; so the fourth step in the new creation of the new man is, that he join the heat of zeal with the light of knowledge; as in the sacrifices, fire and salt were coupled. The fifth day's work was of fishes to play in the seas, and fowls to fly and soar towards heaven; so the fifth step, in a new creature, is to live and rejoice in a sea of troubles, and fly by prayer and contemplation heavenward. On the sixth day, God made man; now all those things before named being performed by Him, *man*, is a new creature. They are all thus like a golden chain concatenated into several links by Saint Peter." Add to your light of knowledge, the firmament of faith; to your faith, seas of repentant tears; to your tears, the fruitful trees of good works; to your good works, the hot sunshine of zeal; to your zeal, the winged fowls of prayer and contemplation; and so *Ecce omnia facta sunt.* Behold all things are made new!—HEYWOOD.

DECALOGUE; *fetched from heaven by Moses, and the opposition he encountered from angelic interference.*

Moses is represented by the Cabalists as having received the law, not as is commonly believed by Christians, by the condescension of the divine Majesty, on Mount Sinai; but by actually ascending into heaven to fetch it. And ample details have been given of the opposition he experienced from numerous and mighty angels, and the means by which he overcame that opposition and surmounted other difficulties and obstacles in his progress through the celestial regions.

DEITY; *hieroglyphically represented.*

Divers nations, but especially the Egyptians, made certain hieroglyphics to express the sole supremacy of the Deity. First, by the stork, which is a bird that hath no tongue; and God created all things in a temperate and quiet silence: inferring from this that man ought not to speak of him too freely or rashly, nor to search too narrowly into his hidden attributes. They interpreted His infinity by a circle, which hath neither beginning nor an end. So likewise by the eye; for as in all other creatures, so especially in man the eye is of his other members, the most beautiful and excellent, as the moderator and guide of our affections and actions; so God is the bright eye of the world who by the apostle James is called the Father of men, unto whose eyes all thoughts be naked and open, who looketh upon the good and bad, and searches into the reins of either.—HEYWOOD.

DEVIL; *the method and ceremony of the homage performed; and the fealty paid to him, according to the ritual of witchcraft.*

First, the magician or witch is brought before the tribunal of Satan, either by a familiar spirit or else by a magi or hag of the same profession, who sits crowned upon a majestic throne, surrounded by a host of other devils, who attend upon him in the capacity and dignity of lords, barons, and princes, richly appareled in the vestments of Tartarean paraphernalia. The palace or parliament-house of his satanic majesty is represented as built of beautiful marble, and the walls of which are hung with gorgeous drapery interwoven with gold and silver and purple covered arras, and designed to augment the pomp of his regality and imperial state. Satan, from his royal seat, casts his eyes round about, as if ready to incline his benign ear, by way of encouragement, to any suitor that may be presented. A devil, of venerable aspect, now steps forth and saith, "Most potent lord and master, great patron of the spacious universe, in whose hands are all the riches and treasures of the earth, and all the goods and gifts of the world, this person I present before thine imperial throne, to follow thy standard, and to fight under the patronage of thy great name and power; who is ready to acknowledge thee to be god and creator of all things, and none but thee. It shall be thy clemency, O most sovereign lord, to vouchsafe this man (or woman) the grace of thy benign aspect and receive him (or her) unto thy patronage and favor." To which Satan, with a grave countenance and loud oration answereth, "I cannot but commend this thy friend, who so cordially hath committed himself (or herself) unto our safe guard and trust; whom as our client and favorite we accept, and promise to supply him with all felicity and pleasure, both in this present life and the future." This done, the miserable wretch is commanded to renounce his faith, baptism, the eucharist, and all other holy things, and to confess Lucifer his only lord and governor; which is done with many infernal and execrable ceremonies not befitting to be here mentioned. Then is the certificate of initiation and reception written with the blood of the left thumb. After which the devil marks him either in the brow, neck or shoulders, but commonly in the more secret parts, with the stamp or character of the foot of a hare, a black dog, or a toad, or some such figure by which he brands him (as the custom was of old, to stamp their slaves and captives whom they bought for money in the market-places) to become his perpetual slave and vassal; and this the wicked spirit doeth, as desirous to imitate God in all things; who in the Old Testament marked his chosen people with the seal of circumcision, to distinguish them from the gentiles, and in the New Testament, with the sign of the cross, which succeeded that of circumcision (according to the testimony of the fathers). And as the devil is always adverse to his creator, so he will be worshipped with contrary rites and ceremonies. Therefore, whenever magicians, and witches, present themselves unto him, they worship him with their faces from, and their backs towards him, and sometimes standing upon their heads with their heels upwards, but what is most beastly and abominable of all the requisition of their homage and fealty, the devil presents unto them his forked tail to kiss; which divers magicians have confessed. Those who put themselves under any certain constellation by which to produce curious and prodigious effects, whereby the work is taken from the creator and attributed unto the creature; and all those operations of conjuration, incantation, abjuration, murmuration, together with those conventicles and nightly assemblies of sorcerers, and other diabolical inventions, have the great devil himself for their author and abettor.—HEYWOOD.

Some of the ancient writers on Sorcery, have affirmed that every magician and witch after they have passed through the ordeal of performing homage to the devil, immediately a familiar spirit is appointed to attend them, and whom they styled *Magister*, *Martinellus*, and that he is sometimes visible with them, in the shape of a dog, a rat, an Ethiope, &c. That Simon Magus had a black dog tied to him with a chain, which, if any man attempted to speak to him, with whom he did not desire any communication, he instantly sprang at him, and the offender was soon devoured.

The knowledge of devils makes them familiar with the virtues of herbs, plants, stones, minerals, &c. They understand the nature of all creatures, birds, and beasts. They possess excellent skill in all the arts and sciences. By their influence they operate on the four elements, stars and planets; are acquainted with the cause of meteors, and can produce miraculous alterations and wonderful effects in the air.—BURTON, *Anatomy*.

The ancient, as well as the more recent sophists, enumerate the following kinds of devils, their particular orders, and point out their respective presidencies—*Fiery* spirits or devils, have control over blazing stars, fire drakes, *ignes fatui*, &c. The *aerial*, keep their quarters in the air, and control tempests, thunder, lightnings, &c. The *water-devils*, preside over naiads or water-nymphs, oceans, rivers, &c. The *terrestrial*, supervise lares, genii, wood-nymphs, fairies, robin-good-fellows, forests, &c. The *subterranean*, are commonly seen about mines, produce earthquakes, are conversant with the centre of the earth and volcanoes, and torture the souls of men till the day of judgment. Their egress and regress are about Ætna, Lipari, Mons Hecla in Iceland, Vesuvius, Terra del Fuego, &c., because many shrieks and fearful cries are continually heard thereabouts, and familiar apparitions of dead men, ghosts, goblins, &c.—BURTON, *Passim*.

FANATICISM; *its natural character and practical effects.*

The fanatic will live on better terms with angels and with seraphs, than with his children, servants or neighbors, or he is one who, while he reverences the thrones, dominions, and powers of the invisible world, vents his spleen in railing against all "dignities and powers of the earth."—ISAAC TAYLOR.

FIRMAMENT; *morally considered.*

If, with Seneca, we contemplate aright in imagination the magnitude and beauty of the orbs of heaven, we shall look down, with a noble indifference, on the earth as a scarcely distinguishable atom, and say, "Is it to this little spot that the great designs and most glorious desires of man are confined? Is it for this, that there is such disturbance of nature, so much carnage, and so many ruinous wars? O! folly of deceived men, to imagine great kingdoms in the compass of an atom, to raise armies to divide a point of earth with their swords! It is just as if the ants should divide their mole hills into provinces, and conceive a field to be several kingdoms, and fiercely contend to enlarge their borders and celebrate a triumph in gaining a foot of earth, or a new province to their empire. In the light of heaven, all sublunary glories fade away, and the mind is refined and ennobled, when with the eye of faith, it penetrates within the veil and descries the splendor of the heaven of heavens.

FUTURE STATE; *its necessity, reality, equality, promise, and moral influence.*

It is indeed a wide ocean, said the abbé, full of waves and dangers, storms and tempests; and like the Atlantic before the adventurous Genoese first crossed it, no one comes back to tell us what is beyond. But as to the eye of Columbus, enlightened by true genius, it was self-evident that to harmonize with the known world in which he dwelt, there must be another continent beyond the broad western sea; so to the eye of the religious man, enlightened by revelation, it is self-evident, that beyond the scenes of time, there must be another world to equalise all that is unequal in this.—ANONYMOUS.

If there be men dignified by the name of philosophers who can hold that the present scene of being, with all its moral evil, and physical suffering, is to be succeeded by no better or happier state of existence, just because "all things have continued as they were" five or six thousand years; their inferences respecting the future state, would not have been less conclusive, or the revealed declaration of the scripture less true, had they based it on a period, even an hundred times more extended.—HUGH MILLER.

"Plato, thou reason'st well,
Else whence this pleasing hope, this fond desire,
This longing after immortality!
Or whence this secret dread, and inward horror—

Of falling into naught? Why shrinks the soul
Back on herself, and startles at destruction?
'Tis the divinity that stirs within us,
'Tis heaven itself that points out an hereafter
And intimates eternity to man."—Addison.

The doctrine of a future state is not merely a speculative proposition to serve as a subject of metaphysical investigation or to be admitted merely to complete a system of philosophy or theological belief. It is a truth of the highest practical importance which ought to be interwoven with the whole train of our thoughts and actions. Yet how many are there even of those who bear the Christian name, who are incessantly engaged in boisterous disputes respecting the nature of faith, who have never felt the influence of that faith which realizes to the mind, as if actually present, the glories of the invisible world. If we really believe the doctrine of immortality, it will manifest itself in our thoughts, affections and pursuits. It will lead us to form a just estimation of the value of all earthly enjoyments. For in the sight of eternity all secular pursuits in which men now engage appear but vanity, and all the dazzling objects which fascinate these eyes, as fleeting shadows. A realizing view of an eternal state dissipates the illusion which the eye of sense throws over the pageantry and splendors of this world, and teaches us that is transitory and fading, and that our most exquisite pleasures will ere long be snatched from our embrace. For not a single mark of our sublunary honors, not a single farthing of our boasted treasures, not a single trace of the beauty of our persons, can be carried along with us to the regions beyond the grave. It will stimulate us to set our affections on things above, and to indulge in heavenly contemplations, for "where our treasure is, our hearts will be also." Rising superior to the delights of sense, and the boundaries of time, we will expatiate at large, on those boundless regions which "eye hath not seen," and contemplate in the eye of reason and revelation those scenes of felicity and grandeur which will burst upon the disembodied spirit when it has dropped its earthly tabernacle in the dust. Again, if we believe the doctrine of immortality, we will be careful to avoid those sins which would expose us to misery in the future world, and to cultivate those dispositions and virtues which will prepare us for the enjoyment of eternal felicity. Between virtue and vice, sin and holiness, there is an essential and eternal distinction, and this distinction will be fully and visibly displayed in the eternal world. He whose life is a continued scene of vicious indulgence, and who has devoted himself to "work all manner of uncleanness with greediness," becomes by such habits "a vessel of wrath fitted for destruction," and from the very constitution of things there is no possibility of his escaping the misery of the future state, if his existence be prolonged. Whereas, he who is devoted to the practice of holiness, who loves his creator with supreme affection and his neighbor as himself, who adds to his "faith virtue, knowledge, temperance, patience, brotherly kindness and charity," is by the possession and exemplification of such graces, rendered fit for everlasting communion with the Father of Spirits, and for delightful association with all holy intelligences, that people his immense empire. The belief in a future state, also, will excite us to the exercise of contentment and reconcile our minds to whatever privations or afflictions, providence may allot us in this world. "For the sufferings of the present time are not worthy to be compared with the glory which is to be revealed." If we believe that the whole train of circumstances connected with our present lot is arranged by wisdom and benevolence, every thing that befalls us here must have a certain bearing on the future world, and have a tendency to prepare us for engaging in its exercises, and for relishing its enjoyment. We will not rest satisfied with vague and confused conceptions of celestial bliss; but will endeavor to form as precise and definite ideas, on this subject, as the position of our sublunary condition will permit. We will search the oracles of divine revelation and the discoveries of science, and endeavor to deduce from both, the sublimest conceptions we can form of the glories of that "inheritance which is incorruptible, undefiled, and that fadeth not away, which is reserved in heaven for the faithful."

GOD; *understood by the works of nature and the volume of Inspiration.*

Saith an old divine: we come by two ways to the knowledge and apprehension of God, by his works and by his word; by his works we learn to know there is a God, and by his word we come to know what God is. His works teach us to spell, his word to read. The first are his back parts, by which we behold Him afar off, the latter represent Him to us more visibly, and as it were "face to face." For the word is a book consisting of three leaves, and every leaf printed with many letters, and every letter containeth in itself a lecture. The leaves are heaven, the air, and the earth, with the water: the letters engraved are every angel, star and planet; the letters in the air, every meteor and fowl; those in the earth and water, every man, beast, plant, flower, mineral, fish, &c. All these, set together, spell unto us—That there is a God.

I am the God of Abraham, and the God of Isaac, and the God of Jacob, in a special sense, not merely as their creator and preserver, which he is to all men, but as their governor, protector, supplier and friend,—not of the dead, which are non-entities. In Scripture, that God is one God, and that we are his people, are correlative propositions.

The works of creation, and every thing around us, manifest the presence of God,—his radiant, life-giving circle. It is neither pantheism nor poetry alone, but the truth of nature exemplified in the variations of the seasons.

> "These, as they change, Almighty Father, these
> Are but the varied God; the rolling year
> Is full of thee. Forth in the pleasing spring
> Thy beauty walks, thy tenderness and love."

Every germ that is evolving, every flower that blooms, presents to us the moving presence of God. Whenever we conceive of the operations of the laws of nature in the world, or disconnected from the power of His immediate presence, at the place where such operations exhibit themselves, we practically deny his omnipresence. It is a beautiful and instructive story of the traveller, amid the emergencies of a journey in the destitution of a desert, attracted by a flower, growing upon a stone in the arid waste, exclaiming, God is here! The blooming flower was the manifestation of his presence.

"Should fate command me to the utmost verge,
Of the great earth, to distant barbarous climes;
Rivers unknown to song; where first the sun
Gilds Indian mountains, or his setting beams
Flame on the Atlantic Isles, 'tis naught to me,
Since God is ever present, ever felt,
In the void waste, as in the city full;
And where he vital breathes there must be joy."

IMMORTALITY; *symbolized by the Tomb.*

It remains for death to exhibit the glory of life. It was a beautiful superstition, that of ever-burning lamps in tombs. To seek for such, imaged well the practice of the Christian, who beholds immortality in the grave.—SLACK.

JACOB'S LADDER; *its prophetic and spiritual meaning.*

The Rabbins have a conceit respecting the ladder which Jacob beheld in his dream, "set upon the earth, and the top of it reaching to heaven, and the angels of God ascending and descending upon it," which they say represents the rise and fall of the four great monarchies; the seventy steps agreeing with the seventy years captivity in Babylon, or two and fifty steps representing the time of the reign of the four Assyrian kings.

In Jacob's ladder figur'd this we see,
(Which ladder Christ himself profest to be),
Of which the foot being fixt upon the ground,
The top to heaven. Thus much to us doth sound,
That in this scale, at such large distance set,
The heaven and earth at once together met.
So Christ's humanity from earth was given,
But his divinity He took from heaven;
As from earth, earthy; as from heaven divine;
Two natures, in one person, thus combine.

HEYWOOD.

JEWS; *touching the prophecies relative to their present condition, and the prospective restoration to their former possession of the divine favor, and return of their national glory.*

In the midst of all changes,—the vicissitudes of time,—the revolution of kingdoms, and the downfall of empires, the Jew abides the same in every particular, the same as when God led him out of Egypt, with one creed, one language, one liturgy, one sorrow, one hope, he is found in every corner of the globe, a severed fragment of that exquisite design which the Lord shall again arrange, as of old, to be the beauty and glory of the whole earth.—CHARLOTTE ELIZABETH.

JOSEPH; *traditionary statement respecting his burial and the journeyings of his coffin.*

Rabbi Nathan affirms that Joseph was buried in the mausoleum of a certain king of Egypt, and that Moses stood near that royal cemetery and said, Joseph, the time is arrived in which God swore that he would deliver Israel; the time is come also for Israel to fulfill the oath which thou didst impose upon them; if thou show thyself, well; but, if not, we are released from our obligation. That Joseph's coffin instantly advanced; and that Moses took it, and carried it off with him, and that during all the year that Israel passed in the wilderness, the coffin of Joseph and the ark of the Lord marched side by side.—ALLEN.

JUDGMENT DAY; *its necessity, equity, and moral influence.*

This is the day that must make good that great attribute of God,—his justice; that must reconcile those answerable doubts that torment the wisest understandings and resolve those seeming inequalities, and respective distributions in this world, to an equality and recompensive justice in the next. This is that one day that shall include and comprehend all that went before it; wherein, as in the last scene, all the actors must enter to complete and make up the catastrophe of this great piece. This is the day whose memory hath only power to make us honest in the dark, and to be virtuous without a witness. *Ipsa sui pretium virtus sibi*, that virtue is her own reward, is but a cold principle to maintain our variable resolutions in a constant and settled way of goodness.—SIR T. BROWNE.

MAGIC; *its author and history.*

Some authors have supposed the art of magic was devised before the flood, by the Devil, who communicated the invention to the giants, by whom *Cham*, the son of Noah, was instructed in the science of sorcery. For this abomination, with the consequences of all manner of iniquities arising therefrom, was the deluge brought upon the world, and which, after the flood, was taught by *Cham* to his son, Misraim, who conveyed it to the Egyptians, Babylonians and Persians, and from them imparted to the other nations of this terraqueous globe.

Other writers on magic derive the words from *Theurgia* or white-magic, *Goetia* or black-magic, or the black-art, otherwise called necromancy. The effect of the first, they imputed to good angels; and the evils of the latter they ascribed to demons; affirming the one to be lawful, and the other unlawful.

Tertullian traces all the chief luxuries of female attire, the necklaces, armlets, rouge and the black powder for the eye lashes, to the researches of fallen angels into the inmost recesses of nature, and the discoveries they were in consequence enabled to make of all that could embellish the beauty of their earthly favorites.

Mesmerism; *a characteristic and medical anecdote.*

Remarks.—The daring follies and satanic delusions of the present day are not entitled to the merit or charm of novelty, as regards either their source, principles, designs, peculiarities or practices; being in spirit—*in facto*—precisely the same as those which existed during the dark and sanguinary period when witchcraft prevailed in England. Fortune-telling is now exploded, and entirely confined to the simplicity of silly and ignorant girls; pronounced by law a misdemeanor, and punishable upon the indictment *of obtaining money under false pretences.*

During the reigns of the Charles's, and the interregnum of the Protectorate, these abominations were rife. Modern Millerism corresponds to the Millenium of the Fifth-Monarchy-Men; whilst other similar vagaries, which have recently startled or seduced the imbeciles of the passing hour, are merely modified to meet the advanced stage of the scientific knowledge of a progressive civilization; putting on the disguise of new names and assuming the different dress of a changed appearance, to distinguish them from such as originated in the dark, superstitious and disastrous times of English history, when the corrupting influence of courtly intrigues, commingled with the subversive errors of a headlong fanaticism, and those heretical dogmas which provoked the outbreak—"the confusion worse confounded"—of those sanguinary and sectarian conflicts which have ever attended the unyielding hostilities, fierce and violent struggles of religious denominations for the ascendency to supreme authority, or the tyranny of despotic power, so dishonoring to the benevolent character of a Catholic Christianity, as well as abhorrent to those essential principles which involve the inalienable and sacred rights of civil and religious liberty, whose safe and solid base alone affords a sure foundation upon which to erect the various and stately superstructures of social, political, and ecclesiastical institutions; rendered most durable and attractive when built according to the glorious order of a divine architecture, and adorned by the chaste ornaments of those plastic and apostolic rules, taught and perfected only in the school of Christ.—G. C.

By the spirits called Lares, or household gods, many men have been driven into strange melancholies. Amongst others I will cite one least common. A young man had a strong imagination that he was dead, and did not only abstain from the use of meat and drink, but importuned his parents that he might be carried into his grave and buried before his flesh was quite putrefied. By the counsel of physicians, he was wrapped up in a winding sheet and laid upon a bier, and so carried toward the church upon men's shoulders. But, by the way, two or three pleasant fellows, suborned to that purpose, meeting the hearse, demanded aloud of them that followed it, whose body it was there coffined and carried to burial? They said it was such a young man's, and told them his name. Surely (replied one of them), the world is very well rid of him, for he was a man of a very bad and vicious life, and his friends may rejoice he hath rather ended his days thus, than at the gallows. Which the young man hearing, and vexed to be so injured, roused himself up upon the bier, and told them that they were wicked men to do him that wrong, which he had never deserved, and told them, that if he were alive, as he was not, he would teach them to speak better of the dead. But they proceeding to deprave him, and give him much disgraceful and contemptible language, he not being able to endure it, leapt from the hearse and fell about their ears with such rage and fury that he ceased not buffeting with them till quite wearied, and by his violent agitation the humors of his body altered, he awakened as out of a sleep or trance, and being brought home and comforted with wholesome diet, he within a few days recovered both his pristine health, strength and understanding.*

"Time is, that I, being a young man, writ of Magical Art three books in one volume, sufficiently large, which I entitled of *Hidden Philosophy;* in which wheresoever I have erred through the vain curiosity of youth, now in my better and more ripe understanding I recant in this palinode. I confess I have spent much time in these vanities, in which I have only profited thus much, that I am able to

* The foregoing incident is extracted from a work containing upward of seven hundred folio pages of doggerel verse and laborious prose, preceded by a dedication to Henrietta Maria Queen, which breathes the gallantry and quintessence of chivalric courtesy; but considering it a literary curiosity I was enticed to proceed over its rugged and unpolished pages even after the fatigue and lateness of business—from occasionally meeting with a brilliant sentiment and diamond thought. The volume is an *omnium gatherum* of astrology, astronomy, cosmogony, mythology, philosophy, sorcery, theology, talmudic traditions, pagan fables, puritanical research and literature. And I am further induced to insert (using modern orthography) the additional remarks of the author respecting himself, as they embrace an admirable moral, and present a pointed and warning rebuke to such whose propensity to waste their time and indulge their fancies and mar their usefulness in the absurdities and wonders of supernaturalism bear an inverse ratio to their belief in the mysteries and truths and requisitions of the Bible.—G. C.

dehort other men from entering into the like dangers. For whatsoever by the illusion of the devil, or by the operation of evil spirits shall presume to divine or prophesy by magical vanities, exorcism, incantations, amatories, enchanted ditches, and other demoniac actions, exercising blasphemous charms, spells, witchcrafts, and sorceries, or anything belonging to superstition and idolatry; all these are foredoomed to be tormented in eternal fire with *Jamnes Mambre and Simon Magus.*"—HEYWOOD.—(1659.)

MESSIAH; *Traditions relating to the Blessings and Celebration of Christ's Kingdom.*

The felicities and glories which will usher in the government of the Messiah is to be celebrated by a royal festival, to which all Israelites will be invited, and seated every one beside a golden table. As all other kings and princes on the occasion of a public festival are accustomed to entertain their guests with spectacles and games; so this banquet of the Messiah is to be introduced by a sportive exhibition. He will amuse the company with a battle between Behemoth and Leviathan, as it is written, "Thus shall the beasts of the field play." Job i. 20. The various feats of Behemoth will be highly gratifying to the Messiah. "These also shall please the Lord better than an ox or bullock that hath horns and hoofs." Psal. lxix: 31. But Leviathan shall advance to the contest armed with his scales, as with a breastplate and coat of mail dreadful to behold. The battle will be fierce; but the combatants being equally matched, neither will be victorious. They will both fall exhausted with fatigue. Then Messiah with a drawn sword shall stab and slay them both. "In that day the Lord, with his sore and great and strong sword shall punish Leviathan the piercing serpent, even Leviathan that crooked serpent." Isaiah xxvii. 1. These huge animals, together with Bar Juchine the enormous bird, are then to be spitted and laid to the fire, and all requisite preparations to be made for the splendid banquet, as it is written: "And on this mountain shall the Lord of hosts make unto all people a feast of fat things, a feast of wines on the lees, of fat things full of marrow, of wine on the lees well refined. Isaiah xxv. 6. Having provided three courses of flesh, fish and fowl; the rabbies have supplied this sumptuous feast of the Messiah, with the customary appendages. The dessert will consist of the most delicious fruits, the produce of the garden of Eden, including some of the fruit taken from the tree of life; the choicest and most exquisite wines of the vintage of Paradise, prepared immediately after the creation, and preserved in Adam's wine-cellar ever since, expressly for this glorious occasion. "In that day sing ye unto her, a vineyard of red wine, I the Lord do keep it." Isaiah xxvii. 2, 3. "In the hand of the Lord there is a cup, and the wine is red, it is full of mixture, and he poureth out of the same." Psalms lxxv. 8. "Since the beginning of the world men have not heard, nor perceived by the ear, neither hath the eye seen, O God, besides thee, what he hath prepared for him that waiteth for him."

Isaiah lxiv. 4. At the conclusion of the feast Messiah is represented as filling a cup, over which, according to usual custom, a grace will be pronounced; that the company giving glory to God will beseech him to undertake the office; resembling that of the cup-bearer—that God will offer it Michael, Michael to Gabriel, Gabriel to Abraham, Abraham to Isaac, Isaac to Moses, Moses to Joshua; that all these declining the office as being unworthy of such high honor, will at last assign it to David; declaring it will be proper for an earthly king to perform this service to the King of Heaven,—that David will say, "Well! then I will give thanks and this office becomes me as it is said," "I will take the cup of salvation and will call upon the name of the Lord." Psalms cxvi. 13. And that this cup will contain two hundred and fourteen gallons, as it is said, "My cup runneth over." Psalms xxiii. 5. The luxuries and provisions remaining on the table will be distributed amongst the guests, who will expose them to sale at the market-place at Jerusalem; that of the part of the skin of Leviathan will be made tabernacles, pavilions or awnings for the just; and that the rest will be spread upon the walls of Jerusalem, diffusing a light to the extremities of the world; as it is written, "And kings shall come to the brightness of thy rising." Isaiah lx. 3. The banquet will be succeeded, and the festival concluded by music and dancing; God entertaining the just, with music and dancing, and will himself sit in the midst of them, in the garden of Eden, and every one will point to him with an outstretched finger. "And it shall be said in that day, Lo, this is our God, we have waited for him; we will be glad, and rejoice in his salvation." Isaiah xxv. 9.—Allen.

Resurrection; *Physically Explained and Illustrated; and Symbolized by Funereal Trees, Ornamental Flowers, and Perennial Shrubs.*

During the life of any animal its particles are in a state of ceaseless change; the organism of to-day is not that of yesterday. When this removal of particles ceases to take place, according to vital laws, the organism decays. But who shall say that the power which brought them together decays also? All that we know is, that we no longer see the same process conducted; but that does not prove annihilation. All action that we are acquainted with produces reaction; and perhaps, if life operates on matter, matter operates on life. This action may, for aught we know, be needful for the development of the soul; but the necessity of that precise mode of it which takes place in what we call a living organism, is only for a time. Death is only one of change, and change has its relation to Time; it is a relation, not an absolute existence. The opponents of the natural evidence of immortality, appeal to the triumph of death in the lower world; but they know not what those triumphs are, nor to what extent they go. Nature is the art of God. It seems a constant plan of nature to build exquisite structures with worthless and often loathsome materials. The brilliant plant and the phosphorescent light spring from putrescence; and among the decay of expectations and the mangled relics of happiness, hope blossoms and shows at once a flower and a star. That in strewing their tombs the Romans affected the rose; the Greeks the amaranthus and myrtles; that the funeral pyre consisted of sweet fuel, cypress, fir, larix, yew, and trees perpetually verdant, lay silent expressions of their surviving hopes; wherein Christians which deck their coffins with bays, have found a more elegant emblem; for that tree seeming dead will restore from the root, and its exsuccous leaves assume their verdure again. Whether the planting of the yew in church yards hold not its original from ancient funeral rites, or as an emblem of the Resurrection, from its perpetual verdure, may also admit conjecture. If in the decretory term of the world, we shall not all die, but be changed according to received translation; the last day will make but few graves; at least quick resurrection will anticipate lasting sepulchres; some graves will be opened before they be quite closed, and Lazarus be no wonder. When many that feared to die shall groan that they can die but once; the dismal state is the second and living death, when life puts despair on the damned; when men shall wish the covering of mountains, not of monuments, and annihilation shall be courted.—SIR THOMAS BROWNE.

Death is as necessary to the constitution as sleep. We shall rise refreshed in the morning.—DR. FRANKLIN.

SAINT PAUL'S *traditional descent into Hell.*

Adam de Ross thus sings of St. Paul's descent into hell. The Archangel Michael performs the office of guide to the apostle. "My good son," says he to him, "follow me without fear and without suspicion." God commands me to show to thee the gnashing of teeth, the pangs and the anguish which sinners undergo. Michael goes first; Paul follows, repeating psalms. At the gate of hell grows a tree of fire; from its branches hang the souls of misers and scandal-mongers. The air is full of flying imps, who drag the wicked to the furnace. The two travellers pursue their way through the desolate regions. The archangel explains to the apostle the torments inflicted for different crimes; from the bosom of an immense forge a vast wave, in which burning furnaces roar and sparkle, issue rivers of molten metals, in which demons are disporting. The further the envoys of heaven penetrate into the bowels of the earth the more terrible become the torments, and St. Paul is filled with pity. They arrive at the mouth of a pit, sealed with the seven seals. The archangel removes the seals, and pushes back the apostle, till the pestilential vapor exhaled from the pit has passed off. From the bottom of this pit ascend the moan of the greatest sinners. St. Paul inquires how long their punishment shall last. "One hundred and forty thousand years," replies St. Michael, "though I am not quite sure of it." The apostle begs the archangel to implore the Almighty to mitigate the punishment of these reprobate spirits. Their prayers, joined by those of other compassionate angels, are granted. God ordains that in future the tortures shall be suspended from Saturday till Monday morning. St. Brandan, in his voyage to the terrestrial paradise, had obtained the same favor for Judas.—CHATEAUBRIAND.

SATAN; *his subtlety, temptations and delusions.*

The devil would persuade me that the brazen serpent was no miracle, but merely operated by sympathy; and to the misapplication of our studies would resolve all phenomena into natural causes. Thus the devil played at chess with me, and yielding a pawn thought to gain a queen from me, taking advantage of my honest endeavors; and whilst I labored to raise the structure of my reason, he strived to undermine the edifice of faith.—SIR THOMAS BROWNE.

The time when the fall of Satan and his angels took place is generally imagined to have preceded the creation of the world; and some have accounted for it by the supposition that the arch-fiend and his angels, being informed of God's purpose to create man after his own image, and to dignify his nature by Christ's assuming it, and thinking their glory to be thus eclipsed, coveted the happiness of man, and so revolted; and with this opinion that of the Mahometans has some affinity, who are taught that the devil, who was once of those angels who are nearest God's presence, and named Azazel, forfeited Paradise for refusing to worship or pay homage to Adam at the command of God. But whatever was the occasion or mode by which it was manifested, pride seems to have been the leading sin, and it ultimately terminated in rebellion and apostacy.

SENTIMENTS *on a variety of subjects, speculative and curious.*

Rest not in high strained paradoxes of old philosophy, supported by naked reason and the reward of mortal felicity; but labor in the ethics of faith, built upon heavenly assistance and the happiness of both beings. Understand the rules, but swear not unto the doctrines of Zeno or Epicurus. Let not the twelve but the two tables be thy law. Let Pythagoras be thy remembrancer, not thy textuary and final instructor; and learn the vanity of the world rather from Solomon than Phocylydes. Keep not in the dogmas of the Peripatetics, Academy, or Porticus. Be a moralist of the mount, an Epictetus in the faith, and Christianize thy notions.

Be not a Hercules Furens abroad, and a poltroon within thyself. To chase our enemies out of the field, and be led captives by our vices; to beat down our foes, and fall down to our concupiscences; are solecisms in moral schools, and no laurels attend them. To manage well our affections, and the wild horses of Plato, are the highest circenses, and the nobles digladiation, is in the theatre of ourselves; for therein our inward antagonists, not like common gladiators, with ordinary weapons and downright blows make at us, but also like retiary and laqueary combatants with nets, frauds, and entanglements, fall upon us. Weapons for such combatants are not to be forged at

Lipara. Vulcan's art doth nothing in this internal militia; wherein not the armor of Achilles, but the armature of St. Paul, gives the glorious day, and triumphs, not leading up to the capitol, but into the highest heavens.

Let not fortune, which hath no name in Scripture, have any in thy divinity. Let Providence, not chance, have the honor of thy acknowledgment, and be thy Edipus in contingencies. Mark well the paths and windings thereof; but be not too wise in the construction or sudden in application. The hand of Providence often in abbreviatures, hieroglyphics, and short characters which, like the Laconicism on the wall, are not to be made out but by hint or key from that spirit which indited them.

We fall not from virtue, like Vulcan, in a day. We are not left without parentheses of consideration, thoughtful rebukes, and merciful interventions to recall us unto ourselves.

It is the heaviest stone that melancholy can throw at a man, to tell him he is at the end of his nature; and there is no future state to come; unto which this seems progressional, and otherwise made in vain. But man is a noble animal,—splendid in ashes, pompous in the grave, solemnizing nativities and deaths with equal lustre, not omitting ceremonies of bravery in the infancy of his nature.

Enjoy the whole world in the hermitage of thyself. Thus the old ascetic Christians formed a paradise in a desert, and with little converse on earth, held a conversation in heaven; thus they astronomized in caves, and though they beheld not the stars, had the glory of heaven before them.

Opinion rides upon the neck of reason; and men are happy, wise or learned, according as that empress sets them down in the register of reputation.

Some negroes who believe in the resurrection think that they shall rise white. Even in this life regeneration may imitate resurrection; our black and various tinctures may wear off, and goodness clothe us with candor. Good admonitions knock not always in vain. There will be signal examples of God's mercy, and the angels must not want their charitable rejoicings for the conversion of lost sinners. The universe is one grand miracle.

Guide not the hand of God, nor order the finger of the Almighty unto thy will and pleasure; but sit quiet in the soft showers of Providence.—Sir Thomas Browne.—*Christian Morals.*

The great advantage of this mean life is thereby to stand in a capacity of a better; for the colonies of heaven must be drawn from earth, and the sons of the first Adam are only heirs unto the second.

I cannot contemn a man for ignorance, but behold him with as much pity as I do Lazarus. It is no greater charity to clothe his body, than apparel the nakedness of his soul.—Sir Thos. Browne.

The poets considered wisdom and virtue the two wings by which we aspire and attain unto the knowledge of God.

A dialogue between two infants in the womb concerning the state of this world, might handsomely illustrate our ignorance of the next; whereof methinks, we yet discourse in Plato's den, and are but embryo philosophers.

As the Son is begotten of the Father, and the Holy Ghost proceedeth both from one and the other; in like manner is the will engendered of the understanding and memory. And as the three persons of the Trinity are but one God, so these three powers, understanding, will, and memory, and faculties of the mind, make but one soul.
HEYWOOD.

The eye of the soul is the mind; it is a substance created invisible, incorporeal, immortal, like unto God, and being the image, *omnia anima et Christi spousa aut Diaboli adultera.* Every soul is either the spouse of Christ or the strumpet of the Devil.—HEYWOOD.

Age is the sauce of a wise man, and a wise man is the meat of age, for not by age, but by travel and industry, wisdom is obtained.

It seems as though in mortal life we behold only images and reflections. It remains for immortality to exhibit realities as they are.

The serpent that tempted Eve had the face of a woman, *quod similia similibus applaudant.* That like might be pleasing to like.
HEYWOOD.

The worlds of matter and of spirit are full of analogies. Indeed matter is only Divine thoughts visible and tangible to human sense.
SLACK.

Pyramids, arches, obelisks, were but the irregularities of vainglory and the wild enormities of ancient magnanimity. But the most magnanimous resolutions rest in the Christian religion, which trampleth upon pride, and sits upon the neck of ambition; humbly pursuing that infallible perpetuity into which all others must diminish their diameters and be poorly seen in the angles of contingency.

Evenus, an elegiac poet of Pharos, was the first it is said, that enunciated the proverb that "Habit was second nature."

It were better to have no opinion of God at all, than such an opinion as is unworthy of Him,—for the one is unbelief, the other contumely.—LORD BACON.

SILENCE; *Figuratively Recommended.*

Nature has afforded us double eyes and ears to behold all objects and listen to all voices and sounds; but to warn us that we should be sparing in our speech, she hath afforded man but one tongue, and that portalled with lips, and portcullised with teeth, near to which are placed the five senses, to signify to us that we ought to speak nothing rashly, without their counsel and advice, with the help of the faculties of the soul, which are reason and understanding, which have their residence in the brain.

Silence is a gift without price, and a treasure without enemies.

SIMILITUDES; *Moral, Devotional, and Allegorical.*

What the pilot is in the ship; what the charioteer is in the chariot; what the leader of the song is in the chorus or anthem; what the law is in the city; the same is God in the world. God, if thou respecteth his force! is the most able; if his features! He is the most beautiful; if His life! immortal; if his virtue! He is the most excellent.—HEYWOOD'S HIERARCHIE.

We have for the sea, the world; for the ship, the church; for our mast, the cross; for the sails, repentance; for our pilot, Christ; for the wind, the Holy Ghost.—ST. CHRYSOSTOM.

Where nature fills the sails the vessel goes smoothly on; and when judgment is the pilot, the insurance need not be high. When industry builds upon nature, we may expect pyramids.

But as eagles when they rest, and the lions when they walk; the one plucks in his talons, the other his claws to keep them sharp, as loath to dull them till they meet their prey; so it is not fit we should trouble our heads, or exercise our wits upon things impertinent, but rather reserve them for things only behoofull and necessary.

Avarice, the offspring of usury and extortion, makes the nobleman mortgage his estates, the lawyer pawn his Lyttleton, the physician sell his Galen, the soldier his sword, the merchant his ship, and the world its peace and happiness. She is drawn in a chariot with four wheels, which are called pusillanimity, inhumanity, contempt of God, and forgetfulness of death. The beasts harnessed to it are tenacity and rapacity, which are guided and governed by the cruel charioteer named a *greedy-desire-of-having*.

Men's miseries, calamities, and ruins are the devil's banqueting dishes.

That in the spiritual building, the foundation below is placed in humility, the breadth thereof is disposed in charity, the height thereof is erected in good works, and is tiled and covered by Divine protection, and perfected in the length of patience.—HEYWOOD.

Nearly every part of the world has its representative in the human frame; for the head is heaven, of which the eyes are the stars; we consist of four elements; in the womb we are curled up into a ball; and when we stretch out our arms, a line drawn around us would be a circle.

SOUL: *Jewish Traditions respecting it, together with a variety of Curious and Mythological particulars, and Classical Allusions;—its Nature, Transmigrations, Modifications and Destiny.*

All the souls of the Israelites, it is said, were contained in the soul of the first man, and were made ready on the entrance of every Israelite into this world. The number of souls of the Israelites are calculated to amount to six hundred thousand, and therefore the soul of the first man consisted of that number twisted together like so many threads. Of these six hundred thousand souls that there is never one man wanting, which shows them to be a model of the upper chariot, in which are to be found six hundred thousand sciences. Another rabbinical work gives the following luminous statement. "The number of souls is six hundred thousand; and the law is the root of the souls of the Israelites, and every verse in the law was six thousand explanations, and every soul is formed particularly out of one explanation.

It is also necessary to be known, according to the doctrine of the Cabalist, says Menasseh, that at the beginning of the world souls were created by God in pairs, consisting each of a male and female; and therefore they affirm that marriage is either a reward or punishment, according to the works which a man has done. For if a man is deserving, and accounted worthy, he obtains his original consort; the person with whom he was created is bestowed upon him as a reward. But if otherwise, he is punished by being united to a person of uncongenial disposition and manners: with whom he is doomed to live in almost continual strifes, contentions and other similar miseries. As there is one mansion for the residence of those souls who never yet descended into the world, there is said to be another, for the reception of those who have departed out of this life, and on the decease of the body have returned to their source and origin." The following passage professes to describe the manner in which a soul is received on its arrival in the latter of these places. When a soul first enters Paradise, particularly if beloved or related to any that are there, it is immediately welcomed by them with pleasant countenances; and as the people of this world delighting to hear news from distant parts, put many questions to strangers concerning them; so do the righteous, who are already in Paradise, welcome the arrival of their friends and kindred, and ask them concerning the affairs of this world.

The doctrine of the metempsychosis, or that one soul animates several bodies in succession, has been generally adopted by the Jews for many ages, and is professed by them to the present day. The revolution of souls from one body to another, says Menasseh, is a matter of justifiable faith throughout our whole community. Nor are there more than one or two rabbies who deny or reject it. But there is another very great party of the *Sages* of Israel who believe it; and they maintain it to be a fundamental or principle of the law, and as we are bound to hearken to the words of these teachers, so we are to embrace their faith, without doubt or hesitation. The rabbies seem not to be very eminent for their gallantry or courtesy to the ladies. "The soul of a woman goes into a man for reward," says Menasseh, "but the soul of a man passes into a woman for punishment—such a punishment comes to pass on account of some heavy sin. The Cabbalists, also, believe that souls are removed out of bodies of one kind into bodies of another kind. The soul of a man passes into a beast if he has committed one more sin than he has performed good works. Some of the builders of Babel are declared to have entered cats and monkeys; and some are said to migrate into noxious reptiles and insects. The soul of a govĕrnor who proudly exalts himself above his people, into a bee. The soul of a cruel and wicked tax-gatherer, for his cruelty to the poor, into a raven in which he was recognized by a sagacious rabbi.

The souls of the righteous, whose conversation is with the law, into a fish. Other souls migrate into vegetables. For certain crimes a soul migrates into the leaf of a tree, sometimes passing from leaf to leaf, through several leaves. The soul of him who utters slanders passes into a stone. Rabbi Isaac Luria went on a time into the city of Tiberias; and passing by the great school of Rabbi Jochanan, who was then living, he showed his disciples a stone in the wall and said to them, "Into that stone has entered a soul that cries to me to pray for her; and this is the mystery of the words, 'For the stone shall cry out of the wall.'"—Hab. ii. 11. The soul of him that sheds blood goes into the water; the height of the punishment being in cataracts. Some souls are said to transmigrate into water-mills. The Jews, doubtless, borrowed the tenet from the Gentiles. It is known to have been widely diffused in the heathen world, from the Druids of Gaul and Britain, to the Brahmins of India. The Egyptians, according to Herodotus, are the first who asserted the doctrine that the soul of man is immortal, but that when the body decays it enters into some other animal which is then born; and that after having passed through all the different species of beasts, fishes, and birds, it again enters into a new born human body, and that the revolution is accomplished in three thousand years.

Know, curious reader, says Menasseh, that there are souls that migrate after a different manner, which among the Cabbalists is called *Ibbur*, or impregnation. The souls of the righteous, without any impairment of themselves, impregnated other souls; darting out sparks for the aid of the generality, or any particular person, of their times, and in this respect resemble candles, suffering no diminution from others being lighted by them. Some have said that the soul of Seth was pure and unspotted, and was, on account of Israel, conveyed to Moses, to qualify him for the delivery of the law. The souls which pass through the mystery of *Ibbur*, may return or depart at any time. The souls of Moses and Aaron came through the *Ibbur* to the soul of Samuel, and through *Ibbur* another spirit entered into Caleb, which strengthened and guided him in the right way, that he might not join the report of the spies.

Pythagoras asseverated to his disciples, that as a peculiar privilege, vouchsafed to him by Mercury, he had been first Æthalides, the reputed son of Mercury; then Euphorbus, who was slain by Menelaus at the siege of Troy, next Hermotimus.

"Even I, who these mysterious truths declare,
Was once Euphorbus in the Trojan war."

The soul of this philosopher is also represented as having been once embodied in a female named Alce, possessing surprising beauty, but divested of all chastity. Empedocles, an advocate of this Pythagorean dogma, started the notion of transmigration into vegetables, pointing out the degrees of preference due to different migrations, having declared that he had previously existed in human bodies, male and female, and also, to have been a bird, a fish, and a shrub. Among vegetables his predilection was for the laurel; among animals, for the lion; but honored mankind by saying that migration into a human body was most desirable of all.

Plato supposed the human soul to be an emanation from the divinity, *Divina particulum auræ*, and that after the purification of various transmigrations it was again re-absorbed into the divine essence. The souls of those that have made their belly their god, and loved nothing but indolence and impurity, into the bodies of asses. Those who loved only injustice, rapine and tyranny, animated wolves, hawks and falcons. Those remarkable for popular and civil virtues, migrate into bees and ants, and again return into human bodies.—*Various Authors.*

The Druids believed in the immortality of the soul, and its transmigration into different objects; and the clouds as palaces for its reception when it departed from the bodies of their warriors and great men.

The Mexican or American Indians indulged in similar fancies respecting the immortality and metamorphosis of the soul. Their chiefs who died in battle, and their wives who expired in childbirth, ascended up to the house of the sun, as the Lord of Glory; every day hailing his beam with demonstrations of joy, and the animation of vocal and instrumental music. After four years, these souls animated clouds, birds, or descended to the earth again. Those who were struck with lightning or died of diseases, and children sacrificed to Thalve, went to a place called Talocan, the paradise of that God. Those guilty of heinous crimes went to Mitchau or hell.—CHESTER.

Some of the ancient philosophers affirmed that spirits were of divers qualities, and operated upon men according to their different dispositions. Those of an ethereal or fiery temperament stirred up to contemplation. Those that were aerial to the business and common affairs of life.

The watery to pleasures; the earthy to base and grovelling avarice; the martial to fortitude; the jovial to prudence; the lunary to fertility of offspring; the voluptuous to licentiousness; the mercurial to policy and wisdom; the saturnine from all things that be evil. Such was the Socraticum Demonium, or genius of Socrates.—HEYWOOD.

They also indulge the conceit that the soul, together with the body, is derived from some seminal principles; others, that God created and infused souls into bodies when they are formed in the womb; others, that God framed them, first, when He created all things, and now assigns them to us, according to his pleasure.

The ancients used music at their funerals, to excite or quiet the affections of their friends, according to different harmonies. But the sweet and symbolical hint was the harmonical nature of the soul, which, delivered from the body, went again to enjoy the primitive harmony of heaven, from whence it first descended, which, according to the progress traced by antiquity, came down by Cancer and ascended by Capricornus. That they sucked in the last breath of their expiring friends, was surely a practice of no medical institution, but a loose opinion that the soul passed that way, and a fondness of affection, from some Pythagorical foundation, that the spirit of one body passed into another, which they wished might be their own.

As the doctrine of the certain existence of another world is one of the chief truths to be enforced upon man, a visible ascension into heaven has taken place in the three stages of development of the great scheme of Redemption. Enoch, Elijah, and Christ, proved to the world, by their ascension to heaven, the truth of the immortality of the soul, and that its future happiness is the object which God has constantly in view under every mode of appealing to his creatures.

I believe that the whole frame of a beast doth perish, and is left in the same state after death as before it was materialed into life; that the souls of men know neither contrary or corruption; that they subsist beyond the body and out-live death by the privilege of their proper natures, and without a miracle; that the souls of the faithful as they leave will take possession of heaven; that those apparitions and ghosts of departed persons are not the wandering souls of men, but the unquiet walks of devils, prompting and suggesting unto us mischief, blood, and villainy, instilling and stealing into our hearts; that the blessed spirits are not all at rest in their ground, but wander solicitous of the affairs of the world, but that those phantasms appear often, and do frequent cemeteries, charnel-houses, and churches, it is because those are dormitories of the dead, where the devil, like an insolent champion, beholds with pride, the spoils and trophies of his victory over Adam.

This is that dismal conquest we all deplore, that makes us so often cry, O! Adam, *quid fecisti!* I thank God I have not those strait ligaments or narrow obligations to the world as to dote on life, or be convulsed and tremble at the name of death.—SIR THOS. BROWNE.

The soul is an inseparable portion of the great universal mind; in other words of Brahma,—like the being from whom it emanates, it is therefore indestructible. It knows no distinction of time, it is free, immutable and eternal. The mind cannot pierce it; water cannot drown it. The earth cannot absorb it.

It is beyond the reach of the elements, invulnerable, invisible, universal, subsisting in all places and at all times, and victorious over death.—*Sacred Books of the Brahmins.*

Our inquiries respecting the nature of the soul must be bound over to religion, for otherwise they will be open to many errors. For since the substance of the soul was not deduced from the mass of heaven and earth, but immediately from God, how can the knowledge of the reasonable soul be derived from philosophy? It must be drawn from the same inspiration from whence its substance first flowed.—LORD BACON.

WOMEN; *prototypes of the absurd and unsexing order of modern Socialism.*

Lastheniæ, of Mautinea, and Axiotheo, of Phylsia, were two female disciples of Plato, who habited themselves like men, because they ridiculously conceived that that unnatural manner of dress best suited the dignity of pagan philosophy.

www.ingramcontent.com/pod-product-compliance
Lightning Source LLC
LaVergne TN
LVHW010240110826
845151LV00004B/1345
9781425524319